"*Poor Richard's Creating E-Books* will answer every question you might have about this blossoming industry. The book is well-written and entertaining, with complicated issues such as copyrights, formats, and contracts explained in laymen's terms (and with generous doses of humor) that can be quickly grasped and understood. This book is a must-read for anyone thinking of entering the e-book arena, whether as a publisher, author, or even a reader! I highly recommend it."

—Cheryl Dyson, Editor,
XC Publishing

"Some people think anyone can create an e-book, but authors Chris Van Buren and Jeff Cogswell tell you how to do it *right*. From nitty gritty details on formats, handheld devices and digital rights management to the requirements of the traditional book industry and leads for online marketing, *Poor Richard's Creating E-Books* tells you everything you need to know in a friendly, easy-to-read style. If you're in the e-book business, you need this book!"

—Mary Westheimer, CEO,
BookZone.com

"Today, there are only two types of publishers: Those in danger of missing the electronic boat and those who do not even know there is a boat to catch. Continuing the *Poor Richard's* series, this book explores, defines and explains the exciting world of e-books. Welcome aboard."

—Dan Poynter, Author,
The Self-Publishing Manual

"As a small publishing firm, we see electronic books as a key technology to reach future readers and expand our market. But e-books come in a bewildering array of formats, business models, and technologies, and good information about them has been tough to find. Until now. *Poor Richard's Creating E-Books* answers all the questions I had about what formats to choose, and how to charge for our products, and how to protect them from piracy. This book is a must-read for any author or publisher who wants to take advantage of the next publishing revolution."

—Dan Newman, President,
Say I Can

Praise for other books in the Poor Richard's Series

Poor Richard's Web Site

"Makes it possible for ordinary people to set up effective business websites without going broke or spending forever online. It's a great read for anyone who wants to build a business site, and it becomes a part of our recommended library."

—CMPnet's Techweb

"A good source with easy step-by-step directions." —*Publishers Weekly*

"Offers clear advice to help you defend against jargon-happy sales people and computer magazines." —Fortune.com

"If you really want to build a functional Web site [this] might just be the book for you."
—CNN Interactive

Poor Richard's Internet Marketing and Promotions

"Reading their advice is inspirational." —Amazon.com

"The book explains many powerful techniques for getting people's attention online. Great reading." —*Amarillo Globe News*

"If you're struggling to get noticed on the Net, don't just take a look at this book—buy it. It's the closest thing to an investment with a guaranteed return that you can possibly make." —Borders.com

Poor Richard's E-mail Publishing

"The single most authoritative and helpful guide an entrepreneur can turn to when it's time to move beyond a Web site." —*The Newsletter on Newsletters*

"Unites commonsense advice with clear explanations of e-mail technology . . .The book is packed with marketing know-how and tells you how to make money with your newsletter . . .Don't click Send without [this book]." —*PC World*

Poor Richard's Building Online Communities

"An extensive course on creating a vital Web community." —Entrepreneur.com

"Create a web community for a business or family using the power of the Internet and this *Poor Richard's* guide, which focuses on inexpensive methods of achieving such a goal. From locating and participating in mailing lists to joining web-based communities for business and pleasure, this imparts the basics of understanding how such groups function." —Review's Bookwatch

POOR RICHARD'S CREATING E-BOOKS

How Authors, Publishers, and Corporations Get into Digital Print

by
Chris Van Buren
and
Jeff Cogswell

TOP FLOOR
PUBLISHING

To all my friends at Waterside Productions, Inc.
Thanks for all your help over the years. —CVB

To my wonderful wife, Rainbow. —JMC

Poor Richard's Creating E-Books
How Authors, Publishers, and Corporations Get into Digital Print

Copyright © 2001 Chris Van Buren and Jeff Cogswell

SAN#: 299-4550
Top Floor Publishing
8790 W. Colfax #107
Lakewood, CO 80215

Feedback to the author: feedback@topfloor.com
Sales information: sales@topfloor.com
The Top Floor Publishing Web Site: http://TopFloor.com/
The Poor Richard Web Site: http://PoorRichard.com/
Cover design/illustration by Marty Petersen, http://www.artymarty.com

Library of Congress Catalog Card Number: 2001088614

ISBN: 1-930082-02-9

03   02   01   6 5 4 3 2 1

ACKNOWLEDGMENTS

A big thank you goes to David Fugate, Margot Maley-Hutchinson, and Matt Wagner for helping with the original outline of this book and for advice and information along the way. Many thanks to Trudy Totty for helping with research and for general input and to Mary Westheimer of BookZone (http://www.bookzone.com/) for many great suggestions. Thanks to all the personal story contributors (Mary, Xina, W.L., and Dan) and our editors Missy Ramey, Jerry Olsen, and Hilary Powers—and Joann Woy, our proofreader and indexer. And thanks to my father, Robert, for teaching me English.

—*CVB*

Thanks to my agent and friend, Margot Maley-Hutchinson (congratulations on the new baby!) and to the rest of the folks at Waterside, as well as my co-author Chris for the great work. Thanks to all the fine folks at Top Floor for doing a great job on this book, especially Missy Ramey, Jerry Olsen, Hilary Powers, and Joann Woy. Jerry and Hilary, you are both by far the best editors I've worked with. And Hilary, I'm sorry you're not related to Tim Powers, but at least we agree he's one of our favorite authors. Finally, thanks to all the great folks I met at the e-book conferences for sharing your ideas with me!

—*JMC*

ABOUT THE AUTHORS

Chris Van Buren has a varied background in the writing and publishing business. He began his career as a computer documentation writer and went on to become an editor at CompuSoft Publishing, one of the first computer book publishing companies in the United States. He later wrote and published several computer industry newsletters, including *The AppleWorks Journal* and the *Microsoft Works in Education Newsletter*, co-published with Microsoft Corporation.

Chris also spent many years as a computer book author and has written more than 15 books, including *Using Excel for the Macintosh*, *The MacWorld Excel 5 Companion*, and *The HTML Quick Reference*. Currently, Chris is a literary agent with Waterside Productions, Inc., (http://www.waterside.com/) and has represented a wide variety of books, including many best-selling computer books, cookbooks, and spiritual books. He is also the publisher of the *E-Publishing Opportunities* e-mail newsletter (http://www.myplanet.net/vanburen/). You can e-mail Chris directly at vanburen@bigplanet.com.

Jeff Cogswell programs computers, writes books, and plays the piano and guitar. Early on he had some ideas for how e-books could be made to happen when his first book went out of print and he continued to get letters from people who wanted it. Being more of a writer than a programmer, he prefers to write about e-books and let other people build the e-book software.

He has written several books including *Simple C++* and *Delphi 32-bit Programming Secrets* (with Tom Swan). He recently rewrote one of his early C++ books, and by the time you read this it should be available as an e-book. His Beginner's Guide to E-books Web site can be found at http://www.geocities.com/jeffcogs/. Jeff can be reached at jeffcogs@yahoo.com.

TABLE OF CONTENTS—AT A GLANCE

TABLE OF CONTENTS

FOREWORD

by Mardi Link, Editor-in-Chief, *ForeWord* magazine

"I would." That has become my enthusiastic answer to the people who still insist on asking me, "Who would read a book on a computer?"

I've downloaded travel guidebooks, collections of short stories, and even classics of literature in the public domain. (I doubt I'm the only one assuaging my reader's guilt by downloading free copies of *The Scarlet Letter* and the like from Web sites like Project Gutenberg.) I've also relished the chance to read new work by one of my favorite novelists before her accompanying hardcover was even out of the printer's warehouse. All these scenarios are possible because I do read books on my computer. And on my laptop, my Casio, and my Rocket.

An avid reader of literary fiction, I make it a point every year to read each of the fiction finalists for the Pulitzer, the National Book Award, and the Booker Prize. Usually I buy my favorites from the bookseller down the street from my office and check the others out from the library. This year, though, when a business trip to the Pacific Northwest coincided with the announcements of the National Book Award finalists, I decided to lighten my bag and download a few to read on the long flight. Imagine my surprise when only one was available as an e-book! I ended up checking the hardcovers out of the library, after all.

These few examples from my own esoteric reading habits offer just a peek at the market for e-books. As an author or publisher, take a moment to envision your ideal reader. By taking advantage of e-books, you can give your readers time (getting it first), accuracy (instant updates), and portability (hardcovers are heavy). If you can solve a reader's problem, you can sell e-books.

Right now is perhaps both the most exciting and the most distracting time to be an author or an independent publisher. Just when The Blob seems to have decimated Publishers Row, gorging itself on formerly respected publishing houses like so many hors d'oeuvres, and eliminating many opportunities for first time authors to be published, hundreds of new e-publishers have set up shop, taking our industry back to its honorable cottage origins. Imagine it! Independent e-publishers and authors have the freedom to publish virtually anything, bound only by their vision and discipline. No chainstore buyer can tell you to change your title; no distributor can demand a deposit against returns.

This earnest freedom comes bundled with, yes, that grown-up word, responsibility. Like it or not, many readers, booksellers, librarians, and reviewers see e-books not as an opportunity, but as a challenge to the traditional book, which was working just fine, thank you very much. As such, the first ones have been and will continue to be judged harshly. It's every e-book author and publisher's job to keep the best of that tradition—meticulous editing and careful selection of manuscripts, for example—while re-inventing the book and finding new readers.

With *Poor Richard's Creating E-Books* you hold in your hands, neither the kite nor the key, but rather the filament to bend a bit of their power your way. It isn't too much of a stretch to imagine Ben Franklin himself formatting files, posting on topical listservs, and e-mailing his ideas to today's revolutionaries.

FOREWORD

by Jim Milliot, Editor, *Publishers Weekly*

Without question, electronic publishing, be it about e-books, print-on-demand or online books, has been the focus of much discussion and debate within the book industry since the beginning of 2000. While publishers had long theorized about an e-book world, they were jolted into action when Stephen King had a huge hit in spring 2000 with the e-book release of *Riding the Bullet*. Afraid that they were in danger of being left behind as an important new delivery channel developed, traditional book publishers jumped-started their e-book operations, while entrepeneurs began testing the e-book waters for them-selves. Throughout 2000 and into 2001 different associations and organizations held scores of seminars dedicated to electronic publishing. Unfortunately, the conclusion that can be drawn in March 2001 about the future of e-book publishing from all the discussions is that nobody has a clear idea of where the e-book market is headed.

There is currently no standardized technical format for how an e-book should be published; there is no single accepted player for consumers to buy to read e-books; there is no consensus on how much e-books should cost; there is a ragging debate over who even controls e-book rights, especially of older works; and there is no agreement about how large the e-book market will be. To try to get a handle about these issues, most of the major publishers have formed e-book divisions, including Random House, HarperCollins, Simon & Schuster, and Time Warner Trade Publishing. Amazon.com and Barnesandnoble.com have established e-bookstores on their Web sites where consumers can download e-titles, and distributors such as Ingram and Baker & Taylor have formed e-publishing divisions geared toward converting texts into digital formats and distributing those files to customers. All of this activity suggests that *something* is happening in the e-book market *today* and that the market is only likely to grow for e-book titles in the future.

Nearly every party that has studied the e-book market, ranging from consulting firms to publishers to industry associations, has had a different view of how fast the e-book market will grow into a major, profitable field. And while the general consensus is that meaningful sales are several years away, there is also agreement that the time is right to begin exploring the opportunities that e-books present.

INTRODUCTION

Who wants to read a book online? As it turns out, lots of people do. And because of this, lots of authors want to put their books online, whether it's on a desktop computer, on a small palm-size computer, or in a format that can be easily printed on demand.

If you're such an author, where do you begin? What do you need to know about the technology and business? And what can you expect in the future of e-publishing?

It's quite possible that the next five years are going to see a radical change in the publishing industry. Never before has it been so easy to self-publish. And never before have publishers paid royalties as high as the ones that many e-books today are earning. In the past, self-publishers were considered "vanity publishers" and scorned by the industry. But worse, it cost them an arm and a leg to get their books printed, while getting self-published books into the bookstores was nearly impossible. Today, with e-books, anyone can self-publish remarkably cheaply and have a chance to reach just as many people as Stephen King.

This book will show you how to make this happen.

Are E-Books Real?

But are e-books for real? Are people really going to read them? Today you may not see many people toting their electronic book devices to the beach for pleasure reading, or flipping electronic pages in their backyard hammocks on a Sunday afternoon, but it does happen. At an e-book conference in early 1999, the inventor of one of the first popular reader devices said he was on an airplane that morning and somebody he didn't know was sitting next to him reading the news on that very product, having no idea that the inventor of the device was sitting next to him.

The e-book revolution is beginning—and by reading this book, you'll be one step ahead of the rest. Electronic publishing is an exploding field with plenty of opportunities for authors, self-publishers, entrepreneurs, and professionals. After reading this book, you'll know just how to go about publishing and marketing e-books and their relatives, Print On Demand books and online interactive books.

In 1999 there were only about 50 or 60 electronic publishers—companies selling electronic books as CD-ROMs or as downloads over the Internet. In 2000, there were over 250 independent e-publishers. Many of these were small companies started by authors who could not get noticed by the print publishing system. At the time this book is being written, there are over 350 e-publishers and many of the big publishing conglomerates have entered the e-book market too—with distinct e-publishing divisions. New e-publishers are being added to the list every week. Even well-known authors such as Stephen King have published e-books. (His book got more than 400,000 downloads over the Internet—you could do only a tenth as well and still make a bundle!) Perhaps more inspiring, several self-published e-book authors have had their books adopted by big-time publishers. All this indicates that e-books are truly getting respect. And the momentum does not appear to be slowing down. The opportunities for both writing and publishing are fantastic.

This book takes you through all phases of e-book writing and publishing—from creating manuscripts and e-book files to marketing and distributing online. You'll get the essential information that you need to know about:

- What makes a good e-book
- How to choose e-book formats
- How to create e-book documents
- Where to find various services for start-up e-publishers
- Where to distribute your e-books
- What to look for in e-book publishing contracts

As you'll see in this book, you have many ways of getting your e-book published. You can work with existing e-publishers to get your own works published and distributed—both electronically and in print. Or you can dive into an e-publishing venture of your own, acquiring manuscripts from other authors, designing covers, and distributing books through various online bookstores. Your business can be as simple or sophisticated as you want it to be.

What Are E-Books Good For?

With e-publishing, you don't have to grovel to the print publishing establishment to get your work noticed. The Internet and e-book technology gives you the power of independence—the power to create your own e-books and sell them online. The only people you answer to are the readers themselves, your customers. And you won't be alone out there. Plenty of online services, agents, discussion groups, and information resources can help you along the way. Indeed, many people have decided to make a business of helping other people start and run their e-publishing businesses. This book will lead you to all these resources and more.

Here are some other things that make e-publishing an attractive alternative to traditional print publishing:

The freedom to do your own thing your own way. You don't have to adhere to the standards of the print publishing world. There's plenty of room online to try new things.

The ability to start small and grow. You don't have to start by opening a publishing company online with dozens of books. In fact, you can start as an author, writing for other e-publishing companies. You can choose to do certain aspects of the publishing process and hire out the rest. If you decide that e-publishing is for you, you can slowly take over more of the process.

Ease of entry. You don't need a huge investment or lots of books. All you need is the desire, the information in this book, and perhaps a Web site to accompany your efforts online.

No printing bills, no shipping, no storage. Selling e-books is a matter of transferring electronic files over the Internet. The economics of e-publishing are much different from those of print publishing.

Easy access to online booksellers and distributors. Small e-publishers can get their books into the major online booksellers, such as Amazon.com and Borders. You don't have to be a member of a secret society to enter the market.

Better author royalties, friendlier contracts. Generally, e-book publishers offer authors more favorable royalties than the ones print book publishers offer. The benefits that the publishers enjoy with e-book publishing are shared with the author.

More control over how your work is published. As an author, you can often participate in the editing, layout, and cover design of your book. Some publishers even let you set the price of your work.

The ability to work from just about anywhere. Most of the process of creating and publishing e-books is done online, over the Internet. As long as you have a decent Internet connection, you can work from just about anywhere.

In This Book

In the chapters to come, you will see not only how to make all this happen, but what software and devices are available for reading e-books. You have lots of reader software packages and hardware devices to choose from, and you will need to know which ones offer what features, along with the pros and cons of each. We'll also talk about the compatibility issues, that is, whether you can copy e-books between the different software packages and devices. We'll also tell you who the major players are in the field, and what they have to offer. On top of all that, you'll learn:

- What the different standards and file formats are for storing e-books on the computer
- Where the different file formats are used
- How to create e-books that use the different file formats
- What sort of copy protections are available, and the philosophical and ethical issues involved

We'll also tell you about industry trends, so you can get an idea of what's happening now and what to expect in the future. To help put things in perspective, we'll compare e-publishing to a similar industry, e-music, and show you where the e-music folks went wrong, what they did right, and how e-publishers are learning from the mistakes of the e-music industry, which is a year or so ahead.

This book also gives you success stories from real authors who have managed to succeed in the e-book business, as well as lists of e-publishers looking for works from authors, businesses looking to provide resources to e-publishers and authors, and sample contracts. The sample contracts should be especially helpful to you, as one of the authors of this book is a literary agent and knows just what aspects of contracts are beneficial to you, the author of an e-book.

How to Use This Book

Although this book was written with the intention of your reading it from front to back, most of the chapters stand on their own and can be read individually. For example, if you mainly want to learn about copyright and protecting your work, you can easily read Chapter 5, "Digital Rights and Copy Protection," by itself without worrying that you might have missed something important.

The book is divided into four main sections:

Part I: Electronic Publishing Overview. This part gives an overview of the technology, a discussion of the various hardware and software available, and an overview of the industry. It gives you the necessary foundation for understanding what exactly e-books are, and how the market works.

Part II: Planning and Creating an E-book. This part takes you through the process of putting your e-book together. Because the choice of e-book software and hardware is so broad, we cover as many of the more popular ones as possible. This section also includes an entire chapter about copy protection—a big issue today, especially after the e-music industry's big fight of 2000, the Napster case. Napster opened everybody's eyes to the issues and helped us see the situation from many different perspectives. Many of us could see how both sides were right in the case. Fortunately for e-publishing, the e-music industry had its problems early on, so we could learn from it. These topics are all covered in this section.

Part III: Getting Your E-Book Published. This part is devoted to e-publishers—the different types of e-publishers, some of the bigger players, and how you can get involved with your own e-publishing venture. It also includes an entire chapter devoted to marketing your e-books, showing you the different approaches you can take, and how to get your e-book noticed.

Part IV: E-Book Business Issues. Whether you're an author or an e-publisher, if you are getting paid (or even hoping to get paid), then you are in business. And with that comes the requirement for knowing various business issues. Before you can really understand your own business issues, however, you need to understand the economics of the publishing industry. The more you understand about the economics, the better you can run your own business, carefully fitting it to today's economy. Therefore we devote an entire chapter to the economics of the publishing industry. We follow that with two nuts-and-bolts chapters about running your business, including the hot buttons and other business issues.

Part V: Real-Life Success Stories and Future Trends. This final part includes a chapter of personal success stories, and a general look at the trends of the industry and where the industry is likely to be headed.

Where to Find More Information

Throughout this book, you will find addresses of Web sites, companies, and occasionally e-mail lists that will help you continue with your e-book publishing ventures. We encourage you to get on the computer and check out as many of these Web sites as you can.

The best way to understand the industry is to get involved in it. Ten years ago, that would have meant flying to New York or Indianapolis and visiting the publishers. Today the Internet makes it all possible without leaving your own house. The more you visit these sites and study the market, the more you will understand it and the better you will be able to plan your next move on marketing and selling your own e-books. After all, it's up to you to make things happen. Between reading this book and studying the businesses out there, you should know everything you need to publish and sell your e-books.

The authors of this book maintain Web sites and mailing lists pertaining to e-books. We would love to hear from you. You can find our e-mail addresses at the beginning of this book in the "About the Authors" section.

PART I
Electronic Publishing
Overview

CHAPTER ONE

Understanding Electronic Publishing

E-publishing is nothing new. Take a look at any site on the World Wide Web, and you see a page that has been published electronically. But even before that, and closer to the world of books, the idea of e-publishing has been around for a while. Early on in the computer world people were tossing around the idea of shipping books on disk instead of in printed form. Unfortunately, a single floppy disk didn't leave much room for an entire book, especially the images. But in the early 1990s, with the increase of CD-ROM drives, several paper-printed books (typically books about computers) shipped with an entire copy of the book stored on an attached CD-ROM. It was the goal of some people to completely remove the paper book altogether and ship only a CD-ROM. But it turned out that shipping only a CD-ROM gave no financial benefits to the publishers over shipping a paper-printed book. They still had to deal with the distribution and warehousing costs. (Key point: CD-ROM distribution provided no financial benefits to the publisher.)

Meanwhile, some publishers (particularly smaller publishers) realized that if they included a CD-ROM with their book, they could provide a total multimedia experience that would be far more exciting for readers than just having the words and text of the book on the CD-ROM. Some publishers ventured into the world of multimedia, but soon realized that while the product was certainly exciting, it (again) wasn't cost-effective. It cost the publishers too much money to produce the big multimedia production for the CD-ROM, and they would in turn have to charge far more for the book and CD combination than what consumers would be willing to pay.

And so the world would have to wait.

Flying Cars and E-Books

So here we are with a new millennium starting, and we're not riding in flying cars and we're still reading almost every book on paper, including books like this one, which is not only about e-books but was typed in using a computer and lived on a computer all the way to the printers. It was essentially an e-book living in its authors' and editors' word processors. Bummer it couldn't stay that way.

But that's not to say electronic books don't exist. As you read this, hundreds of companies out there are working to make e-books a reality. Companies are creating little electronic gadgets and gizmos that are specifically for reading books, much like the things people carry on *Star Trek*. (Not the things they wear on their chest to instantly teleport them miles away. *Poor Richard's Guide to Teleporting About the Universe* is scheduled for print in 173 years. Place your orders today!)

In the sections that follow we take a brief look at the different hardware and software you can buy right now. But first, some thoughts about this whole e-book thing and what it's all about and . . .

Why Would Anyone Want an E-Book?

Being active in the e-book community, we get asked this question a lot. One day Jeff was having lunch with some friends, and one of them didn't know that he had anything at all to do with e-books. She suddenly went on a rant about how she'd heard that some people are trying to take books and put them on the computer. She said, "Why would I want to do that? I don't want to sit there at my computer reading a book!" She was plain mad about the thought that anyone would take her cozy paper books away.

We agree. (But we're not mad.) A few years ago Jeff read an article in a computer magazine that said, "Imagine sitting down at your computer and reading the latest Stephen King book." (It's ironic that several years later Stephen King really was one of the first big-name e-book authors! Maybe the computer magazines have a bigger influence on famous people than they realize?) After reading the article, Jeff scoffed. Yeah right, he said, having recently completed a week-long course titled "Human Factors of Software Design."

Here's the problem (which he learned in the week-long class, so he knew he was an expert!). It's the ergonomics and the screens. First, people don't want to sit at a desk to read the book. To quote Peter Kent, author of *Poor Richard's Web Site*, "Try Kent's Electronic Book Bathroom Test: An electronic book is not a real book unless it can be read while sitting on the can." People want portable books, they don't want to lug around a computer and monitor. And many of us sit in an uncomfortable position when looking at a computer screen. The other problem is the screen itself. The resolution of today's computers is far better than it was, say, in 1992 when Jeff first read that article, but it's still nowhere near as good as a printed book.

Back to lunch: Jeff told his friend what he was doing. She proclaimed him to be directly descended from the Evil One, straight from the bowels of the underworld, where they read all their works on computer screens and paper is nowhere to be found. He realized that she heard that our goal was to wipe out paper books and make all these poor myopic people with back problems sit at their computers and stare into the glowing screen late into the nights. If that were the case, then perhaps she really had reason to call us evil.

But that's not our intention at all. First, we want e-books to be portable, not just for desktop computers. Second, the resolution of computer screens gets better every year. Third, people have pretty much gotten over their unwillingness to stare at the computer reading for hours and hours. Look at how many people surf the Web and read Web pages online for hours. Next, Jeff had the chance to read a book on a little handheld computer, and to his surprise, it turned out to be a rather pleasant experience. He had to get used to the idea of turning a page, where a whole page would appear on the screen with each "page turn," rather than scrolling like most Web pages. And it was great to be able to read in the dark, since the LCD screen lit up. All in all, it was like bowling. Once you've tried it you realize: You know, it really isn't that bad! And finally, we aren't trying to remove paper books. They aren't going away anytime soon.

Jeff explained all this to his friend and to everyone's surprise she became fascinated with the idea of e-books, and her husband is now eager to go out and buy a little handheld e-book device! (We don't know about her, but she doesn't seem to object.)

E-Book Devices

These small devices we're talking about are usually called e-book devices. They range in size and features. Some are slightly smaller than a sheet of notebook paper and an inch or so thick, others are about half that size. Most have no keyboard; instead, the entire front of the device is a touch-sensitive LCD display. Some are in color, others are in black and white. Two such devices that have been very popular are the Rocket eBook and the Softbook Reader. The companies that created these two devices have been purchased by the same company, **Gemstar** (http://www.eBook-Gemstar.com/), which has replaced both devices with equivalents bearing the RCA brand (the same brand that shows up on televisions). The Softbook has been replaced by the model REB1200, and the Rocket eBook has been replaced by the new model REB1100. At the time of this writing, another is forthcoming, one by **Franklin Electronic Publishers** called the eBookMan (http://www.franklin.com/ebookman/default.asp), shown in Figure 1.1. The Franklin eBookMan is an inexpensive reader, which also has "PDA"

Figure 1.1: The Franklin site, showing its eBookMan device.

(personal digital assistant) features; that is, it has an address book, schedule, dictionary, and so on. In Chapter 2, "What's an E-Book?" you'll be seeing more details about these devices.

E-Book Software

Companies are creating software for handheld and palm-size computers, for laptop and notebook computers, and for desktop computers that allow you to view and read e-books on these computers, without the need for a separate e-book device. Some are the huge, well-known companies (Microsoft, Adobe, and Xerox, to name a few), others are high-tech dot-com start-ups pushing forward with nearly as much force as the bigger companies. Some of their software lets you view books saved on your own hard drive, while others let you view books out on the Internet.

Viewable books sometimes make use of sophisticated software to prevent people from copying without paying. If you view such a book, you aren't supposed to be able to give it to your friends. Other books don't have such software and you can freely copy them. It's usually up to the publisher to determine whether you can copy the books or not. Some publishers believe it's very important, in the interest of profits (say it again: *in the interest of profits*), to bar people from copying, ensuring that payment comes in for each and every copy out there. Others believe in the honor system, figuring that if they let people send the books all over the planet, a certain number of people are likely to pay up, thereby maximizing the profit.

A Matter of Principle—Are you starting to see a common theme revolving around the publishers' interest in profit? Because you should. We're not saying that's a bad thing, but we are saying it's important that you understand that fact if you're going to take part in the business. Few companies, especially among the big, monster-size publishers that opened shop 250 years ago, do things out of the goodness of their hearts or out of an excitement for new technology; rather, their major motivation is in making money for the shareholders.

At this point you might be wondering what happened to the big production, multimedia books mentioned earlier on. Where are they? Believe it or not, in this particular area the industry has taken a couple of steps backward. The problem is not a lack of capabilities. Certainly even most laptops and handheld computers are quite capable of fancy multimedia. (For instance, my tiny palm-size Casio E-100 can play videos and CD-quality sound.) The problem is simply the size of the books and the time it takes to download them off the Internet. A full multimedia presentation can take as little as ten megabytes. On a CD-ROM, that's nothing. But when you're using a standard modem, it could take a very long time to download. Of course, the download problem is changing with the increasing popularity of cable modems and high-speed DSL, but still not everybody has high-speed access. When they do, then you can expect to see much bigger multimedia presentations. Until then, plan on seeing books that are mostly in the style of text rather than multimedia.

In Chapter 2 you'll see more detail about the different software available for reading books. But just a quick mention: One that's sure to be big by the time you read this is the Microsoft Reader. Other big ones are Glassbook Reader and Peanut Reader. (As you can see, if you're not sure about the name of the soft-ware package, it's probably called Reader. At least it's clear what the programs do.)

File Formats

So you can see there are lots of different kinds of software and devices for e-books. And as you can probably imagine, there are also lots of different ways for the creators of the e-books to save these books on a hard drive. In other words, there are lots of different file formats they can use. And often, for each file format, you need a different viewer or device. Imagine if every videotape production required its own brand of VCR. You want to watch this movie, you'll need that VCR; you want to watch that movie, you'll need this VCR. So you better check out which movies are available for which VCRs before you buy a VCR.

Now imagine that for e-books. Sound messy? It is. Right now, most of the different companies in the e-book world are either working together or fighting with one another, trying to come up with a standard file format that they can all use. The ultimate dream is to be able to download any e-book and read it on any viewer of your choice, whether the viewer is a handheld device or a piece of software sitting on a desktop or laptop. At the moment, it looks like the industry is narrowing things down to two different standards, called Open eBook (OEB) and Portable Document Format (PDF). OEB is created by a government-headed consortium at the **Open eBook Forum** (http://www.openebook.org), of which **Microsoft** (http://www.microsoft.com) is a major player. (One of Jeff's former co-workers thought he wrote the Open eBook spec. As flattered as he

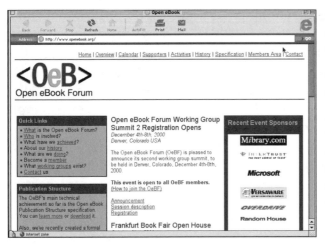

Figure 1.2: The Open eBook site.

was, he actually had nothing to do with it whatsoever.) The Open eBook site is shown in Figure 1.2. PDF, on the other hand, is created primarily by (and owned by) **Adobe** http://www.adobe.com. Each format has its strengths and weaknesses. We'll look at these in more detail in Chapter 4, "The Production Process." And just to make things messier, there are lots of companies doing their own thing, too.

Making E-Books

So how are e-books made? It depends on who you talk to. Typically the companies that create the e-book reader software also produce the tools to create e-books, or they work with some company who produces the tools. These tools range from converting existing printed books by scanning their pages one by one and then carefully converting them, through taking the original computer files for existing printed books and converting them to the necessary file format, to starting from scratch—going straight from the word processor to the e-book and bypassing the printed stage altogether. We'll look at the different tools available in Chapter 4, "The Production Process," and talk about how to create your e-books.

What Can You Do With E-Books?

So now the burning question: What makes e-books better than printed books? What exactly can you do with e-books?

- You can use an e-book device to hold open a printed cookbook while you're trying to follow a recipe.
- When the screen is turned off you can use it as a mirror and see if your teeth are clean.

Okay, funny, funny, but seriously, having a book in an online format makes for a much more powerful approach to reading. For instance, at least one popular e-book software manufacturer (**Glassbook**, http://www.glassbook.com), which makes software for desktop and laptop computers, lets you click on a

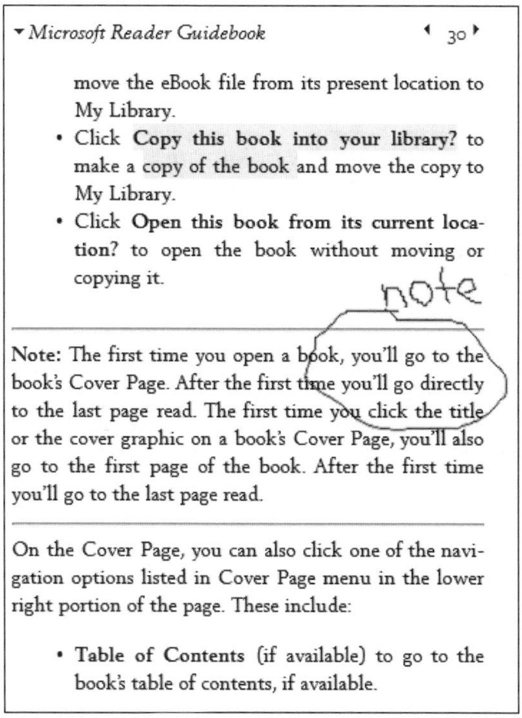

▾ Microsoft Reader Guidebook   ◄ 30 ►

> move the eBook file from its present location to
> My Library.
> • Click **Copy this book into your library?** to
>   make a copy of the book and move the copy to
>   My Library.
> • Click **Open this book from its current loca-**
>   **tion?** to open the book without moving or
>   copying it.

note

> Note: The first time you open a book, you'll go to the
> book's Cover Page. After the first time you'll go directly
> to the last page read. The first time you click the title
> or the cover graphic on a book's Cover Page, you'll also
> go to the first page of the book. After the first time
> you'll go to the last page read.

> On the Cover Page, you can also click one of the navi-
> gation options listed in Cover Page menu in the lower
> right portion of the page. These include:
>
> > • **Table of Contents** (if available) to go to the
> >   book's table of contents, if available.

Figure 1.3: The Microsoft Reader with notes and highlights added.

word in the text and look up its definition. Also, for most e-books, searching is much more powerful than using the limited index in a printed book. How many times have you been reading a book and said, "I remember a dozen or so pages back the author said something about—" but you can't find the item in the index and you're forced to skim through the pages? With an e-book you can quickly and easily search for text, any text, not just what's in the index.

Some e-books let you highlight text and add notes in the margins. The **Microsoft Reader** software (http://www.microsoft.com/reader) lets you do this. So do the **Gemstar RCA** reader devices (http://www.eBook-Gemstar.com/). Figure 1.3 shows this in action with the Microsoft Reader.

E-books also have the benefit that they can hold a lot of information. Typical e-book devices can easily hold dozens of books. Imagine carrying a whole set of paperbacks in a device the size of a single paperback.

They also have other benefits for different areas of work or study. For example, a student might be able to fit several textbooks on a single device, along with some reference guides (a dictionary, a thesaurus, a book of math formulas . . .). This would prove a great asset in an open-book exam.

Is There Anything to Read?

So what e-books are available? At the time of this writing, you can choose from thousands of e-book titles. However, because the industry hasn't settled yet, it's still in a state of disarray, where different titles are available for different software and devices. The e-book industry hasn't standardized the way the videotape industry has, but rest assured that it will in due time. (In fact, early on there were several competing standards for videotapes, two in particular being Beta and VHS, and VHS won out.)

Meanwhile, depending on your hardware and software preferences, you can be pretty sure there are e-books available for you. Some are for free and some are for pay.

***Project Gutenberg**—It probably bears mentioning at this point that over the past thirty years, a group of people scattered over the planet has gotten together with the goal of taking classics (that is, non-copyrighted texts or works for which the copyright has run out) and getting them into an online format for people to read and distribute using the computer. This effort is called Project Gutenberg, named for the guy who invented the printing press. The e-books are stored in a basic "ASCII text" format that virtually all computers can display, without requiring fancy-schmancy e-book software. The project has already converted literally thousands of texts, and all are available for free. The Project Gutenberg home page can be found at* http://www.gutenberg.net/.

A Look Ahead

If you attend an e-book conference, where everybody who has any business related to e-books shows up, and if you listen to the speeches, you will hear dozens of different predictions for where the paper book and e-book industries are headed in the next five to ten years. You'll hear predictions about where technology is headed, what consumers' lives will be like, and how the publishing industry will or won't change. Some of these predictions are, frankly, totally outlandish and unsupported; others are a bit more realistic. Certainly, there's no way to know for sure what will happen, but here we present some of the more likely outcomes.

Not too many years ago, most people did not expect that nearly everyone would one day own a computer. But now people all across the country and all over the world, from all areas of life, do own computers. But it has taken a while to get to that point. With any new technology, there's an enormous leap between just the so-called early adopters using it and every person on the planet jumping in. So contrary to what some of the more radical visionaries proclaim, we can expect it to take a few years before we see all the newspapers on the Boston subway replaced by handheld book reader devices. (And hopefully they won't be discarded on the floor of the train!)

However, it really is happening, although gradually. You are seeing more and more people carrying palm-sized computers. Although most people use these devices primarily for storing phone numbers and appointments, the palmtops are out there and the people who own them really like them and are eager to do more with them. While most people do tend to be a bit wary about reading books on their small computers, they are eager to read the *New York Times* or the *Wall Street Journal* that way. So it's just a matter of time before those same people want to read books and novels as well.

Once it happens, what can we expect? There will certainly be the few "Superpower" e-books designed for technonerd power users; these people will be heard saying things like, "Check this out! My e-book reader is hooked up to my mobile PCS network, and I can create a custom book, where each chapter is generated from a separate book, all of which are the results of an extensive search I just performed on the entire Library of Congress! The book is generated in real time and downloaded to my device as I'm reading it, and it even includes a full index!"

But in the nearer future, we can expect more modest advances in e-books. For example, it should be possible to reorganize your e-books so that you can have a chapter from this book and a chapter from that book. You should be able to do very sophisticated searches (such as "find me the parts of the book that talk about writing and how it relates to the medical industry"). Further, you can expect to be able to do expanded searches among the different e-books available online, just as you can presently do for Web sites (say, "Find me all books that talk about writing for the medical industry").

Certainly as download times shrink and distribution mechanisms become more powerful, we can expect to see more multimedia in these books as well. Such multimedia will be particularly useful in textbooks. Instead of a math book just showing the graph of a particular equation, a figure in the book might be a full-featured graphing calculator, where the student can put in different functions or adjust the numbers. Or a chemistry book might show a revolving molecule in 3D, or a history book might include a short video of Martin Luther King's "I Have a Dream" speech. A literature book might include a video of portions of a Shakespeare play. A foreign language book might allow you to click a paragraph of text and switch between, say, English and French.

As for distribution, some companies are hoping to have alternate means for getting books onto your computer or e-book device. Already, you can go to some Barnes and Noble stores and get a print-on-demand book, where the book is physically printed while you wait. The next logical step is that you'll be able to bring in your laptop or small computer or e-book device and hook it up to a server computer, from which you can get a rapid, high-speed download of several books, and pay for them all at once.

Comparison With Print Publishing

E-book technology opens a whole new set of options that are not possible with print books. But beyond these differences, the actual business of publishing is likely to change as well—although, and we can't stress this enough, very slowly and gradually.

The bigger publishing companies have no intention whatsoever of ditching paper books. At present, they are watching the e-book market to determine how quickly they want to move ahead with e-books—if at all. (Fortunately, virtually all of the large publishers recognize that e-books are going to happen and are either planning on entering the e-book market or have already moved forward in it.) And as these publishers embrace e-books, they will release titles gradually. In other words, they are treating it as a potential line of business and are being cautious about it, like any potential line of business. Like all big companies, they do not simply embrace a new business because it's exciting; rather, they only move if they see a line of business in it with potential profits, all within their own business model.

The publishing business model works in part because it provides a lot of services authors find very useful. The first stage of the creation process for a nonfiction book takes place in the Acquisitions department, where someone comes up with book ideas and then goes out to find authors. Fiction authors usually write their manuscripts and then sell them, but nonfiction authors either get recruited by acquisitions editors or submit proposals to them. Authors often use agents for both sales and proposals, as many publishers prefer not to deal directly with the author.

Nobody Stands Alone—*A good book evolves and grows, thanks to the work of all its editors. It never goes to press looking exactly like it did before the editors worked on it, and that is a good thing. Editors know what a book should look and feel like, what the prose should sound like, what organization, layout, and so on are likeliest to make the author's point to the author's audience. New authors simply don't know these things, and if they refuse to recognize the realities, they are only hurting themselves by self-publishing. E-book conferences draw crowds of people who have the notion that with e-books you can just cut to the chase, removing unnecessary editorial interference. Unfortunately for the self-publisher, editorial work is rarely unnecessary. It's the editors who transform a book into a good book. So please don't think you can skip the editorial process and put out a good book, unless you have years of experience. (At this point you might be thinking the book you're reading evolved and the editors added this Note. But it really was written by the authors.)*

After the acquisitions editors have come up with a book and an author to do the book, they negotiate a contract, often with the help of an agent representing the author. The author now has a book deal. The publisher then assigns the book to a managing editor, who will oversee the writing of the book and the assignment of other editors to help develop the book's content and assure its accuracy. The editing crew can include *developmental editors* who help set the structure and content of the book, *technical editors* who follow the instructions in the text and make sure everything works and is technically accurate, and *copyeditors* who help polish the language so the that message comes across effectively.

The author usually sends each chapter to the managing editor as soon as it's complete, so the production process can move ahead while the book is still in progress. Many publishers now use word processors for everything, so almost every book starts out as something like an e-book. In fact, the actual text you are reading in this book was typed in by us, the authors of the book—it wasn't retyped by someone else at Top Floor Publishing, as it would have been in the old days. The book was developed, checked for technical accuracy, copyedited, and made up into pages all from our original files.

After the editors finish with a file, it goes to the Production department, a group of very talented people who are good at things like understanding how a reader's eyes move about a page. They know where to put a diagram, for instance, so that the reader can easily look at it while reading the text. Most people probably don't realize how much art and psychology is involved in the production process. And again, this is something self-published, first-time authors know little about, unless they have experience in production.

After the layout is complete, the book goes to the printers—and that's where the costs really mount up. Printing is getting more and more costly as paper and other supplies increase in price, and as the specialized equipment grows ever larger and more complex. There's a real economy of scale here—printers tend to charge more per page for little books (because it's just as hard to set up the presses for a small book as a big one) and for short press runs (again because the prep work is the same and there's less product to sell at the end).

And this brings us to an interesting point about e-books: Some publishers are fearful that if they sell a book both as a printed book and an e-book, they will have to cut down on the number of books they print on paper, meaning the cost to print the book actually goes up. Recent studies suggest this might not be true. Still, only time can tell for sure. It's certainly one reason why publishers haven't instantly embraced the e-book world.

What's in Electronic Publishing for Me?

So why would you want to publish electronically? Although even in the late 1990s people had lots of answers to this question, none of them were tested or proven. We now have some solid answers. And over the next couple of years we'll see even more solid answers as people learn the ins and outs of electronic publishing—not by speculating, but by doing.

Consider this for starters: Most of the really big publishers pay authors of nonfiction roughly 8 percent to 10 percent of net sales.

What Does Net Mean?—*The phrase "10 percent of net sales" sounds small enough—and it usually works out to be even smaller than it sounds. Publishers seem to have their own mysterious ways of calculating what exactly net means to bring it down as far as possible. The average $40 computer book brings the author less than a buck a copy.*

Now compare this to an online publisher such as **Fatbrain** (http://www.fatbrain.com). Fatbrain's **MightyWords** site (http://www.mightywords.com), which is now a separate company from Fatbrain, lets anybody upload works to be published electronically from its Web site, and consumers can purchase the documents online and immediately download them. It includes some basic copy protection, and the files are in PDF format. The pay? Fifty percent of gross. A $20 computer book, for instance, would get the author $10 per copy. (Note that it might seem like we're comparing apples and oranges, with a $40 printed book versus a $20 e-book. But that's because right now, it's not clear yet that consumers will be willing to pay full printed-book price for an e-book.) So you, the author, would get $10 per copy, rather than a measly 90 cents or whatever.

But there are drawbacks as well. You're on your own for the editing, layout, and marketing—remember, all that good stuff a publisher gives you. (But have no fear, that's where this book can help. The parts that follow the first four chapters give you loads of goodies about how you can make all that happen for yourself.)

And another drawback is—at least right now—you're unlikely to see sales as high as you would with a printed book. But again, with the marketing methods laid out in Part III, *Getting Your E-Book Published and Sold*, it will certainly be possible.

So those are the drawbacks, but as you can see, $10 per book is a much better deal than under a buck. And the great thing is, even though you're self-publishing, you don't incur enormous printing costs. And since it's electronic, it's easy for you to try out e-book publishing.

These are all arguments that have been made for some time, before the e-publishing business began to prove itself. And they still stand. But there's more. For instance, it's proving to be much easier to get self-published in e-book format. Even some high-profile, well-known authors have had certain works rejected by publishers, but the authors were able to get these works published as e-books. The works were rejected not because they were bad works; rather, the publishers felt they couldn't command a large enough sales volume. And then for some e-books, once the book proved itself as an e-book, traditional publishers were willing to pick it up and carry it as a printed title.

Also, publishers don't have much room for a small novella unless they happen to have a collection that they can put it in. Electronic publishing, however, is an ideal place for smaller works, as the electronic publishers have no economies of scale pushing them to produce the bigger stuff instead.

The Current State of E-Publishing

E-publishing is still brand new, and it hasn't yet settled down. But we can say that it's definitely happening, whether people like it or not—and many people certainly do have opinions about it. And now is your chance to get in on it.

The biggest software manufacturers have embraced it. All of the big publishing houses are talking about adding e-publishing divisions, and some have already started. New and small online-only publishing companies have opened up for business.

So now let's take a look at what exactly an e-book is and go into a bit more detail about the software and hardware that let you view e-books. We'll tackle that in the next chapter.

CHAPTER TWO

What's an E-Book?

It's important to understand what exactly an e-book is. You can't join the fun if you don't know what they're all about.

As we mentioned in the preceding chapter, there are two aspects to e-books: software and devices. In fact, the very term *e-book* sometimes causes confusion. You may have noticed in Chapter 1, "Understanding Electronic Publishing," that sometimes we referred to the text as an e-book: Jim was reading an e-book called *Zen and the Art of Basketweaving*. Or sometimes we referred to the device or software as an e-book: Julie was reading *Zen and the Art of Basketweaving* on her e-book.

In general, we'll use the term *e-book* to describe the actual text (á la the first example about Jim's reading). The devices and software will be called either e-book devices and e-book software or e-book readers and e-book reader software.

Sometimes we'll use the term *content* to mean the text. For some reason, people in the industry like to use this rather dry word, but it usually refers to the collective of works, rather than an individual e-book. In either case, you'll be able to figure out which we mean easily enough.

Types of Electronic Content

Because of the Internet, books now can live in dozens of online formats. Different companies have come up with all different ways to create and view electronic content. And more often than not, it's a matter of the people who create the methods believing dearly that their method is the best and most important. Here's a selection:

- Some people believe books should be read on Web sites, and not permanently saved to your computer.
- Other people believe books should be downloaded to your computer, and permanently saved and not moved.

- Others believe books should be downloaded to your computer, and from there you should be able to put them on any of your computers.
- Others believe books should be downloaded to your computer but only temporarily, as though you'd borrowed them from a library.
- Still others believe the books should be somehow sent electronically to the consumer, but ultimately printed.

And boy do they believe it. If you go to an e-book conference, you will hear people debating about which way is best. (Of course what it really comes down to is the fact that they believe their own way is best because they've gotten venture capitalists to invest millions in their way and there's a lot hanging over their heads!)

E-Books

It might seem silly to talk about the types of e-books and have a section called e-books. But the whole concept of electronic content is very broad and covers different areas, e-books being just one of these.

Typically e-books include books that are read on the e-book devices as well as books that can be read using software specifically created for viewing e-books, such as the Microsoft Reader (for use on Windows and Pocket PC) or the Peanut Reader put out by **peanutpress.com** at http://www.peanutpress.com/ for use on Palm and Windows CE/Pocket PC.

eMatter

This is a trademarked term coined by **Fatbrain.com** (http://www.fatbrain.com) and referring to a type of electronic content available from **MightyWords** (http://www.mightywords.com/), a separate company spawned from Fatbrain, and partly owned by Barnes & Noble. On this site (see Figure 2.1) you can find lots of different kinds of electronic content, including novels, short stories, short technical papers, and longer technical manuals. All the material requires Adobe's Acrobat or Acrobat Reader product, and the files typically have copy protection (except for the free files).

The site used to be a place where anybody could upload pretty much anything, and reap 50 percent royalties. However, just as we were writing this book, things changed. While anybody can still submit anything, it goes through a very strict filtering process to make sure it fits what MightyWords wants to sell. Check out the MightyWords site to find out more information.

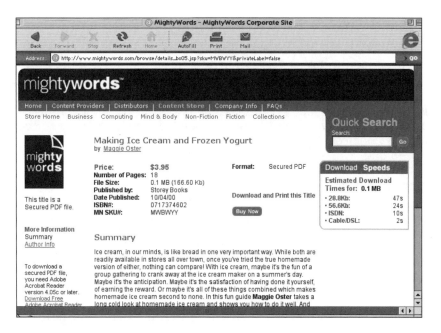

Figure 2.1: The MightyWords site brings a wide array of literature to your screen (and a steady flow of bucks to participating authors).

Print On Demand

There's a new method of book printing that holds a lot of promise, called Print On Demand (or just POD). The idea is that since regular printed books have for some time lived electronically all the way to the printers, why not put small print engines in bookstores, and instead of shipping the printed books, just ship those same files that would normally have gone off to the big printers?

Up-front printing costs would plummet, and there'd be no waste or returns. You, as a consumer, would simply go to the bookstore, request a book, and *shazam!* someone would print up the book for you right then and there.

This technology already exists, and several companies are working on it. Interestingly, the main players are the printing and distribution companies, such as **Ingram** (with its Lightning Source company, http://www.lightningsource.com/) and **Baker & Taylor** (http://www.btol.com/). If you think about it, it makes sense, since POD has the potential to compete with the printing companies, as you'll note we said earlier, "just ship those files that would normally have gone off to the big printers." So instead of losing business, the printing companies are embracing the new technology and complementing their business.

The plan is that POD kiosks (dare we say POD pods?) will eventually be in all the bookstores. And the really cool thing is that these books are virtually indistinguishable from the normal printed version.

In Chapter 3, "New Ways of Publishing," we'll take a more detailed look at Print On Demand, as this is a big technology coming quickly, and deserves a bigger mention about how it relates to the writing and publishing business.

Book-Fame! I'm Gonna Live Forever!*—Right now there's a problem brewing in the industry. Many older book contracts talk about giving the publishers rights to the book until it goes out of print, at which point the rights go back to the author. But what if a book can live indefinitely—forever, even—via Print On Demand but sales drop to one or two books per year? Agents are scrambling to make sure that authors are protected from this.*

Online Libraries

One rather unusual use of the e-book concept is the online library. There are a few out there, the biggest one probably being **NetLibrary** (http://www.netlibrary.com/).

NetLibrary's concept will sound familiar: You go to the library, find a book you want, and check it out. While you've got it, nobody else can read it. (It's checked out to you, after all.) Then, before the due date, you return it. After that, somebody else can check it out.

That all sounds familiar...except it's all online. It's an e-book. It's all done electronically. You download the e-book and can read it, and while it's checked out, other people cannot download it and read it. After you check it back in, you can't read it anymore. The site is shown in Figure 2.2.

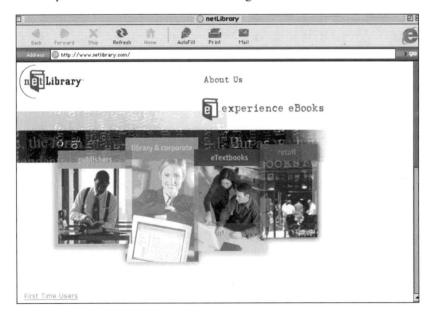

Figure 2.2: At the NetLibrary site you can read your fill—assuming nobody's beaten you to the book you want.

Online Knowledgebases

A slightly modified version of the e-book concept is the online *knowledgebase*—basically a pile of information that you can search through. This is something that we won't talk a whole lot about here because it's not quite in the e-book world, but it should probably be mentioned because of its relationship to e-books.

Several companies are putting up knowledgebases these days. The idea behind a knowledgebase is that you go to the Web site knowing what information you want to look up. You start with the site's search engine, in which you type a couple of words or a phrase representing the topic. You click Find and receive a list of matching entries for you to click.

What we just described may sound a bit like a Web search engine (such as **Yahoo!**, http://www.yahoo.com/). But it's not the same. Whereas a Web search engine searches through Web sites, a knowledgebase searches through information typically stored on a single Web site, and normally you'll be searching for information, not for Web pages.

Some examples of online knowledgebases include

- **Merriam-Webster's** site (http://www.m-w.com/), where you can look up any word in a Merriam-Webster dictionary or thesaurus.
- **Encyclopaedia Britannica** (http://www.britannica.com/), which includes the full text to the famous encyclopedia as well as hundreds of popular magazine articles.
- **Microsoft's Encarta** (http://www.encarta.com/), which contains an entire knowledgebase and online learning center. This site is shown in Figure 2.3.
- **Infoplease Encyclopedia and Dictionary** (http://www.infoplease.com/encyclopdict.html), which gives you a wonderful encyclopedia, dictionary, and several almanacs.

Online Courseware

Right now, the e-book industry and the electronic courseware industry are, for the most part, disjoint. They even have their own conventions (e-courseware tends to meet in Los Angeles, e-books tend meet in New York and San Francisco). Seriously.

As you can imagine, the e-courseware industry has a lot going on now that nearly everybody owns computers and most schools are filled with the things. There's a whole world of possibilities for online learning, from using the Internet for remote classrooms with students scattered all about the world to classrooms

Figure 2.3: Microsoft's Encarta site—way more than an encyclopedia.

where the students sitting beside each other can do interactive learning exercises on their own computers at their desks.

However, because the folks in the courseware industry are more interested in how people learn and how people can have interactive experiences, they aren't doing as much in the textbook industry. The e-book people, however, are moving forward in the textbook industry, working to get textbooks (without the multimedia experience yet) onto the screens of the students.

The worlds will certainly converge, but right now the technologies are spread out a bit. If both e-books and online courseware are your cup of tea, hang in there, because the two will come together within the next couple of years, once the technologies are firmly in place.

If you're interested in studying more about online courseware, here are a couple of books, which you can find at **Amazon.com** (http://www.amazon.com/).

- *Building Learning Communities in Cyberspace: Effective Strategies for the Online Classroom,* by Rena M. Palloff and Keith Pratt.
- *The Online Teaching Guide: A Handbook of Attitudes, Strategies, and Techniques for the Virtual Classroom,* edited by Ken W. White and Bob H. Weight.

On the Web, a good starting point is the **Web-based Education Commission,** at http://www.hpcnet.org/webcommission/.

Other Online Information

You'll find several different philosophies about how books should be presented online. Should you read books online using your Web browser and Internet connection, or should you be able to download them and read them when you're disconnected? If you can read them only online, what do you do if you want to read while you're on an airplane? But if you can download them to your computer, what is to stop you from giving them to friends?

The copy protection issue makes for some particularly interesting problems and issues. One approach is that before you can open a document on your computer, your computer sends out a request to some other computer (called a server), which either grants or denies your rights to read the document. Or, it might grant a partial right, allowing you to see only certain parts of the document. It also might track which pages you access and for how long you have them on your screen. (But if you think about it, that's not very useful in determining how much time it took you to read it: If you had a page on your screen for two hours it might be because you went to lunch and left it open but never actually read it!)

Sound like Big Brother? (Not the TV show; George Orwell's charming head of state!) It does to a lot of people. As it happens, this form of the technology is finding its way mostly into online corporate documents, as the e-book community has little interest in it. Most people who write e-books are not interested in tracking such information—and the creators of e-books also read e-books and don't want somebody tracking their every move. Further, if e-books did track consumers, the people would certainly be very unhappy about it, and e-books would probably be a flop. Therefore, most of the companies that have created such technologies have modified their software to work on a more personal level—that is, a level where you can download items to your computer and take them on your laptop on the airplane, and they maintain their copy protection. Companies that have created various forms of copy-protection technologies include **ContentGuard** (a spin-off company from Xerox, at http://www.contentguard.com/), **InterTrust** (http://www.intertrust.com/), **Softlock** (http://www.softlock.com/), and **Reciprocal** (http://www.reciprocal.com/).

For other online approaches, some companies are exploring ways to let you read parts of books on the Internet until you pay, at which point you can read any of the book on the Internet. You can't download the entire book in one shot; instead, you can only view a page at a time. (They figure you won't bother to save each page as you download it until you've got the entire book.) A slightly alternate version of this can be found at **books24x7.com** (http://www.books24x7.com/), which is an e-publishing source primarily for technical books that have already been published on paper. This company allows you to sign up for a free trial. During the free trial you can read any page of a book, until you reach a certain number of pages. After that you can continue reading, but portions of the book will be scrambled. Once you pay, then you can read any part of the book. Books24x7.com works on a subscription basis.

A similar company is **iBooks.com** (http://www.ibooks.com/). You can purchase books and read them online, all within your Web browser. You can also do a full-text search of all the books on the site. If you haven't purchased a book, you can still do a search and look into a book, but some of the text will be garbled on the pages that you view. (For example, some sentences will be gibberish, like "Kon cuemjke, htc uhsnfnmh kwrmksns.") Like books24x7, iBooks.com primarily publishes books that have already been published in paper format, and it receives these books through arrangements with the publishers.

One interesting company in this area is **Bookface.com**, http://www.bookface.com/. Like the others discussed in this section, you can read online using your Web browser. But Bookface books are free. The site's claim is that reading books online is like watching TV: It's financed through advertising. For the authors, this might not be the best arrangement. Imagine a whole world like that: Eating at a restaurant would be free, but you're forced to watch ads that appear on your dinner plate. And the companies that advertise on the dinner plate? Their products are free as well, but come with ads for other companies. Sort of like a painting of a painting of a painting of a painting....

Some other companies take the photocopy-machine-in-the-library approach. These people feel you should be able to read and print any page or several pages and pay for only the pages you access, say, at a dime per page—sort of like taking a pile of dimes to the library and photocopying only the pages of the articles and books you want. These companies are primarily appealing to readers of scientific journals.

Downloadable E-Books

In contrast to the companies providing methods of letting people read books online over the Internet using their Web browsers, there are companies whose approach is to let you download the books to your computer, save them on your hard drive, and read them at any time. Typically these books are not read using a Web browser, primarily because Web browsers don't provide much in the way of copy protection. Normally the downloadable books require a proprietary piece of software—that is, you can't just use any e-book reader software to read the book. You have to use a particular piece of software, either one developed by the company that sold you the book or one from a big-name company such as Adobe or Microsoft.

What Makes a Good E-Book?

Now that you've seen the variations in online publishing, you need to know what makes a good e-book. What sells? What doesn't? Throughout this book you'll be reading about different business approaches to making sure your books sell. But all those tips and advice will be for naught if you don't have a good e-book. Here we give you lots of tips on how to make your book an excellent book.

First things first, and this might seem trivial: You want something that's as good as a printed book. Just because getting an electronic book published is easier to arrange than getting a print book published doesn't mean you don't have to work hard. In fact, since e-book publishing is so accessible, we're about to see a flood of e-books. Next time you're at the bookstore (the walk-in kind, not the online kind), head over to the computer book section. You'll quickly see what the latest hot topic is—and that every publisher has a book about that same topic. Think the printed book market is flooded? Just wait until the editorial filters are gone, and everybody who has an idea or thought about a topic publishes it. The flood will be big, and your book is going to be just another one of the 3,000 different titles available for that topic alone.

And that's for nonfiction. Fiction is likely to start out not quite as bad—but rapidly get worse when all those authors who can't sell their works realize they can easily self-publish on the Internet. Soon after the nonfiction market is flooded, the fiction market will get flooded even more than the nonfiction market.

So how do you make your book stand out? First and foremost, it shouldn't just be good. It should be great. And it certainly needs to be better than all that unedited, self-serving junk that surrounds it. (Are things really going to be that bad? Unedited, self-serving junk? We certainly hope not, but fear that it will be. We've both been around the block on this one—Jeff as an editor and Chris as a literary agent—and we know firsthand how much more material is looking for a home than can find one on the printed page. All those rejected books have the potential of finding their way into electronic media.)

And how do you make your book great? You need to learn how to write well.

Forgive us if that's a bit blunt or condescending, but there's always more to learn. Personally, we're always looking for ways to improve our writing, and even the best writers are, too. Times change, writing styles change, and what's considered good today may not have been considered good last year.

So now let's take a look at some general guides on making your e-book the best it can be.

Study, Study, Study!

If you're interested in learning the nuts and bolts about professional writing, subscribe to **Writers Digest Book Club** (http://www.writersdigest.com/). Order the books that interest you. Most are excellent, especially those that are written by well-known authors and established editors. And while you're at it, you might subscribe to the *Writers Digest* magazine as well. *The Writer* is also a good magazine. Buy them. Read them. Learn them.

Second, follow the advice a great writer once gave Jeff: Buy William Zinsser's *On Writing Well* and memorize every word. (Thanks, Tom Swan!) You can find it on **Amazon.com** (http://www.amazon.com/). Come to think of it, Jeff realized while writing this that he needs to go back and reread it and save this book's copyeditor some work. He recently used some of Zinsser's advice while writing a magazine article: Go through the draft and remove the unnecessary words, trimming it down so that it says the same thing in as few words as possible. That was a good idea, considering he went way over the word count, rambling on and on. (Editors really don't like it when you go over word count, because it throws off their page count and layout.) So Jeff needed some advice like that. He went through and trimmed and trimmed. He took adjective–noun combinations and replaced them with a single, more powerful noun. He cut out redundant phrases, replacing things like "I felt the software product—" with "The software—" and so on. Soon he had the article well within the limit. He submitted it, and the editor sent back an e-mail note congratulating him on what a great article he had written. Now Jeff knows the real reason the editor felt that way. It wasn't that it was really all that great (it was just a short product review, really), but Jeff took care of the polishing instead of leaving it to the editor. Instead of having to mark it all up and trim it down to make it fit, the editor felt it was *already* perfect (that is, it looked the way the editor would have made it). It really wasn't that hard to follow Zinsser's advice—and in the end, Jeff was getting calls from the editor for more articles.

Practice, Practice, Practice

Jeff recently found the files of one of his first magazine articles from several years ago. He was shocked. Was his writing really that bad back then? He suspects in ten years he'll look back and say the same thing about his writing today.

We improve by doing. Sure, you can read a book about swimming. But it's not until you've jumped into the pool—not once, but hundreds of times—that you actually improve. Same with writing. Practice. Write. Do it. Often.

Be Humble

Never turn away a good editing job. Think of it this way: If somebody takes an hour or two out of their busy life to completely cover your work with red marks, consider it a compliment. Think how much better your work will be after you make all the changes.

Next, respect the readers. They know best. After all, they're the ones paying you. And a million people can't be wrong. Deliver what they want and your wallet will be happy.

If your ego just can't allow you to submit to such things, look at it this way: It's the readers who are filling your bank account. If you have to give in to their silly expectations, then do so, remembering that you have a better copy sitting in the "version 1" folder on your computer's hard drive, which you can get out anytime you want and read it in the self-gratifying privacy of your own home.

Good Grammar Is Your Friend

Imagine if you opened up this book you're reading and you saw this gem: *Me and the other authors of this bok have includee alot of good advice on publshing e-books.*

Depending on your feelings toward such grammar and spelling problems, you might just shrug it off and keep reading—or you might cringe and choke. But either way, it will leave a lasting impression on you regarding the credentials of the authors, Top Floor Publishing, and the publisher's employees. And once you start wondering that, you'll be likely to question the technical accuracy of the information in the book. If the people can't even spell correctly or use good grammar, how can they possibly know how to write and market a good book?

And so it is with all books. You need your grammar and spelling to be correct. How can you get it right? First, keep a grammar guide handy. Some people like the *Chicago Manual of Style*. Others like the *New York Times Style Guide*. They're both good, and they're both reputable. And if there's a disagreement between two guides, and you find yourself arguing over whether to put quotes around words following *so-called*—then it sounds like you're in pretty good shape with your understanding of the English language. So get a copy of one of these books and use it.

A Good Editor Is Worth a Thousand Misspelled Words

Okay, cute title for this section, but a good edit job versus a bad edit job can make or break your book. Having no edit at all is likely to kill it completely.

So what do we mean by "edit"? As you may have seen in Chapter 1, "Understanding Electronic Publishing," there are actually several different kinds of editors who work for a publishing company. However, here we mean more along the lines of a copyediting job—often miscalled proofreading by those who aren't sure what goes on with either. While many authors can certainly benefit from a full edit, including content editing and so on, for most self-published authors, that's a bit out of reach due simply to the cost involved in hiring such an editor. (Most freelance development or content editors of computer books charge over a thousand dollars—sometimes well over—per book.) But every book can benefit from a good copyedit, correcting misspelled words and grammar problems along with other high-level problems such as saying "in the next chapter we talk about—" and then forgetting to talk about it.

In other words, get a good second pair of eyes, at the very least. But if you can afford to fork out some cash for more than the bare minimum, you should consider hiring a professional copy or manuscript editor. This person can go through your book and fix many problems that you are unlikely to catch for yourself.

Writing Courses

You can find writing courses in many different places (such as universities and community colleges), but since you're interested in e-books, you might be interested in online courses.

One e-book company, **iUniverse.com** (http://www.iuniverse.com/), provides a whole series of online courses, found at http://www.iuniverse.com/marketplace/ learn_online/wri_university.asp. We have not personally taken any of them, so we cannot vouch for them. However, you'll find a wide range of courses that you can browse through—take a look at the course outlines, and the prices. The prices are quite reasonable when you compare them to, for instance, a university course.

Hyperlink Overload

Since your book is online, and not just printed, you should consider adding certain online features such as hyperlinks. However, consider this before you venture in and add a gazillion hyperlinks in your document: It's easy for people to get lost or confused if there's too much bouncing around within a book. Jeff was reading a book online and the page he was reading was filled with underscored words, each one a hyperlink to another page in the same book. As he got to each one, he wasn't sure if he was expected to click on the hyperlink to understand the rest of the chapter. "Click here or you'll be confused" was what it seemed like, although it wasn't clear. So he clicked the first one and ended up on another page somewhere in the book, and that page was filled with hyperlinks. Soon it felt like he was surfing the whole Internet, bouncing from page to page and getting completely lost, yet staying within one book. It was frustrating. He eventually realized the people who made the book thought it would be nice if the every word that had any relation to another page of the book were hyperlinked to that page. But the truth is it made for a very messy, unmanageable book. So here's the moral: Don't go overboard on the hyperlinks. You might think you are doing your readers an extra service, but really, you aren't.

Click Here, I Dare You

Another tidbit about the online experience is this: Make sure your book is still useful when printed. Plan that eventually it might find its way into a printed medium, whether it's your consumers' own home printers or an actual print publication with a first run of 10,000 copies. If you add hyperlinks where the user is required to click, or if you refer to the hyperlink without giving the address, you could have a problem when it's printed. Have you ever printed up a Web site? You might see something like this:

Click here to send me mail.

Go ahead, click it. Obviously you can't if you're reading this on a printed page. But the online version has my e-mail address hidden behind it. What's my e-mail address? When the page is printed, it's gone and nowhere to be found.

A better approach would be something like this:

If you want to send me e-mail, my address is jeffcogs@yahoo.com.

The e-mail address is clickable in the online version, and for the print folks, it's clearly written out.

From Rags to Online

The same book that had too many hyperlinks also had another problem: It was clear the publisher had simply taken the files for the printed version of the book and saved them in a hypertext format, adding a gazillion hyperlinks. Whoever did the deed overlooked a problem, however. The whole thing was arranged in order by page, with no notion of chapters. There were statements such as

See the next chapter for more information.

all over the place. And wouldn't you know, this time...there was no hyperlink! So how could one get to the next chapter? There were no chapter headings, nothing, only page after page after page. In other words, there was absolutely no way to know where the next chapter was. All you could do was read on and hope to one day see it on the side of the road.

Different Reader Software

Although it's true that almost all the reader software packages are named Reader (Microsoft Reader, Adobe Acrobat Reader, Glassbook Reader, and so on), it's also true that they do not read the same file formats—and they handle different issues differently, such as the placing of figures and the pagination.

Further, there's the possibility that in the future when you write an e-book, you'll save it in one format, and from there it will be viewable on several different reader software packages and on several different computers, from tiny palm-size computers to desktops and everything in between.

Look at a recent printed textbook with lots of diagrams and figures. You'll notice that when you open the pages, the publisher was very aware that you would be looking at the whole spread of the two pages. Figures will be placed carefully, with text appearing around them to set them off and enhance the message. Other times you won't get a sense of what comes first and what comes next. Some photos or figures will spread across both pages—either helping you follow the text or making it harder, depending on how well the designer thought through the layout.

Now think about what it'll take to put that online, so it can be read on a small palm-size computer with a two-inch by three-inch screen. It's not going to be easy, and there are no solid answers yet about what's best. Online book companies and publishers are still pondering the problem. Some suggest having just the text. Some suggest having the whole page and letting you scroll within it. Others say have the images, but let them be clickable.

Since you're going to be doing your own layout, the following sections take up a couple of these problems.

Pagination

Since you're making sure your book can be useful in both print and online formats, you need to be aware of a problem in going between the two: pagination. When Jeff (the primary author for this chapter) looks at this page as he's writing, because of the zoom factor he sees as the top line the sentence that says, "The e-mail address is clickable—" (just above the "From Rags to Online" header) and the bottom is the line that follows this one. But as you look at the book, unless there was some printing miracle, chances are you see a very different set of first and last lines. The printed page is almost always a different size from the page viewed on the screen.

Different reader software packages handle this problem differently. Some assume the page is bigger than the screen or window, and require a human to scroll within a page and then click a button to get to the next page. Others will completely repaginate the document.

Repagination is typically not a problem with fiction, since it's rare the text will refer to itself. Nonfiction, however, is another story—it tends to be full of references to other paragraphs, pages, or chapters. In an e-book, it's still okay for the author to refer to what someone just read in the preceding paragraph. But because of the possibility of repagination, it's best not to refer to the next page or the preceding page. Instead, refer to section and chapter headers.

No, This Image, Not That Image!

Just as with pages, it's unwise to refer to images by their position in the text. Don't say, "The figure to the right shows—." Instead, number your figures and refer to them by number. That way you'll be ready for nearly all the different kinds of online layout, should your book end up living in multiple formats. Further, it's a good idea to put enough information in your text so that it will stand on its own if the figures get dropped by a reader device that doesn't support anything but words in a row.

Reader Devices and Software

The devices and software have their own little tricks over and above the problems you get into with formatting. It's useful to explore these things in a little more detail here, and then we can put it together and talk about the pagination and image-handling issues and how they fit together with these devices.

Hardware Devices

At the time of this writing there are a few popular devices on the market; two of the most popular are the Softbook Reader and the Rocket eBook. The two companies that make these devices, Softbook Press and NuvoMedia, used to be separate companies; in early 2000 they were both purchased by the same company (Gemstar International Group Limited, which also owns *TV Guide* magazine). Since that purchase, Gemstar has phased out the original Softbook Reader and Rocket eBook and replaced them with two new models that bear the RCA name. The Softbook model has been replaced by the model called REB1200, and the Rocket model has been replaced by the model called REB1100.

The different brands of hardware devices share many elements. One common gripe people have about many of these devices is that they lack organizer software such as calendars, address books, and so on. However, in late 2000, Franklin introduced the eBookMan, which includes such software.

Nokia and other mobile phone manufacturers are always present at the e-book conferences. Supposedly they have plans to put some sort of e-book software on the tiny little displays of their cell phones. When they mention this, some people applaud, others scoff at the idea of reading book pages the size of matchbooks. As of late 2000, however, such devices do not yet have reader software.

The following sections discuss the two mentioned products from Gemstar and the one from Franklin.

Gemstar REB1200

The REB1200 from Gemstar, the successor to the Softbook Reader, is a handheld device with a display that's 8 inches measured diagonally, weighing in at 33 ounces, slightly more than 2 pounds. The Softbook Reader came in a protective leather case that gave it that "executive look" (for better or worse); the new REB1200 is bare. It has a touch-sensitive screen, and you use a stylus to point to it. Whereas the Softbook Reader had a grayscale screen (meaning it showed several shades of gray), the REB1200's screen is a full-color, VGA screen, 640 pixels wide by 800 pixels tall. The device includes both a built-in rechargeable battery and an AC adapter for plugging it into the wall. It includes 8MB of RAM, with a CompactFlash slot, which is the same kind of memory expansion slot found in digital cameras. Using this slot, you can put up to 128MB of memory in the REB1200.

The software installed on the REB1200 is proprietary reader software; it only reads files created specifically for that type of device; these files were formerly called Softbook Editions. The claim is that it's based on the Open eBook standard, although you can't just suck in any file created to this format. (We'll be talking about file formats in more detail in Chapter 4, "The Production Process.")

The device also has a built-in 56 Kbps modem, along with a 10Base-T Ethernet adapter. The Ethernet adapter means you can hook it into a network like the kind found in most corporations as well as home networks. Using the modem, you can dial out onto the Internet and connect to a special site to buy and download books without the need for a computer—which makes this device especially valuable for readers who want to use it on a stand-alone basis, say, because they're traveling light. Or, if you have the device hooked into a network, you can do the same thing over the network connection, provided the network is connected to the Internet.

Like most of these devices and software packages, the REB1200 opens to a library screen showing the different books currently installed in the thing. It seems every single software package and device has this feature, although each company that makes these devices and software takes particular pride in its own library. The basic gist is that the library screen displays the books installed on your device, and you can click a book's title to open the book. With the REB1200, this library is actually a double library. You can have books stored on your own device, and you can also have books stored on your own private "online personal library" at the mentioned site on the Internet. Unfortunately, you cannot transfer books from your PC to the REB1200; in fact, such books never live on a PC. So how do you get books between your PC and your REB1200? Get ready for this: You upload it from your PC over the Internet to your private "online personal library" and then you hook your REB1200 device up to the phone line, dial in, and download it—or, if you're on a network, transfer it over the Internet down to the REB1200.

While reading books, you can use the stylus to scribble notes and images on the pages; the device saves your scribbles in its memory. However, you can't *type* notes, so you have to at least try to write legibly. Unfortunately, when using a stylus on a touch-sensitive screen, that's easier said than done. One demo REB1200 at a conference had all the scribbles of the hundreds of people passing by, and most of it was indecipherable. But if you write carefully, your writing will be readable.

Gemstar has lots of books available for the device. The books range from popular fiction (Stephen King, Mary Higgins Clark, and many others) to popular nonfiction (travel, sports, and so on). You can also subscribe to news magazines and papers, such as *Time* and the *Wall Street Journal*.

Gemstar REB1100

The Gemstar REB1100, formerly the Rocket eBook, is similar in many ways to the Gemstar REB1200. Originally, it was a competitor, until Gemstar bought both companies. One benefit to having both products manufactured under the same umbrella is that now we can hope there will be some compatabilities soon. In the past, neither device could display the other's e-book files. Unfortunately, that is still the case, although Gemstar claims to be investigating ways to share text between the two.

The REB1100 looks similar to its big sibling, the REB1200. The REB1100 weighs about half as much, at 17 ounces, slightly more than a pound. The screen has a greenish tone to it, but unlike the REB1200 is not in color. (Technically it's "monochrome," meaning it doesn't have gray scale; it only shows two different colors.) It does, however, display graphics, and the graphics are reasonably clear and easy to follow. The REB1100 has a touch screen, through which you can highlight text and enter notes.

The REB1100 includes a 56 Kbps modem, just like the REB1200, so that you can download e-books. Unlike the REB1200, the REB1100 can be hooked up to a desktop computer (PC or Mac) using either a USB or infrared connection, through which you can transfer e-books. Normally you visit a Web site on your desktop, and when you find an e-book you want to download, you enter a special code that represents your REB1100. This code tells the Web site a particular encryption key for your particular device, and the book is encrypted and then downloaded to your desktop computer. You then transfer it to your e-book device using a software program called (you guessed it!) Librarian. Because the encryption uses a code specific to your device, if you hook up a different REB1100 to your desktop, you cannot transfer the same book to that device. You have to download a new copy, entering the new code. This may or may not mean paying extra money, depending on whether the content is free or for purchase.

The REB1100 includes 8MB of memory, and can be expanded up to 128MB. Unlike the 1200's CompactFlash, the 1100 uses SmartMedia, which is a different form of memory card.

The REB1100 supports the same format that was used in the former Rocket eBook, called Rocket Editions. Gemstar has said it plans to support the Open eBook standard for both its devices, but (as noted earlier) as of this writing it hasn't gotten around to doing so.

Franklin eBookMan

The **Franklin eBookMan** (http://www.franklin.com/ebookman/default.asp) is a new player in the e-book device field, created by a company that has been making organizer software and devices for some time.

The eBookMan is much smaller than the other devices—only about 5 inches by about 3½ inches—with a 200 × 240 pixel screen. Like the older Softbook Reader, it has a grayscale display—not a color display, but not monochrome either. The screen is small, like a Palm Pilot (in fact, it looks a lot like a Palm Pilot).

This device comes with the reader program from Microsoft, called (unsurprisingly) Microsoft Reader. This means that you can read any book created for Microsoft Reader, which also runs on Pocket PC computers and Windows desktop computers.

The eBookMan is sort of a combination of PDA (Personal Digital Assistant) and e-book. The device comes with a set of organizer software, much like other handheld devices and unlike most e-book devices. One particularly cool thing about this product is it has full multimedia sound. You can listen to audio books, too.

Since the device uses Microsoft Reader, creating content for it is easy; you create content the way you would for any Microsoft Reader. We'll look at this in the next section on software.

Reader Software

This section will explore some of the different software available. As the industry is still quite young, there are only a few readers that have established themselves as leaders in the field; these are the ones that we mention here. As most people would expect, Microsoft has already helped lead the way with its own Reader, which is free of course. For each reader, we look at the features and consider how it relates to your work as a self-published author.

Microsoft Reader

It's no surprise that Microsoft has entered the game, and that its product is already doing quite well. (Partly because it ships automatically with small computers that have Pocket PC on them.) As we've mentioned earlier, Microsoft Reader is available for Pocket PC and for Windows computers, and it's also found on the Franklin eBookMan. This alone make it an attractive option for self-published authors.

Microsoft Reader has several features that you would expect in a reader program. When you start it up, you get an attractive library page, from which you can open the different books you've downloaded. When you open a book, you can highlight selections and make notes. The pages appear as individual pages, and when you "turn" the page, it's like a real book: You get another screenful of text. This is unlike a standard Web browser page where you might have one long page requiring the use of scrollbars.

But this program is interesting when run on a laptop or Pocket PC—that is, any computer that has a color LCD screen. It uses a special technology that Microsoft calls Cleartype. This technology allows the fonts to look smoother than regular fonts on the screen. To some people, however, the technology simply makes the fonts look slightly blurry. However, when we compared it to text rendered with standard font technology, we found that the text really does look more like a printed page than most text. Figure 2.4 shows a screen capture of the Microsoft Reader for a desktop computer.

On the PC, where there's a monitor instead of an LCD screen, the Reader also has some special

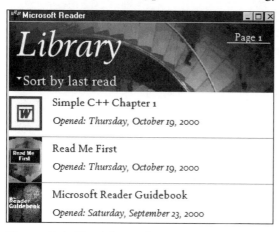

Figure 2.4: The Microsoft Reader gives you a decorative library page.

font-smoothing technology that lets the person using the software choose the type of smoothing from a list of several options. In our opinion, on the desktop computer the fonts do tend to look rather blurry.

Like the various hardware devices, Microsoft Reader claims to support Open eBook. However, also like the devices, it stores files in its own format. Microsoft Reader includes some copy protection to allow you to download e-books that you've paid for, without letting you pass them around.

So There!—*Even though the Gemstar devices and Microsoft Reader all support Open eBook, you cannot transfer files between them. So much for standards. To the manufacturers' defense, though, we should add that the Open eBook standard does not specify a particular file type; instead, it's a standard way of noting certain things internally, like who the author of the book is and such. These things are called metadata.*

There are already lots of titles available for Microsoft Reader, and you can buy them online and download them to your computer. The **Microsoft** site devoted to the reader (http://www.microsoft.com/reader/) has links to sites where you can buy books.

To create books for Microsoft Reader, right now there are a couple of options available. One is to download a free add-in for Microsoft Word, and the other is to download a free program from **Overdrive Systems** (http://www.overdrive.com/), which worked closely with Microsoft in the creation of the reader software. Overdrive also makes several other packages for publishing electronically, but these are primarily intended for big publishing companies.

Peanut Reader

The Peanut Reader from **peanutpress.com** (at http://www.peanutpress.com/; recently acquired by NetLibrary) is for palm-size computers, specifically the Palm, the Handspring, and the Windows CE and Pocket PC computers. Like the other readers, this one has the usual things you would expect from a reader, including copy protection.

The Peanut Reader supports its own file format, with its own copy protection system. For this reason you cannot take a book created for the Peanut Reader and copy it to, say, the Microsoft Reader or any others mentioned in this chapter. So here we go again; no standards and all the players have their own type of reader and their own file format.

To create books for the Peanut Reader, you use a free program from peanutpress.com called MakeBook. MakeBook is actually a Java program, which means you have to install the Java system if you don't have it already. And to use it for the whole job, you need to know how to *mark up* your book's manuscript, which means you need to type in special characters for things like italics or bold. Sounds a bit cumbersome for the people who are not programmers, something like creating Web pages manually.

Fortunately, peanutpress.com also has a macro for Microsoft Word that will insert all the correct markup items into your text for you, making that part a good bit easier. You still have to run the MakeBook program afterwards to convert the book to the Peanut Reader format.

The MakeBook utility and the Word macro are available for free from the peanutpress.com Web site.

Unfortunately, you cannot create books with copy protection in this format. So when you consider whether you want your content to be available for Peanut Reader, remember that people will be able to freely copy anything you create for it.

MobiReader

The MobiReader from **Mobipocket.com** (http://www.mobipocket.com/) is another reader for small computers, including the Palm OS (Palm, Visor) and the Windows CE and Pocket PC computers.

Jeff particularly likes the MobiReader software, because it's easy to configure. You can choose the font size, the font type, and the screen color as you're reading. He prefers a blue background with light blue text, which is easily configurable—and not the sort of thing any manufacturer is likely to come up with as a standard offering.

When MobiPocket started out, the company took the stand that books should be free. Therefore, all the books were free, and there was no real copy protection in the software. However, as we write this, the company appears to be changing this model and planning to sell commercial works, which would make it necessary to charge for the books. Check the site to see how this is coming along.

As with the others, you can create e-books for the MobiReader using software downloadable from the company site. We're not sure at this point if you'll be able to encrypt your works, or if you're stuck making freebies. Check their Web site for updates to see if this situation changes.

Infinite Ink

Infinite Ink started as a small company that made its voice heard throughout the industry. The two guys who run the company are active on standards committees and eager to give energetic talks at conferences. However, their product has not yet gained widespread acceptance. And despite their role on the standards committees, their software does not yet support the standards. Instead, it uses its own file format.

Infinite Ink software presents books much like a Web browser would, with long pages rather than a page-by-page metaphor like the Microsoft Reader. It features a rather powerful search engine, however, where the user can search for words and easily navigate through the book.

This software was one of the first to support a purchasing approach that goes like this: Before you buy a book, you can look at it in a preview mode, where you can only see certain portions of it. The parts you cannot see are blocked out with little square boxes. (Apparently the creator of the work can choose what the blocked-out portions will look like.) When you decide you want the book, you go online, give a credit card number, and download a "voucher" to your computer. This voucher is specific to your computer; once it's present, you can view the entire book. If you attempt to put the voucher on another computer, it will not work, meaning you cannot copy the book to another computer. In other words, the book has copy protection.

As it happens, although this software has not taken off (perhaps due to marketing issues) the technology did capture the attention of a company called InterTrust. InterTrust has created (and patented, so be warned!) a similar technology that's primarily used in music. The InterTrust folks license the technology to various companies. They apparently liked Infinite Ink's technology, because they bought the company.

Although the software includes many good features, you'll want to weigh it like any others in terms of e-book availability and general features such as its Web browser look (possibly a negative) and excellent search engine (a definite plus).

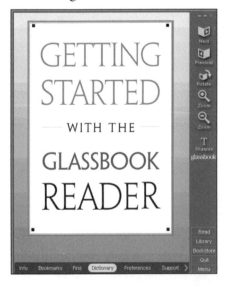

Figure 2.5: The Glassbook Reader—all the world's PDF files in your hand.

Glassbook Reader

The Glassbook Reader, from **Glassbook** (http://www.glassbook.com/) is the Cadillac of the e-book world. It features a user interface that most people would hesitate to call anything but classy or even beautiful, as illustrated in Figure 2.5. The people at Glassbook have gone a long way in making it easy to use.

The Glassbook Reader does not support Open eBook; instead it has full support of the PDF standard created by Adobe. In fact, the Glassbook Reader, in addition to offering its own copy protection and encrypted file format, can open any PDF file. You can use it as your default PDF viewer, in place of Adobe Acrobat Reader. (We talk about Acrobat Reader in the next section.)

Like the others, this reader has several good features: A library that shows what books you own and makes it easy for you to navigate through the books, a search engine, and a highlighter. Plus, the Glassbook Reader has a "sub-pixel" font rendering system, similar to Microsoft's ClearType.

There are actually two different versions of the Glassbook Reader, a free version and a bigger one that's not free but has more features, including a full *American Heritage Dictionary* from the Houghton Mifflin Company. When you double-click a word, the reader shows you the definition. For self-published authors, Glassbook Reader includes a highly sophisticated copy protection and book management software package that was created by Glassbook. This package is called EBX (which stands for Electronic Book Exchange), and it even supports advanced features such as loaning, borrowing, and timed limits as with a library. The company claims that this is a standard and will be free for all to use in other software. At the moment, it's not clear whether this is exactly the case, because Glassbook has patented portions of the standard.

However, aside from the political issues that almost certainly arise during a discussion of Glassbook and EBX, the company is on the right track by attempting to create a standard. If other companies can indeed implement EBX in their readers, then the standard could become a reality.

There are several big titles available from Glassbook, as the company is working closely with several book distributors including **Lightning Source** (http://www.lightningsource.com/) and **NetLibrary** (http://www.netlibrary.com/).

As it happens, Glassbook caught the attention (big time) of **Adobe** (http://www.adobe.com/), which has since acquired Glassbook. At the time of this writing, it's unclear how the Glassbook Reader will fit into Adobe's line of products, but we can be assured that it will become bigger and we will see it on a lot of computers.

Adobe Acrobat and Acrobat Reader

Acrobat and Acrobat Reader are siblings. Acrobat Reader is a scaled-down version of Acrobat. The two programs both let you view PDF files.

It's likely that you've seen PDF files already, because a lot of documents on the Web are saved in PDF. It's a big standard. In fact, a lot of online e-book retailers have opted for PDF, including Fatbrain's **MightyWords** (http://www.mightywords.com/).

Acrobat Reader lets you view PDF files, while Acrobat lets you view, create, and manipulate PDF files. If you have Acrobat, you don't need Acrobat Reader. Acrobat Reader is free, but Acrobat is costly, coming in at over $200.

Acrobat itself doesn't (yet) have a Web site associated with it where you can buy e-books—its creator, Adobe, is specifically a software company (a big one, at that). However, Adobe recently acquired Glassbook, which does let you download and purchase e-books.

CHAPTER THREE

New Ways of Publishing

Because of the new technologies of publishing, there are new ways of doing business in the publishing world. New companies are forming in Silicon Valley to provide e-publishing services or software or both; big publishers are adding e-books to their product lines; book distribution companies are getting into the game. New print technology has arrived along with e-books, as well, and companies are getting into that game, allowing bookstores to print up books instantly and either ship them to you immediately or even print them while you wait.

The traditional publishers (the big ones, those that have been around for hundreds of years) are beginning to publish some of their content electronically. However, remember that with these big publishers it will happen very slowly. After all, the big publishers are well-established businesses and they don't just leap at the latest newfangled technology craze. The last thing on their mind is ditching their old, tried-and-true business models for new models. In this case, they aren't about to dump creating paper books. Instead, they view e-books as a possible new thing to try. Fortunately, many of them *are* trying it.

For instance, Simon & Schuster, a huge name in publishing, has made big plans to add electronic books. As we write this, the folks at S&S are working on going digital with dozens of titles. Their titles will be available for numerous readers, including Microsoft Reader, Glassbook Reader, peanutpress.com, and the RCA devices. They have big names such as V.C. Andrews, Jimmy Carter, Mary Higgins Clark, and Stephen King lined up for electronic content. (**Simon & Schuster** has an e-book Web site at http://www.simonsays.com/ebooks.)

Some of the traditional publishers are creating entirely separate e-book editorial groups, with a new set of editors all the way from acquisitions through final editing, while others (such as Simon & Schuster) are using the same editorial staff to edit both paper books and e-books. It's possible that this is because they see e-books not as a separate thing with a separate set of contents, but rather as just another "print" form that happens to be digital. That implies they will be taking books and creating them in both formats, rather than creating some books as paper books and others as e-books. (That means also that authors will have to go the traditional route of getting published electronically with Simon & Schuster and other companies that take this approach.)

Time Warner Books, on the other hand, has created an entirely separate division devoted to e-books, called **iPublish.com** (http://www.ipublish.com). The news and press releases say that this group functions totally separately from its paper-based counterparts. A visit to iPublish.com gives you press releases, as well as a link to the site where you can download the e-books, (http://www.twbookmark.com/ebooks/index.html). This site reveals that the company carries several books in both printed and e-book form. So it appears Time Warner is also still testing the waters with different ways of working the e-book business.

Incidentally, there is an interesting note on the iPublish.com site that says it cannot currently accept submissions until the site "is launched" (whatever that means). That implies that while Time Warner does not yet accept submissions, we can expect that someday it will. As for how Time Warner will go about it when it does, we can't yet say; will the editors accept just anything or will they require authors to follow careful submission procedures and wait for acceptance? You will have to watch the Web site to find out the answer to this.

The New E-Publishers

As with any new technology, Silicon Valley is bubbling over with new dot-com start-ups related to e-book technology. But in addition to the technology companies, several companies (not just in Silicon Valley) are essentially publishing houses that will publish books electronically.

In the late 1990s many of the new companies were forced to create their own software, since quality software just wasn't yet available. They wanted to see themselves as traditional publishing companies that happened to distribute their books electronically rather than in paper form. However, they found they had to act like software or technology companies because the tools they needed for their chosen field simply hadn't been invented yet.

Now that several respected software packages finally are available, the industry is starting to show signs of a separation between those that make software and those that publish books electronically. Microsoft and others are offering reader software and devices, and new companies are springing up that publish books using these products.

Such a division is probably a good thing, because there's an inherent conflict of interest if an e-book software company also publishes books. Other publishers that might be interested in publishing in the software company's electronic format are apt to veer off for fear that the software maker might use its technological know-how to enhance its own published products and interfere with the success of those of competing publishers.

In the sections that follow, we look at what exactly some of these new e-publishing companies do. We also explore a little about how e-book technology is finding its way into corporations other than publishers.

Self-Publishers

There have always been what people in the industry used to call vanity publishers. They were for authors who chose to foot the bill and publish their works themselves. This typically involved paying a publisher to edit and publish a work, although it could also mean paying a printer to print up a book, with the author doing all the hard work of editing and layout (or hiring somebody to do the editing and layout). In the world of paper books, this is no trivial task, mainly because it takes bucks to get your book printed and sent to the bookstores. And it also takes business relationships with distributors and bookstores.

But with the new e-book world, most of those expenses are gone and now it's much easier to self-publish, mainly because anybody with a computer and the right software can convert a book to an electronic format and upload it to a site that distributes self-published material. Or people can just put it on their own Web site and sell it. There's still the issue of getting an e-book into the standard places to sell it—**Amazon.com** (http://www.amazon.com), for instance—although that do-it-all site now has an e-book division of its own.

In the summer of 2000, Stephen King self-published a work in e-book format. He wrote a novel called *The Plant* (about scary things happening at a traditional publishing company!) and he did it entirely electronically and sold it through his Web site, **Stephen King: the official Web presence** (http://www.stephenking.com), shown in Figure 3.1, with the help of Amazon.com. People could download the book for free, and when they were ready to pay for it they headed over to Amazon.com. By the end of 2000, Stephen King said he chose to end *The Plant* temporarily, because of other commitments. He did say that the payments had started to drop off, but strongly implied he was planning to return to the book a year or so later.

Corporate Publishers

Corporate publishing has always been a big market for printers. Corporations produce a lot of documents that they need to publish either for internal reading or for the outside world. They have internal manuals such as employee handbooks; they have external manuals such as the ones that ship with their

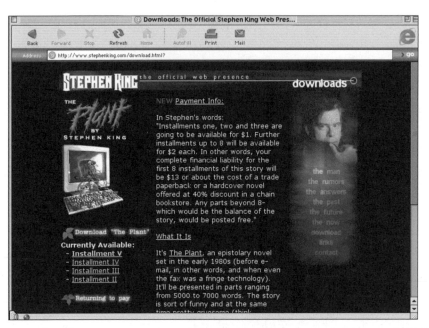

Figure 3.1: Stephen King started to self-publish a book through his own "official Web presence."

products to teach customers how to put together the thingamabob in ten easy steps using only the small tool included.

Corporations discovered some time back that it's easy to publish documents electronically on internal intranets. (An *intranet* is just like the Internet, with files called *pages* and a Web browser that lets people look at them, except the pages are only viewable from computers within the company.) Many companies now put all their internal manuals on their intranet. The reason, of course, is that it saves them tons of money since they don't have to print everything.

Many corporations have also taken to publishing their external documents online. Of course, most of these companies specialize in computer hardware and software, but even some companies outside the computer world have their manuals online. Recently Jeff had to fix his garage door opener. (And incidentally, as he writes this his house in Florida is for sale if anyone wants to buy it!) The garage door opener had broken down (okay, so that's not quite true; it didn't just break: Jeff broke it himself.) Happily, the company that made it—**Genie**—has a terrific Web site (http://www.geniecompany.com). As Figure 3.2 shows, it offers all sorts of online technical support guides. He was able to quickly read the information he needed and figure out that a wire had come loose—and learn how to fix it himself, without having to call a repair person.

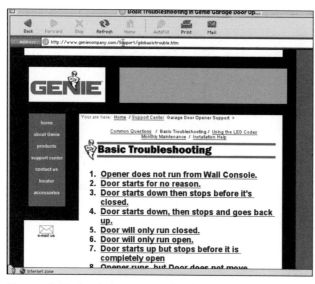

Figure 3.2: Genie has a good online support system.

Corporations may put their manuals on the Internet as Genie did, or, in the case of software companies, they may send a CD-ROM with all the information on it. Some companies don't even send manuals anymore. For years, Borland (now called **Inprise**, http://www.inprise.com) has been including manuals on CD-ROM in PDF format. Recently, Jeff bought some products from Microsoft where all he got was a CD-ROM and a little sheet with installation instructions. The manuals were, of course, on the CD-ROM. (Perhaps it's only a matter of time before Genie starts shipping a CD-ROM with every garage door opener!) Microsoft documents aren't yet available in Microsoft Reader format (because the format is brand new) but perhaps soon Microsoft will ship books in Reader format. Many companies also use Adobe PDF format, requiring Acrobat Reader.

Corporations, then, are faced with many of the same development issues that e-book authors and publishers are dealing with. For example, they might want to prevent certain manuals within their organization from being copied and distributed outside, such as manuals containing trade secrets. Or, if the manuals they ship to customers contain proprietary information, they might not want the customers to be able to make copies and send them to their friends. (In Chapter 5, "Digital Rights and Copy Protection," we cover the different technologies for protecting documents.)

Publisher-Distributors

Another new business model is the company that is both a publisher and a distributor. Even some authors who have published with traditional paper publishers may not realize the role the distributor plays. The distributor gets the books to the bookstores. But sometimes, the distributor is also the printer—that is, it has a contract with the publisher to print the book and then ship it to the bookstores.

With e-publishing, this model changes just a bit, mainly because there's not always reason to ship the book anywhere. It can go right from the publisher's

Web site down to the consumer's computer or to the Web site of a retailer set up for Print On Demand. In this case, the publisher has become the distributor—unless, of course, the publisher uses a third-party retailer such as **Barnes & Noble** (http://www.bn.com) or **Amazon** (http://www.amazon.com) to sell the books. In that case, the book goes right from publisher to retailer, again skipping the distributor.

The idea of publishers selling directly to consumers has problems in itself. Some publishers may not be set up in a business or financial sense to deal directly with consumers. While they might have a Web site, their accounting department might not have systems and processes in place for selling directly to customers, such as processing credit cards and dealing with sales tax. Or, they might not want to deal directly with consumers, because that's not what they do: They publish books and let others deal with the consumers. In those cases, the publishers will require a relationship with a retailer or distributor.

But what role do distributors have in the world of e-books? In early 2000, it was looking like the distributors were more or less out of luck in the e-book world. At the e-book conferences, they were scoffed at by many people and considered unnecessary. But it turns out that in late 2000 the distributors started finding their niche in the e-book industry, doing what they've always done, playing the middleman between publishers and retailers. In late 2000, Ingram—one of the biggest movers of paper books from the publishers into the bookstores—launched its e-book division called **Lightning Source** (http://www.lightningsource.com, shown in Figure 3.3). Ingram doesn't publish e-

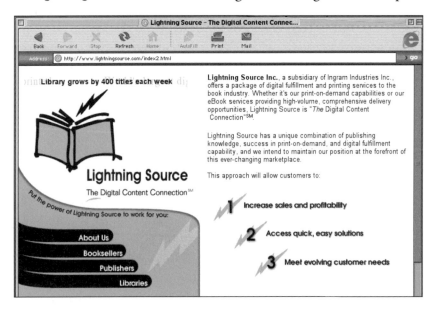

Figure 3.3: Lightning Source has added Print on Demand to distributor Ingram's list of services.

books itself; instead it contracts with e-publishers and helps get the publishers' e-books into various online retail spaces, such as Amazon.com.

Consumer or Customer?—*We use the word consumer to refer to the person who purchases a book to read it or give it away. The word customer doesn't really work, because it means someone different depending on whose customer you're talking about. For example, often the publishers' customers are the distributors and the distributors' customers are the bookstores, while the bookstores' customers are you and your fellows, the consumers. Sort of gives new meaning to the phrase "the customer is always right."*

One-Stop Shopping

The tried-and-true stream of publisher→distributor→retailer→consumer works quite nicely for consumers. If a friend tells you about a great book called *1001 Ways to Download an E-book*, you don't want to have to first dig up the name of the publisher so you can go to its Web site and finally find the book. Quick, who published Stephen King's classic *Salem's Lot*? Imagine if you had to know that first before you could find it. Instead, it's nice to be able to go to any retailer to find books from all different publishers, and it would be nice to know that the different retailers have, for the most part, the same set of publishers. If you want a good book you can drive down the street to either Barnes & Noble or to Border's, and it's likely that both will have it, or that both will be able to get it. Or you can go to Amazon.com and find it online without having to know the publisher. The same should be true for e-books.

While we started this section with ideas about new ways of doing publishing business, we ended it with the old, tried-and-true ways. The truth is that with e-books we're going to see not only the good old ways, which are likely to continue to work in the electronic world, but also new ways. Gradually they will probably come together with a model that offers the best of both worlds.

Print On Demand

In addition to the various ways of bringing e-books to the consumer's computer or reader device, there's another new way of publishing that's closely related to e-books. Big hardware companies, such as IBM, have taken printing technology and advanced it to the point where it's now possible to print books far more quickly and cheaply than it used to be. Using some of the new printing equipment, it's possible to print one single book at the same printing cost per book as it used to cost to print books in batches of thousands. Because of this, companies and even some retailers are now purchasing these printing systems and providing a service called *Print On Demand*.

We briefly alluded to Print On demand (or POD) in Chapter 2, "What's an E-Book?" So what is POD? Not to sound like one of those "imagine if—" ads, but imagine if you go to your neighborhood Barnes & Noble, ask for a book, and it's not there—so the clerk goes to a machine that looks kind of like a laser printer and prints one up for you right then and there. That's Print On Demand, and several companies are already building such systems. Today, the production is mostly done offsite from the bookstore, so the consumer still has to order the book and wait for the order to reach the POD site, and for the POD people (sorry, couldn't resist) to print it and ship it out. As of this writing, however, there are a few experimental on-site POD systems in various bookstores in some of the bigger cities.

POD, whether onsite or off, allows publishers to print only as many books as there are sales. As books are ordered, they are printed...on demand. This benefits the publishers because they don't have nearly as many returns—and the authors, too. Under the old system, bookstores would order books based on a catalog, and if the books didn't sell, the retailers would send them back to the publisher—after tearing the front cover off so that the book becomes worthless and cannot be resold. (That's why you may have noticed warnings in some books that if the front cover is missing the book may be stolen.) Reducing such returns is good for the publishers, because returns have always been a major expense. As far as publishers' accountants are concerned, books are sold when the book gets sent to the bookstore. But if bookstore owners order too many copies, they have a choice. They can discount the extras, or they can send them back. After the books are returned, the bookstores get their money back, and the publisher takes a loss on that book—and passes a share of it along via the author's royalty statements, too. Using POD, the bookstore orders or prints up just as many copies as are needed. Some people have even speculated that there might be a day when bookstores are simply showrooms where the consumers can browse the books, but the copies they look at are not the actual copies they'll be buying. Instead, when they're ready to buy the book, the bookstore prints up a copy for the consumer to buy.

Another advantage to POD is that it allows publishers to try books that they think are likely to have a smaller run. In Chapter 1, "Understanding Electronic Publishing," we talked about how publishers are unwilling to do small-run books because of the high per-copy cost involved. With POD, the cost could go down. Not considerably, because there are still other costs, such as editorial and layout and marketing, but the high expense of printing low-run books goes down enough to make it slightly more attractive to publishers.

In the rest of this chapter we talk about various aspects of Print On Demand. We cover the things you should know if you're interested in publishing your work with this technology, who the major players are, and some of the problems you'll need to deal with.

POD and Author Rights

Unfortunately, there are rights issues. Think about this: Most author contracts say that when the book goes out of print, the rights will revert back to the author. But if a book can be printed any time somebody wants a copy, when will it ever go out of print so that the author can get the rights back? And while it's still technically in print with a copy or two sold per month, is the publisher going to spend any time marketing such a book? Most likely, not. Thus the book would be effectively held hostage by the publisher. Normally the reduction of sales to a trickle is the classic situation for an author to regain rights to the book, to either find a new publisher for it or begin marketing it directly. This same problem occurs in the e-book world as well, and we have a whole chapter devoted to rights and contracts—Chapter 10, "Hot Button Issues in E-Book Publishing Contracts." If you're an author you definitely want to read it.

Converging Technologies

When it comes down to it, almost all new books spend some part of their life in a digital format. This book you're reading was typed on a computer—as most books these days are. It was laid out using sophisticated desktop publishing software.

Because of that, companies, such as book distributors in particular, have realized that there's no reason a single book, stored as digital data on a computer somewhere, couldn't be printed at the printers and sent to bookstores, set up for Print On Demand, or transferred directly in the form of an e-book. One file could be used for all three things. And that's what the hope is with some of the newest technology. Big distribution companies such as Ingram (with its Lightning Source company) are working toward this. They ultimately want you to be able to pick which book you want, and, as they say, "How would you like it?" If you want it printed on paper form, cool. If you want it in e-book form, not a problem. Pick the format, and that's what you'll get.

However, this is easier said than done. There are several different file formats. As it happens, traditional printed books are usually laid out using a specialized program—Quark or FrameMaker or some such. These are powerful software packages, but not yet very e-book friendly. One format might be used for the printing. Another format might be used for Print On Demand. And then you have the dedicated e-book formats, such as Glassbook, Microsoft Reader, or one used by the hardware devices. They don't match, and they don't mix.

Fortunately, companies are aware of this and are working on this problem. Ingram's Lightning Source division is determined to come up with a solution to the problem. And Simon & Schuster has decided to support most e-book formats. That's fine too, provided everybody is happy. But standards are coming, and we'll get there.

Big Names in the Business

As you can imagine, the big names in the business are taking part in the Print On Demand technology. As we noted in the preceding section, Ingram is doing so through its Lightning Source division.

Baker & Taylor, another huge book distributor, has similarly moved toward Print On Demand. Instead of going it alone, however, it has joined up with another company that already does it, called Replica Books. Replica Books receives orders for books in its database and immediately prints and binds them. The printing is done in black and white, except for the cover. Books can be bound in either softback or hardcover. Then they get shipped out. That's it, done deal.

Replica Books has several different ways to work with publishers to get books printed. Normally it deals in out-of-print books, keeping the book alive. (That could be a problem if you're an author. Make sure you read Chapter 10, "Hot Button Issues.") Replica has different plans with which it can work with either a publisher or an author. Under one plan, the book gets a new ISBN through Replica Books, and under another it keeps its ISBN if it's currently in print.

Replica Books makes the books known to *Books in Print* and *Title Source*, two big databases of books. Bookstores and libraries access these two databases to find out what books are available. That means that while your book is available through Replica Books, if consumers go into a bookstore and ask for it, the people at the bookstore will be able to find your book on the computer and submit an order.

***Books in Print**—If you're not familiar with* Books in Print, *you probably should be.* Books in Print, *published by R.R. Bowker* (http://www.booksinprint.com) *is the standard guide listing all books currently in print. It's used by libraries and retailers and allows quick access to determine what books are available. It's available as a book, as a CD-ROM, and on the Internet. (You need a password to access the Internet site, and it's rather costly for an individual—upwards of a couple of grand.)*

The short story is that having your book listed in Books in Print *makes it far more likely to sell. That's because once it's in* Books in Print, *it becomes available all across the world. If it's not in* Books in Print, *people assume it's not in print.*

Other Players

Smaller companies are also getting involved in POD. One such company is **Xlibris** (http://www.Xlibris.com/), whose site is shown in Figure 3.4. Its model is simple: You, the author, write a book and have it edited (Xlibris doesn't provide editorial services). You submit the manuscript; the folks at Xlibris do the layout and design. As they receive orders, they print copies to fulfill the order on demand. They have several different services, from free to premium services that can cost a couple of thousand dollars. With the free services, you have limited control over what your book will look like, but if you're just trying to get your book in print, this can be a pretty good plan for you. The royalties are quite good, too, at 25 percent of cover price. They also register your book with Amazon.com, Borders.com, and *Books in Print*. We cover Xlibris in more detail in Chapter 6, "Checking Out the E-Publishers."

Another company that's quickly becoming a big player is iUniverse (partly because of an investment from Barnes & Noble.com, which now owns 49 percent of the company). **iUniverse**, found at http://www.iuniverse.com, provides a whole set of services for getting a book published and, like the others, printed on demand via order. The basic plan is free for a previously published but out-of-print book; another basic plan for new books is $99. The company has several other plans, too, with reasonable prices to help you get your book into print,

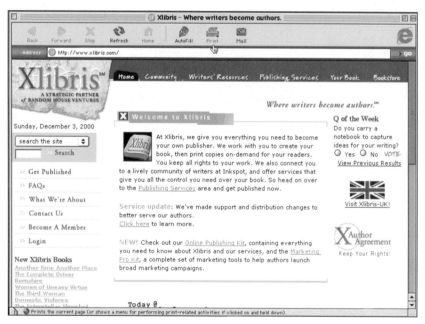

Figure 3.4: Xlibris has taken Print On Demand and made it accessible to authors.

each with its own imprint (that is, the name of the publisher that appears on the cover of your book). And like the others, it will get your book into *Books in Print* and other databases.

Like the others, iUniverse does not provide editorial services. But it does have extensive layout services, including a four-color cover design. For out-of-print books, if you own the rights to the cover art, iUniverse can even print it with the original cover art.

As for inside art, it can either use the art you provide or line up professional (that is, for-pay) services to help you design the art.

As with Xlibris, we give more information about iUniverse in Chapter 6, "Checking Out the E-Publishers."

Problems With Print On Demand

We already mentioned that there are rights issues, wherein Print On Demand can effectively keep a book in print forever, with a book or two per month trickling in, and the author unable to get the rights back. Another problem with Print On Demand is that consumers would not be able to preview the book before buying it. For this reason, if you are considering publishing a book through a Print On Demand company, you will want to make your own efforts to let people see the book. Often this means putting a sample chapter on your Web site and letting people read it online or perhaps download it. You might also put the table of contents online, and any other information you think would help the consumers decide they want your book.

Of course, that means you probably want to have your own Web site. There's a good book out there in the same series as this one—*Poor Richard's Web Site,* available from **Top Floor Publishing** (http://www.topfloor.com/)—that can help you there.

For a nice example of how one author, Elisabet Sahtouris, has managed to get her book into a Print On Demand form and created a Web site to go with it, check out **LifeWeb** at http://www.ratical.org/LifeWeb/. She offers her book in e-book form from the Web site and also includes a link to iUniverse where readers can obtain POD copies. We've grabbed a sample of her Web site and put it in Figure 3.5. And just to round out the picture, Figure 3.6 gives you a companion image: the iUniverse page that offers the book to those who want hard copy without the bother of printing it for themselves.

Preparing for Print On Demand

Since this book is about how you can do electronic publishing, it's useful to talk about how you can use Print On Demand. POD can help you in two areas:

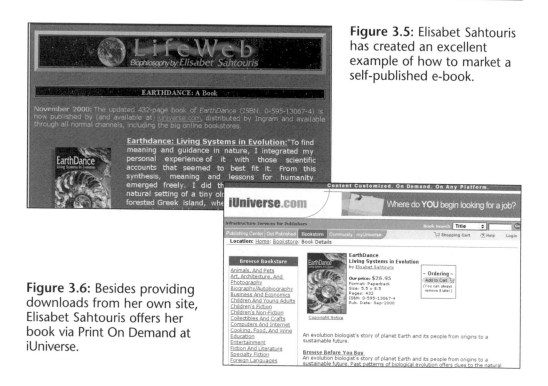

Figure 3.5: Elisabet Sahtouris has created an excellent example of how to market a self-published e-book.

Figure 3.6: Besides providing downloads from her own site, Elisabet Sahtouris offers her book via Print On Demand at iUniverse.

- If you have an out-of-print book that you want to get back into print
- If you have a new book that hasn't been published and you want to do it yourself

Remember, if you have a book that's in print, you have to have the rights to do a separate POD deal. Most likely, you don't have those rights. Check with the publisher or your agent (if you have one) before you send out your book, because otherwise you'll be in *violation of the copyright of your own book.*

Once you've got the rights nailed down, you need to select a Print On Demand company. Take a look at Chapter 6, "Checking Out the E-Publishers," along with Appendix A, "E-Publishers," to see who the players are, and carefully check out their Web sites. Make sure they accept submissions from authors (that is, don't bother with a company if it only works with publishers). Then find out about their different options. Typically, if you're willing to pay, you get more services and more control. But even the free ones are attractive for getting your book into print. Also, find out where the book will be available. Will Amazon.com customers be able to get it? Borders.com? BN.com? And what about brick-and-mortar bookstores (the kind you actually drive to and go inside, remember them)? Will it show up in databases such as *Books in Print*? Can consumers order the book directly from the site? Will the book be available through other distributors such as Ingram?

And what about artwork? Will someone do the cover art for you, or do you do it yourself? And if they do it, do you have any say in what it will look like? If it's an out-of-print title you're getting republished, and you own the rights to the cover art, will the company use the original cover art?

What about illustrations? Most of these Print On Demand companies do not use color, so find out for sure if you have something you think requires color. And how many illustrations do you get? Many allow up to 50, but find out. Do they let you design your internal artwork? Will they do it for you if you can't? And if so, do they charge and how much?

And what about author review? Will you get to see the book before it goes to print? Will you review a printed galley proof copy or will you have to review it online, and are you okay with that? Will you have final say and be allowed changes? Remember, since most of these places do not do editing, they expect edited copy when you submit the manuscript. Therefore, they place a limit on how many edits you can make during this review phase, after they've done the publishing setup but before it goes to print. What about after the book goes to print and you want changes; what are their policies (and fees) for changes then?

What about marketing? Do they do any? If so, do they charge a fee? (Most do charge a fee.) Most likely, you'll end up marketing the book yourself, but what other perks does the company include? Do they give you space on their Web site to help you promote your book? Do they provide you with free marketing tips and advice, probably through their Web site?

Once you've picked a POD publisher, download the instructions and follow them carefully. Each of these sites offers an author kit of sorts that gives you step-by-step instructions. (You might even download the instruction packets from different sites when deciding which POD publisher to go with.) Treat the instructions seriously, because you want to make sure your book ends up looking its best. This is, after all, actually getting your book printed and sold through bookstores and over the Internet.

Make sure you have and use the correct software. You don't want to send in files that the company cannot use. And make sure your images, if you submit any, are in the correct format.

Once you find out the answers to these questions you will be able to make an intelligent choice about which POD system is best for your particular needs.

PART II
Planning and Creating an E-Book

CHAPTER FOUR

The Production Process

Getting a book from idea to manuscript to e-book and into the online bookstores is no small task. Many issues and processes affect not only the e-book's appearance but its sales and marketability as well. For example, suppose you want to sell your e-book through some of the usual venues such as Amazon.com. What do you need to include with your e-book that gives Amazon.com the necessary cataloging information? And beyond that, how do you somehow associate the cataloging information with your e-book or deliver that information with the e-book?

If your book will be handled by a publisher, it's quite possible that the publisher is already familiar with these issues. But if you're self-publishing, then you need to know about this stuff yourself.

This chapter will help you cover all the bases, ensuring that you can get your book all the way from manuscript onto the e-book readers of consumers across the world. For example, we talk about how to get a unique number for your e-book (called an ISBN, the same numbering used for paper books), and whether you need another unique number (called a DOI) specifically for digital information. After that we talk about how to get your e-book from word processing document into the right format.

A Unique Number for Your Book

Most people who have read a book—almost any book—have heard of an ISBN, which stands for International Standard Book Number. ISBNs provide a unique identifier for each book. As we noted in Chapter 3, "New Ways of Publishing," ISBNs are issued by R.R. Bowker, the same company that produces the *Books in Print* database. Typically a single edition of a book will have an ISBN. If a new edition of a book comes out, it will have a new ISBN. Further, the ISBN agencies recommend that each form of the book (hardcover, paperback, e-book) should get a separate ISBN. The number is 10 digits long (but moving to 13 digits in 2005), and it identifies the country or region of the world where the publisher is located, who the publisher is, and then the book itself. Normally a publisher applies for a batch of ISBN numbers (such as a thousand of them), and pays a fee; when the publisher receives the batch of numbers, which all start with the same five digits or so, the publisher assigns one to each book. R.R. Bowker doesn't assign the individual ISBNs to the books; that's up to the publisher after receiving the batch. (It's interesting to note that this is, in fact, how the ISBN agencies define who the publisher is: According to these agencies, the entity that assigns the ISBN is the publisher of the book or e-book.)

After the publisher assigns ISBNs to books, it is expected to report the assignments to R.R. Bowker; this will ensure the addition of the book to databases and catalogs such as *Books in Print*. Publishers can now report this information online via the **BowkerLink Publishing Access System**, at http://www.bowkerlink.com/, shown in Figure 4.1.

So What's an ISSN?—*The ISSN, or International Standard Serial Number, is another identifier commonly used in the publishing industry. Publishers assign ISSNs to serials such as magazines and journals. The ISSN goes with the entire journal, not a particular issue or volume. Normally e-books would not get an ISSN.*

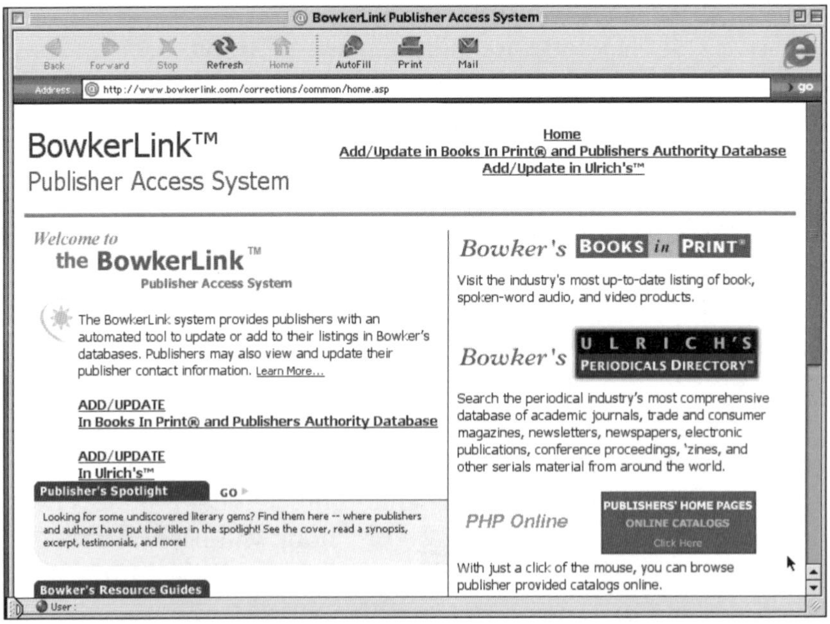

Figure 4.1: The BowkerLink Publishing Access System lets publishers update the ISBN cataloging information for a particular book.

In the early days of e-books, there was some question as to whether e-books should get ISBNs. After it became clear that e-books should indeed have ISBNs, in 1999 the agencies agreed to let publishers assign them to e-books in addition to print books. That is also when the agencies decided that publishers should assign an ISBN to separate e-books from their print editions.

You can find out about ISBNs at R.R. Bowker's **International Standard Book Number** site, http://www.bowker.com/standards/home/. This site includes all the official information about ISBNs, along with the proper application process, including an online application system for getting a batch of ISBNs.

Remember, if you're having a publisher carry your e-book, most likely that publisher will go through the work of assigning your book an ISBN and you won't have to do so. But if you are going to be your own publisher, it's wise to have an ISBN for your book, as most catalogs and online retailers require it as the unique identification for the book.

Therefore, if you are publishing or self-publishing e-books, you will want to go through these steps:

- Apply for a batch of ISBNs with R.R. Bowker.
- Assign an ISBN to each of your e-books.
- Notify R.R. Bowker of that assignment through the BowkerLink site.

A Unique Place for Your Book

Although ISBNs provide a unique identifier for your e-book, the very concept of digital information has opened up new ways of storing your books online, and it turns out that a unique number simply isn't enough. If you want to make the most of the new technology, you need to have not only a number that uniquely identifies your e-book but one that identifies where it can be found in cyberspace, even if you move it to a different site on the Internet.

As one example, suppose you are up late, surfing the Web, and you come across a really great Web site called The Beginner's Guide to E-Books. You decide you'll want to visit the site again, so you bookmark it. Six months later, you're digging through your bookmarks and you come across the title. You click it and end up at a site that's selling organic aftershave. Turns out the publisher of The Beginner's Guide to E-Books moved the site to a different address on the Internet and somebody else moved their site into the place The Beginner's Guide used to occupy. What do you do? Unless you can find it on a search engine, you're pretty much out of luck. You won't find it again. For that matter, you probably won't even know if it's still on the Internet.

Here's another example. Suppose you are taking a class and using the professor's own e-book. The professor handed out an early draft of the e-book just as the term began. But as the term goes on, the professor keeps revising it. The professor wants to make sure that whenever you open the e-book you get not the one sent out at the beginning of the term but the latest and greatest.

To handle such situations, members of the publishing industry have created a technology known as Digital Object Identifiers, or DOIs. A DOI, created by the **International DOI Foundation** (http://www.doi.org/, shown in Figure 4.2), is similar to an ISBN, except that it doesn't just uniquely identify a book; in addition, it provides a number that is sort of a cross-reference to the book. Here's how it works. Imagine a couple of hundred years from now how the U.S. Postal Service might have advanced—maybe to a point where to send a package all you need is the name of the recipient, or perhaps some unique number such as a Social Security Number or taxpayer ID number. The Postal Service would then have a huge database that connects the number to an address. It looks up the correct address in the computer database for the number and delivers the package to the address. Addresses would still exist, and the post office folks would still use them, but the person sending the package wouldn't need to know the address, just the unique identifier for the recipient. Then if the person or business moves, they would simply register the new address with the post office. People sending packages to this person or business would continue using the same unique number as before. The Postal Service would know the new address and deliver the package accordingly. As it happens, telephone numbers in many cities already have this feature; when you move you can often keep the same phone number and people don't need to know where you are when they call you. It's the same idea.

DOIs present this concept for e-books and other digital information, such as Web pages. Every Web page or other piece of digital content gets a DOI, which is ultimately a unique number. When you want to visit the Web site, you don't type in the standard style of Web address, such as **Top Floor Publishing**'s http://www.topfloor.com/, nor would you click a link that has that address stored in it. Instead, you would type in a unique number or click a link that has that unique number stored in it. The unique number represents the Web site. The browser connects to a database, sends it the unique number, and gets back an address for the site. The browser then goes to the correct site. If the owners of the site move it to a different place on the Internet, they would update the database. As long as everybody keeps up with the pieces of the job, the end result is no more broken links on the Internet.

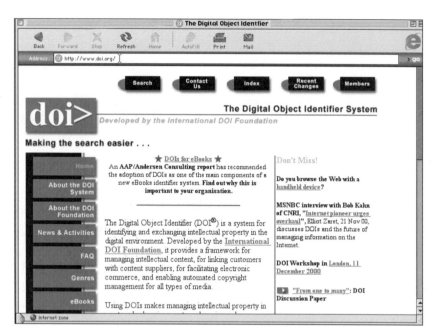

Figure 4.2: The DOI Foundation has created a way of identifying and locating e-books and other digital content.

If you're familiar with the way the Web presently works, where every Web address gets converted to a number, you might wonder how DOIs differ from this current scheme. The difference is that DOIs can refer to specific content on the Web, not just the site where it happens to reside at the moment. Going back to the Postal Service analogy, the DOI is what ties the content you're trying to reach (its identity, its "name," if you will) to its current "street address" on the Web.

DOIs and Handles—This DOI system we just described is really based on something called Handle technology. You can learn more about that at the **Handle System** *site,* http://www.handle.net/. *The Handle System was created by the Corporation for National Research Initiatives, or CNRI.*

So how does this relate to e-books? As time goes on, you are likely to see more dynamic e-books that get downloaded automatically piece by piece as you read them, instead of having you download them once at the beginning. This will happen as more and more people get high-speed Internet access such as cable modems. An e-book you are reading will have a DOI associated with it. When you wish to read it, the e-book reader software will go out on the Internet, find the location of the e-book, and automatically download the most up-to-date version of the part you wish to read. That will guarantee that you always have the latest version of the e-book.

This has great benefit to consumers as well as authors and publishers because it ensures that updates such as spelling corrections or technical corrections would make it to all the consumers, not just those people lucky enough to buy the book after its first print run. Further, the DOI concept allows e-books to be broken into smaller portions such as chapters, and for each portion to have its own DOI. In this manner, custom books could one day be created consisting of chapters from various books.

Part of the idea behind DOI is to remove the notion of absolute places in cyberspace. For example, this book you are reading is filled with Web addresses. While those addresses are unlikely to change drastically any time soon (since they are typically company names), many addresses you might come across on the Internet are likely to change. For example, Web sites under popular Web hosts such as Geocities or Tripod tend to move around a lot. Bookmarking these sites is handy, but there's always the chance that the site will have moved and your bookmark will no longer be valid.

It'll be awhile before the Web completely adopts DOIs, and for now they're primarily used within the e-book world. But because of this, many of the navigation problems plaguing the Web will not be a problem with e-books.

If you are a publisher or self-publisher, the **Association of American Publishers**, http://www.publishers.org/, recommends that you obtain both an ISBN and a DOI for each of your works. You might also consider assigning a DOI to individual portions of your e-books. To find out more about this, visit the **DOI Foundation** (http://www.doi.org/).

---

*The APP and DOIs—In late 2000, the **Association of American Publishers**, completely embraced DOIs for e-books.   At* http://www.publishers.org/home/ ebookstudy.htm *you can find a PDF document (which can be read in Acrobat Reader) called Numbering Standards for Ebooks that completely describes the organization's plans to standardize DOIs in the e-book publishing world. Since the AAP is the primary publishing industry group—all the major publishers are members—this means the major publishers are ready to embrace DOIs. The AAP intends for electronic publications to have both a DOI and a legacy identifier, such as an ISBN or ISSN. This document also gives the details on how DOIs will be used in e-books, probably in a more useful form than the **International DOI Foundation** Web site (*http://www.doi.org/*), which is more technically oriented.*

Metadata

Before e-books existed, publishers were already working to bring computers and the so-called Information Age into the publishing world. Part of this meant finding a way to transmit data about books from one business to another. For example, companies that provided catalogs of books, whether in print form or online, needed to know the necessary information about a book to put in the catalog. It would be too arduous for the people at the catalog company to read and scan every book in their catalog if the catalog consists of more than a few hundred books. For huge catalog products, such as those used by libraries or those used by retailers to locate books for consumers, the information must arrive prepackaged, ready to put into the computer. It's generally up to the publisher to provide the information about its books. This information about the books is called *metadata*.

Since most publishers deal with multiple companies that require metadata, and since companies that receive metadata typically deal with multiple publishers, it was important that everybody agree on the same way of organizing and transmitting this metadata. For example, it would be a problem if one cataloging company is expecting a portion of the information simply called "author" while another is expecting "author last name" and "author first name" as two separate items.

So Much for the Computer—*Although metadata has been around for some time, the truth is that as recently as the late 1990s, many companies were still not transmitting metadata over phone lines or with the help of computers. Publishers were actually printing the metadata on a standard yellow sheet and mailing it to catalog companies, distributors, and retailers. The people who received it would then* **type** *it into their computers. Fortunately, this is quickly changing, thanks to the impact of the e-book world, because with e-books have come standards for such things as transmitting metadata. These standards are helping the print book world as well.*

To standardize the metadata for books, a few different organizations supported by the publishers came together and created the ONIX system, which stands for ONline Information eXchange, found on the **EDItEUR** site at http://www.editeur.org/onix.html, shown in Figure 4.3. (Don't just search the Web for ONIX, though—several other companies use the same name to stand for basically the same thing. These are separate from the ONIX we're talking about here.) The groups that created the ONIX system are EDItEUR, the Book Industry Communication, and the Book Industry Study Group. These three organizations all deal with the technical end of the book publishing industry.

ONIX is continually being enhanced, and recently the AAP has helped update ONIX to be useful for e-books as well. You can find out what the organization has to say about ONIX and metadata in various documents on the **Association of American Publishers** Web site at http://www.publishers.org/.

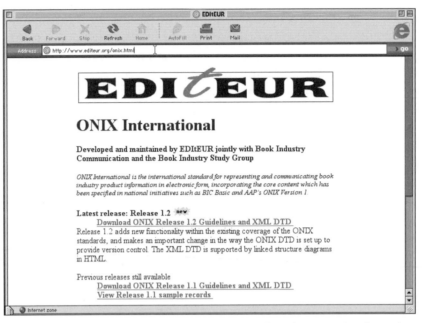

Figure 4.3: EDItEUR's ONIX system handles the metadata for most books today.

As ONIX has been upgraded to support e-books, many new ideas have come up for how consumers can benefit. For example, different portions of books will have different metadata associated with them, allowing consumers to search online catalogs for individual portions of books, not just entire books. With the help of DOI, these individual portions could be connected into a single, custom-made e-book. Or these individual chunks could be sold as single entities. Further, the specification allows publishers and retailers to use custom metadata, such as specific copyright and print rights. (We talk more about digital rights in Chapter 5, "Digital Rights and Copy Protection.")

Because e-books are likely to be searched online using various subject matter and retail search engines, the folks who put together ONIX have realized the importance of distinguishing a certain portion of an e-book's metadata as discovery metadata. *Discovery metadata* includes the name of the book, a description, the author's name, and biographical information on the author.

Other metadata for e-books as specified by the ONIX system include optional reviews, back-cover copy (the text you would normally see on the back of a printed book), and separate descriptions for bookstores and libraries. The entire ONIX system is comprehensive, and once all the e-book publishers, distributors, and retailers have finished adopting it, people can expect some wonderful advances in the online searching and buying of e-books. Plan on this happening in the first few years of this century.

Book numbering and metadata are vital to the publication process. Most publishers already take care of these issues for their authors. But if you're self-publishing, you'll want to be very familiar with these two topics. The more you make use of them, the more likely you'll be able to sell your e-book in all the big venues. The best starting place on the Internet to find out the technical details is in the various e-book sections of the **Association of American Publishers** Web site at http://www.publishers.org/.

Most of the software for creating e-books allows you to enter metadata, which gets stored in the e-book file. Although this information is rarely used at present, we encourage you to enter it anyway—as the technology grows, it will be used more and more. Further, if you are going to work with a distributor or retailer to market your e-book for you, you will want to find out what metadata the people at the organization require in your e-book and in what form they require it.

From Manuscript to E-Book

When you create an e-book, you have to start somewhere. Most likely you'll start with word processing software such as Microsoft Word, so you need to know how to use that without driving yourself crazy. Further, you need to know how to use the various tools for converting a document to an e-book.

In the following sections we discuss how to get your book into the various formats. We're not making any assumptions about whether you're self-publishing or if your book is going to be carried by an e-publisher. If you're self-publishing, this section will help you understand how to convert the files. If you're going through an e-publisher, you'll want to find out if the editors there expect you to convert the files yourself, and if so, what format they require. If they'll be doing the converting for you, then you'll need to know what format they want you to use for the initial documents. However, if the publisher lets you convert, you may want to do so, because that will give you a better idea of what the final product will look like.

This is actually a little different from the way traditional publishers do things. In publishing for paper books, the author submits text and art either chapter by chapter or for the whole book, and the production staff does all the layout. This book you're reading has gone through that same process. We, the authors, really won't know what the final book will look like until we see how the production team actually lays it out.

Because of the nature (and size) of many e-publishing companies, the author is either free to or expected to do the layout for the e-book. Many such companies will accept books in a basic word processing document format and convert them for you (possibly charging a small fee, such as $15). But if you go that route, you won't have much control over the final layout. This is especially true for books that have previously been published, gone out of print, and the rights have reverted to the author. There are many e-publishers out there that will publish your out-of-print book in e-book format, and you have the choice of doing the layout and converting it or letting them do it for you, again for a small fee.

So the moral is that if they let you do the layout, then you should probably do so. That way you will have total creative control, making sure that the sizes of the headings, the placement of the figures, and even the choice of fonts all promote the message you want to convey. If you care about such things, now is your chance to have it the way you want it.

Word Processing

The majority of publishers use Microsoft Word for word processing, even those with Macintosh-based systems. Of course, Word is far from the only software available for writing—but if you insist on using something else, you've got some extra work to do. Make sure that whatever software you are using to convert to e-book format can handle the documents created by your word processor.

On balance, you'll probably find that it's easiest to go with the flow. You'll have the least trouble if you use Microsoft Word—and make sure you're proficient in it. Although you probably don't need to know things like how to make your headings begin automatically with Roman numerals, at a minimum you need to know how to format the text and how to use Word's built-in Style feature. Most publishers that use Word make heavy use of the styles. Further, the different tools that convert Word documents to e-books use the styles as well. Therefore, understand styles and learn to love them. You can find a great book on Microsoft Word, as well as lots of good Word hints, at Word Central on the **J.W. Olsen** site (http://www.jwolsen.com/).

Choosing a Text Format

After your book is written, you need to choose a format for it. As of the early 2000s, we are a long way from having a single e-book format that every e-book reader device and program can read. Therefore, you need to be familiar with the different formats available. Chapter 2, "What's an E-book?" covers the different types of readers on the market. In general, for each reader there's a different format.

In the sections that follow we talk about creating e-books for some of the more well-known formats.

Microsoft Reader

Microsoft has gone to great lengths to make sure that people not only have easy access to the Microsoft Reader but can get to software that lets them create books for that format. The software can be downloaded from the **Reader** site at http://www.microsoft.com/reader/. Note that many of the tools expect your document to be in HTML format, since at the heart of it, Microsoft Reader uses HTML. (Really it uses XML, which includes HTML.)

With the Microsoft Reader format comes all the features of Microsoft Reader. (We discussed this product in Chapter 2, "What's an E-book?")

Open eBook Everywhere—*Because Open eBook (OEB) is a standard and not a particular company or product, various reader software and hardware manufacturers are quick to say that their product supports the OEB standard. Microsoft Reader is one such format. But that doesn't mean Microsoft Reader can display books intended for other readers that support OEB. The reason is that OEB doesn't specify a file format; it only specifies a format for "marking up" the book, providing various levels headers, footers, chapter numbers and titles, and other formatting marks. Eventually the specification will hopefully specify file format as well, providing more compatibility. But at present, buyer beware: don't be fooled by manufacturer claims.*

As of late 2000, the Microsoft Reader format was supported by two e-book readers, the Microsoft Reader software itself, and the **Franklin eBookMan** (http://www.franklin.com/ebookman/default.asp). The Microsoft Reader software can be downloaded free of charge for desktop computers running Windows. It also comes preinstalled on the small Microsoft Pocket PC computers. (You can find out more about Pocket PCs at Microsoft's **Pocket PC** site at http://www.pocketpc.com/.)

Primary Pros and Cons—*The major advantage to using Microsoft Reader format is the fact that at its heart it is HTML. HTML is extremely versatile and allows consumers to resize their windows, with the text automatically reflowing. With Microsoft Reader, the users also have greater control over the fonts. But this can all be a disadvantage as well, because books such as textbooks often require a fixed layout.*

For converting to Microsoft Reader format, there are two different approaches you can take. One is to use a product from Overdrive Software, and the other is to use one called Read In from Microsoft. Each includes a template, which provides Microsoft Word with a set of styles. (You can find information about both of these by going to Microsoft's **Reader** site, http://www.microsoft.com/reader/, choosing Publish, and then Self-Publish.) This will ensure that in the end you'll be using the correct fonts and page size. Then stick to only those styles given in the templates. It's important that you do not pick the fonts manually, otherwise the consumers reading your book won't be able to use the options they choose for the Microsoft ClearType fonts. Using the software is rather straightforward, but you'll want to follow the onscreen instructions carefully to make sure you do it correctly.

PDF

PDF is probably the original online book format. Adobe created it with the intention of putting books online. Soon after it reached the market, software companies began shipping their manuals on disk in PDF format.

A Poor Man's PDF Conversion—*While Acrobat is rather expensive, many simpler tools are either free or inexpensive, and there are even some Web sites that can convert your documents if you upload them. The best place to find such tools is at* **Planet PDF**, *http://www.planetpdf.com/, shown in Figure 4.4. However, remember that you get what you pay for. While many of the products are good, they aren't as powerful as the real thing, Acrobat from Adobe.*

If you really need Acrobat and can't afford it, there's another alternative: Acrobat can be found on most rental computers at Kinko's, a popular chain of copy shops, many of which have entire computer rental centers.

Converting to PDF is probably the easiest conversion of any e-book creation. However, easy does not imply inexpensive, because before you can create PDF you need to purchase Acrobat from Adobe, which isn't cheap. You can get

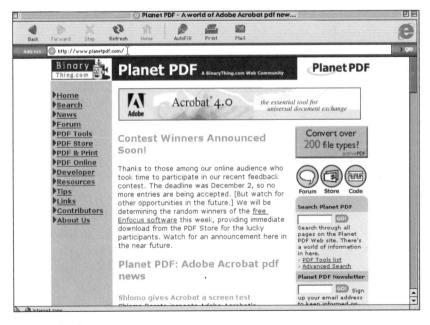

Figure 4.4: Planet PDF is the ultimate source for all things PDF.

Acrobat Reader from Adobe for free (which makes PDF files popular with users), but that doesn't let you create PDF files. You can find information on this at the **Adobe** site (http://www.adobe.com/).

So how do you create a PDF file with Adobe Acrobat? It's easy: You print your document. But instead of selecting the laser printer or inkjet printer, you choose the Acrobat Distiller. Distiller is the piece of Acrobat that does the conversion for you. When you tell your computer to print your document, instead of going to the printer, it goes into a PDF document, so to speak. Then when you open up the resulting PDF document in Acrobat or Acrobat Reader, you will see pages printed on the screen that look exactly as if you had printed the document to paper. So if you know how to print documents, you can easily create PDF documents.

Because of this interesting way of creating PDF documents by "printing" to the PDF document, virtually any software can go to PDF, provided it can be printed. Any word processor that includes a print dialog box will see Acrobat Distiller and think it's just a printer. Or other programs that print as well, including spreadsheets and graphics programs, can print to a PDF document.

Once you've printed to your PDF document, you can open it up in Acrobat Reader and do some simple editing on it. You can't change the text and graphics on the document, but you can remove pages or separate out pages into their own PDF documents, or combine multiple PDF documents into a single document.

Primary Pros and Cons—*The main text describes the major benefit to using PDF: It's extremely easy to create. But the primary disadvantage is the static layout. You'll notice that when you open a Web document (not a PDF document) in a browser, normally, if you resize your window, the text will reflow accordingly, preventing the need for a horizontal scrollbar at the bottom of the window. With the current generation of PDF, this isn't the case. The layout of each page is fixed, and if you make the text too big, you will get a horizontal scrollbar. If you've ever tried to read long documents while having to scroll every single line left and right, you'll know what a headache this is. But at the same time, this disadvantage can be an advantage to the creator of the e-book: You can specify exactly what you want your book to look like, and it won't be reformatted when the consumer opens it up. For many textbooks, for example, a fixed layout is very important.*

Glassbook Reader

The Glassbook format is simply a specially encrypted PDF format. If you are publishing for the Glassbook reader, you will need to get your documents into PDF format. See the preceding section in this chapter for more information on converting to PDF.

If you are self-publishing for the Glassbook Reader, most likely you will not be selling your books yourself, primarily because selling an e-book in Glassbook

Reader format requires the use of specialized Web server software available only from Glassbook. While you're certainly free to purchase such software, it's rather pricey and a bit of overkill for a single author to do so. (You can find out more about the server products at the **Glassbook** Web site, http://www.glassbook.com/. Click Publishers when you get there.)

If you prefer to let an e-bookseller or e-publisher sell your works for the Glassbook Reader, you can find companies that do so from the Glassbook Web site in the Authors section. One such company is **CyberRead**, http://www.cyberread.com/, shown in Figure 4.5. CyberRead accepts documents in PDF format and gets them into Glassbook Reader format for you. This will be the case in general, as the software to convert to Glassbook Reader format comes with the server software.

Glassbook and PDF

As noted, the Glassbook Reader uses PDF under the hood, so this section applies to both. However, if you are publishing for Glassbook Reader, you will want to check out your final PDF in the Glassbook Reader to make sure it looks okay.

With PDF, you have absolute control over the final layout. Everything you choose for the layout will hold regardless of what software the final consumer uses. Therefore, you will want to be sure you carefully choose the fonts and the margins, page size, and so on.

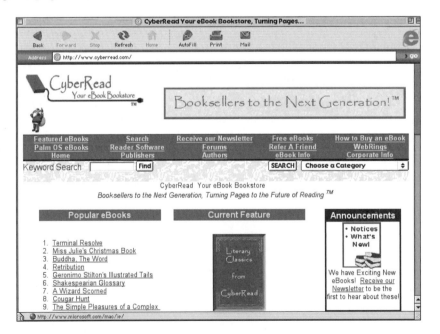

Figure 4.5: CyberRead sells e-books created for the Glassbook Reader.

Most PDF viewers (including Glassbook Reader) let you vary the size by zooming in on the document. While this might seem to mean that it's okay to make your fonts as small as you like, it doesn't work that way. A page is extremely difficult to read if the fonts are so small that the zoom factor causes each line of text to be wider than the computer screen.

A good rule of thumb, then, is to set your page size to 6 inches wide by 9 inches long, and your fonts to somewhere from 11 to 13 points in size. Remember, you set these items in the word processing software such as Microsoft Word. However, the Acrobat Distiller printer driver that lets you print to PDF has various settings as well, such as color versus black and white, and so on.

For many people, laying out a document so that it looks great in PDF is more of a learned and practiced skill than an instinct. Much has been written on the topic and it's all great information—but the truth is you can never be sure until you practice with the different settings available in both the word processor and Acrobat Distiller. Practice, tweak, and check until you like what you have.

HTML (and XML)

HTML and XML formats are mainly for Web work rather than for e-books, but there's a possibility that you might need to use either or both of them, as some of the online-reading e-book Web sites use one of these two formats.

If you're not familiar with XML, you can think of it as a new enhancement to HTML, and anything you create that is HTML can also be considered XML (but not vice versa). Not all Web browsers support XML. However, by definition all Web browsers support HTML. So in general, if you must choose, you're better off with HTML. Eventually all browsers will support XML, but until they do, your best bet is to go with HTML.

Getting to HTML

So how do you convert to HTML? On the surface, converting to HTML seems even easier than converting to PDF. Most word processing programs for either Windows or Macintosh systems have a "Save As HTML" feature that takes the document, converts it to HTML, and saves the resulting coded text.

Unfortunately, life isn't that simple in HTML. Often the resulting document looks best with only one browser, and how it will look in an e-book viewer that uses HTML is anybody's guess. So the most important thing you need to do is test it. After you've saved your e-book as HTML, open it in the particular software application it will ultimately live in, whether it's a Web browser or some other HTML-based software package. If it is destined for a Web browser, you'll also want to make sure you open it in as many browsers as possible, with the bare minimum being Microsoft Internet Explorer and Netscape Navigator. If it looks great in both browsers or in the destination software, then you're good to go.

But what if it stinks? Many times we have saved a document to HTML only to find it looks horrible in the browsers. This is especially true if you have a lot of custom formatting, tables, or columns, and it's almost guaranteed to be true if you have images, particularly images with text wrapped around them.

If it does stink, then your best bet is to get hold of a software package intended for creating HTML and Web files, such as Microsoft's FrontPage or Macromedia Dreamweaver, a fine tool available from **Macromedia** at http://www.macromedia.com/. (A good starting place to find HTML editing shareware is on the **WinFiles** site at http://www.winfiles.com/). Using your HTML software, you might try opening the messed-up HTML file and see if you can make it look better. However, it might be a lost cause. A better bet would be save your book as raw text or ASCII format. Once the file is saved, you can rename it with an .html extension, and then open it up in the HTML editing tool. If you've got a good HTML tool it will see that it's looking at raw text and render it appropriately. Or, if you prefer to skip saving as text, you can often get away with selecting all the text from the file in your word processor, copying it to the Clipboard, and pasting it into the HTML editing tool. From there you can redo all the formatting the way you want to.

Wait! Did we just say to redo the formatting?

Yuppers. While this might seem like a daunting task, the truth is that at this point in time it's often a good idea to format e-books and printed books separately. We still aren't at a point in the technology where the two formats are one and the same. What looks good on paper probably won't look good in e-book format and vice versa.

Fortunately, the more you do this type of thing, the better you'll get; you'll start to see what works well in the word processor for both printer output and e-books, and your job will become easier and easier. For starters, if you stick to basic layout, using the predefined heading levels (and *use them*—don't just set font sizes), and don't use sophisticated columns and fancy font sizes, then you'll probably be in pretty good shape. The problem there, of course, is once you get it into HTML format it's likely to appear quite boring. And that's why once again you'll want to have a good HTML editor on hand.

Therefore, in general it is not a good idea to trust the "Save As HTML" feature, or at the very least, be highly skeptical of it. And find a good HTML editor that you like. You might even want to learn a little HTML so that you can get into the details and have complete control over your work.

***Raw HTML**—If you do want to edit raw HTML, first make sure you completely understand HTML, or at least the bits of it you're using. Hundreds of books can teach you HTML. Once you know HTML (or if you already know it) you'll want to make sure you only use tags that the final reader software or browser can understand. Stay away from things like Dynamic HTML, JavaScript, and certainly more advanced things like Java and ActiveX controls. While these might all make for really awesome Web sites, the chances of their being supported by the reader software are very low.*

Margins and Layout in HTML

When converting to HTML, many of the notions of margins and page size get thrown out the window. HTML browsers have evolved totally separately from printed pages and e-books, and HTML has its own way of doing things. It's certainly possible to set margins and page size using advanced features in HTML (and if you use the Save As HTML feature of Microsoft Word, you'll see an attempt to set margins and page size), but in general these are not good for browsers.

Various features in HTML give you different layout capabilities. For instance, the Cascading Style Sheets (CSS) feature includes some absolute positioning, letting you state exactly where on the page you want certain text boxes and images to appear. While that's a great thing to be able to do, not all browsers support it. And when you open a CSS document in a browser that doesn't support it, it looks terrible. Your best bet is to steer clear of CSS and other advanced features such as Dynamic HTML (DHTML).

However, it's possible that the particular reader software you're creating for uses HTML at its heart and possibly supports CSS or DHTML. If you're not sure, contact either the e-publisher you're working with or, if you're self-publishing, the manufacturer of the reader software.

Instead of using CSS or DHTML, another possibility is to use HTML tables for sophisticated layout. If you're editing raw HTML, you'll want to study up on HTML tables, column sizing, row sizing, column spanning, and row spanning.

Some HTML editing tools automatically use CSS or DHTML. You'll want to check the manual and options to be sure, so that you only use them if you know they're safe for the reader software you're aiming at. Macromedia Dreamweaver is one such tool, but it has an option that lets you use HTML tables instead of CSS.

Other Formats

There are lots of other reader software packages out there, such as one by **peanutpress.com** (http://www.peanutpress.com/), and one by **Mobipocket** (http://www.mobipocket.com/). There are lots of such companies out there, and generally you can download publishing software from their sites. (Both peanutpress.com and Mobipocket have such software available.) However, sometimes this software doesn't give you the ability to create e-books that are ready to be sold via the sites that created the reader software. In fact, often these sites make it quite difficult for authors to sell e-books through their sites. (Mobipocket lets you upload your own e-books, but they are given away for *free;* they are *not sold.* If your goal is to be paid for your books, this isn't the place for them!) It is certainly possible, however, to get some of these organizations to sell your e-books if you are dedicated, and your best bet is to contact the companies directly over the telephone. If you do, you will want to make it clear that you are a *publisher* (and therefore have ISBNs for your e-books, as well as appropriate metadata), and not just a no-name author trying to make a quick buck.

Some Thoughts on Converting

After you've picked the format you prefer or require, and you've found the tools for getting your book into the format, there are several things you need to do to make sure that the book will look good and be useable in an e-book format.

Before listing them, here's the most important rule: *Practice makes perfect.*

It's very possible that the first time you convert a bunch of files to an e-book format, it'll look horrible. As with any task that doesn't go right the first time, don't despair. Look over all the software options, and tweak this and that until you get it into something that looks good. And the corollary to the first rule: If you don't want to practice, hire somebody who's already done it. The information in this section is useful whether or not you want to go through the work for yourself, but it's reassuring to know that you don't actually have to do it yourself. For a list of for-hire conversion services, see the "Getting Into E-Book Format" section of Chapter 7, "Assembling Your E-Publishing Venture."

Now the second most important rule: *Look at your e-book with every reader that will display it.*

Of course, if you're converting your book to Microsoft Reader format, it doesn't make much sense to see what it would look like in Glassbook Reader, since they're separate formats. But it is realistic to see what your Microsoft Reader e-book will look like on both the desktop version and the Pocket PC version of the software. Just because it looks good on one doesn't mean it will look good on the other. It might also help to see what it will look like on the Franklin eBookMan, since that's also a Microsoft Reader platform. While you probably won't own every kind of computer and PDA that has Microsoft Reader, the more you test it on, the better. To find out what platforms are available for the particular software or format, go to the Web site of the manufacturer of the e-book software you're planning to use.

If you'll be publishing in PDF or HTML format, you probably have too many options to realistically test it out on all of them. However, PDF pretty much looks the same on every platform (because the layout of your pages doesn't change from platform to platform), and with HTML your best bet is to at least look at your book in both Netscape Navigator and Internet Explorer on a PC. You might also try it out on a Mac if you have one available (and vice versa if you're a Mac person).

Next, you'll want to follow the tips in the "What Makes a Good E-Book?", section of Chapter 2, "What's an E-Book?" These tips will help you make sure the book is useable and good.

But there are other issues, such as page size, margins, fonts, styles, and so on. How you set these depends on the final format. In general, stick to one column for your output. Having multiple columns does not lend itself well to e-book readers, especially the palm-size and handheld readers.

Graphics Formats

Regardless of which text format you're using, you'll want to pay special attention to your images—diagrams, photos, and whatnot, collectively called graphics files. Graphics files can quickly pile up like dust mice—before you know it, what started as a short book has ended up in the tens of megabytes because of all the beautiful pictures.

In general, it's a good idea to give the images as few colors as possible, even if it means reducing the colors using some graphics software. (A good one is Paint Shop Pro from **JASC Software**, http://www.jasc.com/.) Further, make sure they fit on the page. This is especially important if you're creating an e-book that will be used on a small handheld or palm-size computer. Images that look great on the desktop PC might well be too big for the tiny screens. The e-book software on the little computer will have no choice but to either scale the image down so it fits or leave it too big for the screen—showing only a portion of it and requiring the consumer to scroll and pan to see the whole image. If the image gets scaled down, it's quite likely that the scaling down will make the fine details—including any text the image may contain—unreadable.

You must also choose an image format. The most popular formats are JPG (pronounced *jay-peg*), GIF (pronounced by most as *jif*) , and BMP (sometimes pronounced *bump* or spelled out, *B-M-P*). The only way to know which format is acceptable is to find out which ones the reader software or device prefers. Most readers will take both JPG and GIF, although some take BMP as well.

(Microsoft Reader does not support BMP.) Another factor is whether the images will get compressed or not. BMP files can be huge unless compressed. JPG and GIF both have image compression built into them, and compressing again usually accomplishes nothing. Probably your best bet is to try converting each image to all of the different formats, and see which one looks best and has the smallest size.

Images with PDF are a bit different. If you can drop a particular image into the word processing or layout document and print to PDF, then you'll see the image in the PDF document. But size is still a problem, and sometimes JPG images get compressed down so far they end up looking pretty bad. If you're struggling with images in PDF, you might want to check out the **Adobe** Web site for tips (http://www.adobe.com/) or drop by **Planet PDF** (http://www.planetpdf.com/), which is where all the PDF experts hang out. They can give you the best advice on dealing with images in PDF.

General Tips for Spiffy E-Books—*Keep the following general tips in mind when creating documents that will end up in e-book form:*
- *Stay clear of multiple columns. Stick to one column.*
- *Keep your basic fonts from 11 to 13 points in size. Headers can be bigger, of course, but you should probably stay clear of anything over 24 points.*
- *Keep the page size 6 inches wide by 9 inches tall for PDF; for Microsoft Reader, use the default that comes with the template. For others, check with the manufacturer of the e-book software.*
- *Keep your images small in size and in the number of colors they use.*
- *Choose JPG or GIF over BMP for images—and experiment to see which format works best for each image while minimizing file size.*
- *For HTML, avoid advanced features such as Cascading Style Sheets and Dynamic HTML unless you have a good reason to do otherwise.*

Copy Protection

In Chapter 5, "Digital Rights and Copy Protection," we discuss many topics of copy protection. If you desire to prevent your works from being copied, we encourage you to learn about the issues involved.

But how do you create an e-book that cannot be copied? For all the readers described in this chapter, the actual process of encrypting the e-book and preventing it from being copied takes place during the sales transaction. The work is done by the servers that handle the sale. This ensures that the item is protected for a specific reader software installed on the consumer's particular computer.

For authors going through an e-publisher, this means you really don't have to do much about the copy protection, as it will be handled by the sales channel. However, you will want to make sure that the e-publisher is selling your book through online retail stores that actually do encrypt it.

If you are a self-published author, you have a couple of choices. If you are selling your book through an online retail center, you will want to make sure that the retailer has the appropriate software to encrypt the e-book. But if you are going to sell the book yourself through your own Web site, your only real choice is to obtain the necessary (and pricey) software that will handle the encryption. This is typically the same software that handles the sales of the e-book as well.

Software for selling e-books is available from the manufacturers of e-book reader software. Microsoft makes an entire server system called the Digital Asset Server (DAS). You can find out about this server at the **DAS** site, http://www.microsoft.com/reader/das/default.htm. **Glassbook** makes similar software, and you can find out about it at the company site, http://www.glassbook.com/.

From E-Book to Online Retailers

If you are self-publishing, the final step you need to know is how to get your e-book into the online retailers such as **Borders** (http://www.borders.com/), **Amazon.com** (http://www.amazon.com/), and **Barnes & Noble** (http://www.bn.com/), as well as any number of other online retailers. This section will give you a quick introduction to the subject—for more detail, see the "Selling E-Books" section in Chapter 7, "Assembling Your E-Publishing Venture."

The easiest way to get your e-book into these channels is by going through a distributor. In the same way that publishers of print books use distributors to get books into brick-and-mortar bookstores, distributors now help publishers get e-books into online retailers. Ingram's **Lightning Source** (http://www.lightningsource.com/) does just that.

The only catch is that different retailers sell e-books for different formats. For example, Microsoft Reader is the primary format on Amazon.com. The RCA reader devices are the preferred formats for BN.com.

More About RCA—*Originally, the Softbook and Rocket eBook devices had all the necessary software for creating e-books for these two devices. The software was available at the respective Web sites for the Softbook and Rocket eBook. But in early 2000, the companies that create these two competing devices were both purchased by Gemstar and given the RCA brand name. At the time of this writing, the old software for creating Softbook Editions and Rocket Editions is no longer available, even though the new RCA REB1200 device that replaced the Softbook still supports Softbook Editions and the REB1100 device that replaced the Rocket eBook still supports Rocket Editions. Unfortunately, Gemstar has not yet announced any tools for creating e-books for the new RCA e-book devices. Your best bet is to watch the* **Gemstar** *e-book site, at* http://www.gemstarebook.com/.

To get through this step with Lightning Source, you will need to register with Lightning Source. You can find out more information at the Publisher section of **Lightning Source** at http://www.lightningsource.com/publisher.html; click How It Works.

If you prefer to skip the distributor, you will be in for quite a job, because you will have to contact each retailer and negotiate a deal separately. (That's the purpose of the distributor, really, to contact all the retailers for you.)

Finally, remember something we mentioned in the "From Manuscript to E-Book" section earlier in this chapter: If you're working with a retailer or distributor, make sure you include the required metadata in your e-books, as the business may need it for its database and cataloging.

CHAPTER FIVE

Digital Rights and Copy Protection

Suppose you're going to make a living as an author. You've written the novel of your life, and it's going to make you a millionaire and famous. You're going to live your dream as a writer, with a house in the mountains.

And how would you feel if for each person out there who bought your book, five people just photocopied its pages—five people who really liked your book, fans of yours, and never paid you a dime for your work?

It probably wouldn't make you too happy. That's a pretty easy one.

Have you ever gotten a book out of a public library or borrowed a good paperback from a friend and read the book cover to cover? Did the author get paid for your reading? In the case of the library, if you were the only one who ever got it out you could argue the author got paid for that one copy. But that's not likely; more likely lots of people got the book out, too, and the author only got paid once.

The truth is, the author doesn't make any money when people borrow and share paper books. The same is true with e-books.

Digital information is extremely easy to copy, while books are difficult to copy. You could get the information out of a book by running it page by page through a photocopier, but that could get expensive, and the quality degrades with each copy; further, you don't get the nice paper and the handsome cover. Further, as books get passed around and loaned to people, they tend to degrade. But digital files are easy to copy or attach to an e-mail message and send to somebody else, and the files don't degrade or change or lose anything. It all stays there. So you can imagine what might happen if the world were let loose with e-books with no copy protection. It would be terrible for us authors, because we might sell only ten or so copies, they would go out on the Internet, and millions of people would read our work and not pay a penny for it.

Or would they?

In this chapter we look at the different thoughts behind copy protection in the e-book world. First we give many different perspectives on it, and then we talk about what is being done, and finally about what you as an e-book creator should be aware of regarding copy protection.

Lessons From the Past

Think about software. If software were easy to copy, everybody would do it, and Microsoft and the other big names would go belly up. Thank goodness they protect it.

But wait! Is that true? Is software protected? Actually, most is not. If you purchase Microsoft Word and install it on your computer at home, there's nothing stopping you from loaning the CD-ROM to some friends and letting them install it on their computers. And then they could do the same, and so on. Has this hurt Microsoft? Bill Gates may have lost some income, but he certainly isn't hurting. Why is that? Because most people don't copy software.

Did you know that you can get absolutely any software you want for free over the Internet? It's true. There are newsgroups and Web pages where hackers post any software you can think of. So why don't people download the software for free? Two reasons, and which one matters more depends on the person: fear and honesty.

Some people are just plain scared that they might get caught. Fines are particularly hefty when a business gets caught with pirated software. (Like in the hundreds of thousands of dollars, and we're not exaggerating.) Some people are nervous that pirated software might turn out to be incomplete or contain viruses. Others are, frankly, honest. They don't care to download software without buying it.

The software companies have learned this the hard way. Depending on your age, you may remember the early 1980s when personal computers were brand new. Software publishers went to great lengths to prevent disks from being copied. Some would sell software that would install itself onto a hard drive and then cause the install disk to self-destruct. Some would purposely corrupt an unused portion of the disk so it would cause disk copy software to fail. These are only two of the tricks of the trade; there were many more copy protection methods.

And for every method there was a *crack,* a version of the software that some hacker created by removing the copy protection. These cracked versions of the software would float around on computer bulletin board systems (the dial-in 1980s precursor to the Internet) and people would download them for free. They were everywhere. I remember seeing one program that opened with a message from one hacker to another. It seems the second hacker had been hired by a company to create a copy protection. The first hacker found this when he cracked it, so he added a message that would appear when the cracked version of the software loaded: "Nice try, Jim, but not good enough!"

Eventually the software companies had a revelation. They realized that the harder they tried to copy protect their software, the bigger the challenge they were giving to hackers to crack it. And the hackers *would* crack it, and the free software would float around. But the software companies found that if they took a different approach, one that provided for an inherent trust in the general population, then the hackers would have nothing to do. So that's the way it is for a lot of software today: The software is not copy protected. Sure, there are free copies floating around on the Internet, and if you're really determined to steal software, you can get it. But there are loads of honest people out there, and most software companies are surviving just fine.

Software companies have even taken this concept a step further: They offer free trials known as *shareware*. Many software companies now let you download a free copy of their software. The software will either have certain features disabled until you buy the real thing, or it will have a reminder that it's shareware, like the one in Figure 5.1. Or it may be fully functional, but will no longer work after some time period, such as thirty days. So if you like it, you send in a credit card number and you'll get the real thing. Some companies will send you a new, full version. Others just send you a little license file that will unlock the demo and turn it into a full version. The license file concept is particularly nice, because

Figure 5.1: This shareware notice piles on the guilt, saying you've been using the program since whenever-you-started-using-it until you pay up just to shut it up.

you don't need to download an entire new version of the software, and you don't need to completely reinstall it. Instead, you just copy this license file in and you're ready to roll.

The license file concept is also beneficial to the software companies. It's efficient—the simple existence of a license file may be enough to unlock the demo software and turn it into a full version (or the license file might contain the necessary information to do so)—and the software company can also put more information into the file, such as your name.

We remember seeing this a few years ago in CuteFTP, a nice software package designed for copying files across the Internet (available from **CuteFTP** at http://www.cuteftp.com/, in case that's just what you're looking for). This software uses exactly this license method: You can download a demo for free and use it. For the most part, the demo is fully functional, although there are a couple of things here and there that it cannot do. But then when you're ready to buy it, you send in a credit card number, and the owners send you a license file that you copy to a particular place on your computer. Now when you open up the program you get the remaining features, and the splash screen says "Licensed to" followed by your name, as in Figure 5.2. This same method has also been used by a lot of other software companies for some time.

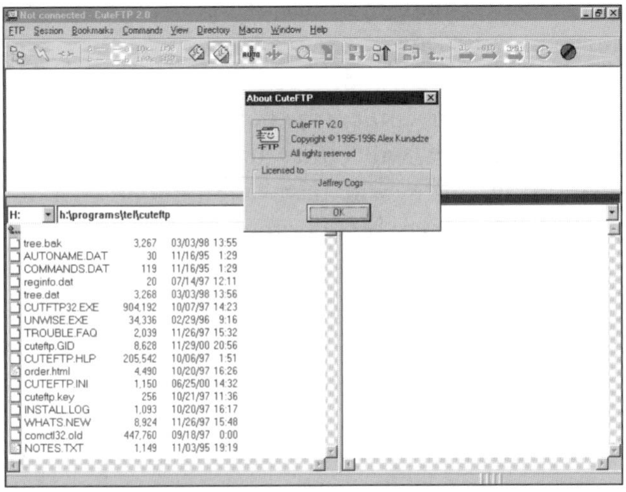

Figure 5.2: Now that Jeff has paid for the software, he has a license file and a notice to prove it, even if they spelled his last name wrong.

We don't know what happens if you copy the license file to somebody else's computer. But it will probably do exactly as it did on the computer it was intended for: It will unlock the software, and the software will now function in full. And when it starts it'll say "Licensed to" followed by the original licensee's name. That's important: It will have the same name on it, not somebody else's. So it's obvious who the culprit was in copying it.

So the software industry has learned. Strict copy protection doesn't pay off; a simple copy deterrent does.

Free Music on the Web!

The music industry was the next big operation to attempt strict copy protection. Over the past few years, companies have gone to great lengths to come up with ways to protect digital music on the Internet. Patents have been filed, and software has been created. And now everyone has music on their computers that cannot be copied. Right?

Wrong. Not on our computers, anyway. We don't have any copy protection preventing us from copying downloadable music files. Do you? It's doubtful. Most people don't. The reason is that the software never made it anywhere.

But the original idea was nice: People could download individual songs and would not be able to copy them. They would pay a minimal price per song, and what they got (that is, the *rights* that they received) would depend on how much they paid. They might have paid a little and only get to listen to the song once or twice. Or they might have paid a premium and could listen to the music as much as they wanted.

Other software took a different approach: You would download the song, and listen to it all you wanted. And at the end of the month you would get a bill. Sounds kind of like Big Brother, but whatever floats the boats (or yachts) of the big record company executives....

Meanwhile, all these different techniques had one thing in common: The downloaded music could only be played on a particular computer. They all used different methods of making this happen, but they all prevented the file from being copied.

Sound like fun? Many people think it's a total distrust of themselves, the consumers. They don't go around copying CDs, records, and cassettes. They also don't try to copy all the VCR tapes they get from the video store and snarl at the ones with copy protection. They don't record songs off the radio and sell them. And they don't like being treated with the assumption that they're criminals.

Because so many people felt the same way, there was an immediate resistance and outcry to such copy protection, especially to monitoring your usage of the songs and billing you at the end of the month. Besides the question of having their listening habits tracked, people felt there were too many ways to get ripped off as a result of anything from bookkeeping glitches to power failures. In the end, the whole thing was a total flop and as of the year 2000, strict copy protection on digital music has not become a commercial reality.

But meanwhile, some software people came up with something called an MP3 file. This was a file format that provided CD-quality sound on your computer. MP3 files had no copy protection, and could therefore be traded over the Internet. They could be copied freely, and the sound was great. Now *that,* people loved.

And so even though most people are inherently honest about not copying software, people did start copying—and copying MP3s. One company that has been in the news a lot as we write is **Napster** (http://www.napster.com/), which gave people software that made it easy to share MP3 files between their computers, over their Internet connection. It was actually quite a remarkably simple idea (the best kind!) that was created by a college student, and he soon found investors and got a whole company going. Figure 5.3 shows the Napster site.

Soon a bunch of record companies (and several musicians, including the rock band Metallica) became upset and sued Napster, alleging that it was helping people copy music illegally.

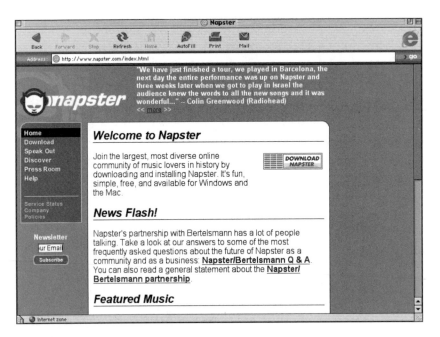

Figure 5.3: The (in)famous Napster site.

So there were two extremes in the belief set: The record companies wanted strict copy protection. The people wanted freedom to copy. And there were fights and fights, and a great big mess. Since the war isn't over yet as we write this, we can't say what the outcome will be. But we can say that the e-book industry can learn from the flap.

Most likely the biggest mistake was the paranoia. The recording industry was so paranoid that it created technology that was far too tight. The people responded by going to the other extreme, embracing something that allowed for total freedom to copy. Much better for all sides if they could have come up with some reasonable middle ground before they got too irritated to see straight!

Lessons From the Paper Book Industry

Now think back to the paper book industry. We mentioned at the beginning of this chapter how difficult it is to copy a paper book, although possible. But we also mentioned the ease with which you can just hand the book over to somebody else who can then get a full read out of it. So think about this: Because you can just trade books around or get them out of the library, in a sense, it really *is* easy to copy books. You may not be physically producing a new copy of the book, but the end result is the same: Two or more people read it, but only one pays for it.

Has this hurt the publishing industry? Have libraries and people trading paperback novels put the industry out of business? Hardly. Although the publishers certainly don't want us to encourage people to pass books around, it does indeed happen. (And it gives us authors a good excuse for inflating the number of copies we say our books sold!) And though we cannot say publishers haven't suffered, we can say that they have managed to build a business model that takes this additional loss into consideration—a business model that has succeeded for a couple of hundred years.

So if that's the case, why are publishers afraid of e-books? Because computer files are *so* easy to copy. While paper books can be passed around to a few people, or a few dozen people can borrow them from a library, computer files can be posted on the Internet and downloaded by hundreds, thousands, or even millions of people.

The Publishers Speak

Some publishers are open to using low-level copy protection on e-books, but others have stronger feelings. Many publishers are terrified of the prospect of their content being freely distributed throughout the Internet, ultimately putting them out of business. Remember, unlike magazines and television, which give out content practically for free and rely on income from advertisers, book publishers don't sell ads. (Who wants to read a novel filled with ads like a magazine?)

So while passing around a magazine increases circulation and therefore the prices the publisher can charge for ads, passing around books causes lost revenue, the very bread and butter of the book publishing industry.

In 1999 the **Association of American Publishers** (an industry group—see http://www.publishers.org/) put together a committee on copy protection issues. The committee worked with various industry groups and companies and developed a methodology for analyzing how secure various copy protection approaches are; they also developed a "report card" showing just how secure various devices of the time were. It's pretty clear from this group's mandate that publishers are very concerned about the potential copying, and will not tolerate the idea of producing e-books with little or no copy protection. You can view the report card and related documents at the AAP's Web site, shown in Figure 5.4.

Superdistribution and Previews

Superdistribution is sort of the positive way of looking at copying digital media such as e-books. The idea is that if people can easily copy works, why not allow this and take advantage of it?

Really, this is not much different from the idea of shareware distribution in the computer software industry, which we described in the "Lessons from the

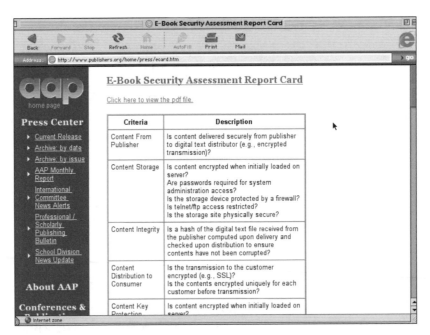

Figure 5.4: The Web site of the Association of American Publishers analyzes the security of various copy protection devices according to these and other criteria.

Past" section earlier in this chapter. Shareware was big primarily in the 1980s and 1990s when a lot of small software companies found that since they couldn't afford big marketing and production campaigns for their products, it was easier to allow people to copy their software and pass it along to friends (hence the notion of *share*ware), and send in a check if they wanted to keep it.

The shareware industry was quite successful by relying on the idea of superdistribution: If every person gave a copy of the software to ten people, then in little time thousands or even millions of people would have a copy of the software. And if all those people who liked it paid for it, the software company would profit. Even if only 10 percent sent in the money, the software company could still potentially profit, given the minimal advertising and distribution costs.

The people of the e-book industry have talked off and on about the idea of superdistribution. However, like software, this technology relies on sending out either fully functional versions of the books or limited versions, which the e-book world calls preview versions.

As you might imagine, the publishing industry is not at all interested in the kind of superdistribution where people can pass around full versions of the books and pay on the honor system. This frightens most publishing companies in the same way it would frighten a store owner to think about letting customers come in and take things home and share them freely and only pay if their conscience tells them to. The store owner would soon go out of business. The shareware approach often works for software, which can be duplicated at little or no cost, but it won't work for material goods that require whole factories to copy such as the items in a retail store. Although e-books are like software as far as ease of copying goes, regular books are not—and regular books are the main product of publishers. Publishers are not yet used to the idea of products that can easily be duplicated and, therefore, superdistributed.

The preview approach, however, has gained some acceptance, although the bigger e-book software and device companies are yet to support it.

Who Wrote This E-Book?

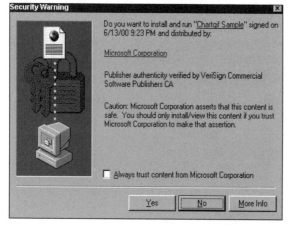

Figure 5.5: A digital certificate verifies that the creator of a document is who it claims to be.

Publishers have raised another concern about e-book distribution, which also has a parallel in the software world. Suppose you receive an e-book and the front page says it came from Top Floor Publishing. How can you be sure it really came from Top Floor? There's nothing stopping people from putting somebody else's name on an e-book. There are great liability issues here, because a publisher doesn't want to get sued for something someone else said but attributed to the publisher.

Further, suppose you receive a book that really did come from Top Floor, and it says so on the cover, but the text of the book has been changed in some way by someone other than Top Floor? One could imagine scenarios of people sabotaging books by adding pornography or other offensive material to them, and again, causing the publisher to get in trouble.

The software industry has solved this problem by using what are called digital certificates. These certificates use encryption technology to be sure that the software could only come from a certain organization holding a certain secret number. Another organization called a *trusted third party* handles administrative issues of verifying that the company is who it says it is, and then issuing the company its own secret number. One well-known trusted third party is **Verisign** (http://www.verisign.com). Figure 5.5 is an example of a certificate in action.

The technology works and has been quite successful in the software industry. Some people have proposed doing the same for e-books, although few of the big e-book software and devices are doing this yet.

Do You Want Copy Protection?

So far in this chapter we have presented a lot of scenarios and ideas. Some people say that since copying has not hurt the computer software industry, and borrowing and trading paper books hasn't hurt authors and publishers, then clearly copying e-books won't hurt authors and publishers, either—so we don't need copy protection. But others say that e-books are too easy to copy and download, and authors and publishers will be hurt. But as we write this, we still don't have enough information to say which is right.

Therefore, as an e-book author or creator, you need to consider this: Do you want copy protection? Probably some. But how much and what kind? Our goal with the first few pages of this chapter was to get you thinking about the different issues in copy protection, and whether you need it. We're not saying you don't need copy protection, but we're not saying it's a definite yes either.

In the following sections, we talk about the different kinds of copy protection available—what they are and how you can use them.

How to Copy an E-Book in Three Easy Steps—*In the early days of software, hacking was rampant. And presently, e-book companies are headed down the same path. They are working hard to make extremely strict copy protection...which makes breaking that protection a tempting challenge. So how do you copy an e-book in three easy steps?*

Step 1. Wait for the book to be released.
Step 2. Wait for the hackers to get hold of it.
Step 3. Download it off the Web.

Okay, that was too cheap. We really can't give you the details of how to copy, because we're not expert in such things. But we can tell you that most likely hackers will find a way. So if you really want to copy a protected e-book, just wait and somebody will.

Kinds of Copy Protection

The world of copy protection falls into a bigger world known as *digital rights management* (DRM). The idea behind DRM is for companies to come up with ways for software to manage what you read, and whether you can copy it or not.

Consumer Rights

In this context, "consumer rights" are the specific things consumers can do with an e-book—not the things an e-book should or should not do with them (amuse them, bore them, mislead them...). These are the specific acts (which may be permitted or forbidden for a given book) in question:

- Copying the book to another file
- Giving the book to somebody else
- Copying text to the Clipboard and pasting it into another program
- Copying a single image out of the book and saving it to a file
- E-mailing a book, text from a book, or images from a book
- Printing a book (once, unlimited times, or a particular number of times)
- Paying for and viewing only portions of a book

Passwords and the Web

The simplest form of digital rights management is to simply protect content with a password. This is commonly done on Web sites where the content isn't very valuable (or the webmasters didn't know any different). With this method, people visit a Web site and are prompted for a password. If they enter a correct password (sometimes in conjunction with a user name) they can access the content.

This approach really doesn't provide any copy protection, because all the big-name Web browsers let you save a Web page to disk, and from there it's not much trouble to print up the site or e-mail it to somebody else. Further, all the major Web browsers let you select text and copy and paste it into another program such as a word processor. However, some companies have been known to follow this practice, particularly online journals.

Big Brother and Persistent Connections

Some DRM systems are extremely complex (borderline cumbersome) and are more suited to documents found in a corporation than among consumers who read e-books at home. These systems usually involve a central computer (called a *server*) that essentially dishes out the documents (or even individual pages of a document) to the users' computers. The corporation might have thousands of people working at different computers, and different people have different levels of what they're allowed and not allowed to read. For example, the people in Human Resources might have access to documents that involve personal information about certain employees, information that isn't for public viewing. But there might be other documents that everybody can read, provided they're reading it from a company computer.

As each person tries to read a document, the server will first ask for a user name and password, and from there decide whether the person is authorized to see the particular document. If so, the server will then send the document. If not, the requester might be given a message such as, "Sorry, you are not allowed to view this document." Or, the person might not even be able to see that the document exists at all—that is, its name won't even appear in the list of available documents.

Some similar systems even take this all one step further by either limiting how long the user is allowed to read the document or monitoring how long the user spends on each page. It's hard to come up with a particularly valid reason why a company would need such information, but perhaps some people could.

Of course, all the systems in this category have strict rules on whether the documents can be copied or not. Typically they let the creator of the document or the person running the server decide whether a document can be copied, and if so, by whom.

Finally, often these systems require PDF documents, which are documents that can be read with Adobe's Acrobat or free Acrobat Reader software, available from the **Adobe** Web site at http://www.adobe.com/.

It's unlikely that you, as an e-book author, would need DRM systems such as these. Probably the biggest reason to ignore them is not the possibly overly strict management but the requirement for a central computer that consumers would need to connect to before being granted access to the books. In the case of the users logged into Internet, this would mean their Internet connection would have to be active and they would need to dial out and connect over the Web to the central server before they could read the book—not just the first time, but possibly each time they wanted to read it. That could be annoying to them, particularly if they wanted to read their books on a laptop or PDA while on an airplane. For this reason, sometimes the term *persistent connection* is used in reference to this sort of DRM system.

Of course, if you're creating e-books for internal use within a large corporation, you may well want this sort of security. Or if you're creating premium content (such as analyst reports and such) then you might also need such strict copy protection, even if it's over the Internet.

One company that makes a system such as this is **ContentGuard** (a spin-off from Xerox, found at http://www.contentguard.com/, shown in Figure 5.6). As it happens, ContentGuard also has additional features that let people disconnect from the persistent connection and take their books and documents on the airplane; however, they still need to first get the rights granted from the central computer.

Persistent, but No Big Brother

Another method of preventing the copying of content is to put the content on the Internet, probably on Web sites, and allow it to be downloaded to a

Figure 5.6: ContentGuard provides a full-featured digital rights and security system.

computer, but not allow the person to copy it. Using various technologies associated with Web browsers (in case you're technically savvy, we're talking about Java here), software companies have come up with ways to make sure that you can only view certain information (such as e-books) in your Web browser, but you can't print it, select the text and copy it, or save it elsewhere on your hard disk. It just sits there in your Web browser. Further, using password protection, they can limit who can access it. Of course, the password concept isn't very good because it's easy for people to just give out their passwords to anyone they feel like letting into the file.

One site that employs this technique is **WordPop.com,** http://www.wordpop.com/. (This site used to be called Netbooks.) If you visit this site, you can view some free books by clicking the Free Books icon on the front page. When you read a book, a window opens that displays the book's text. Although the text appears in the window, you cannot select it with the mouse and copy it to the Clipboard as you can with a normal Web browser window. The window gives you buttons for controlling the size of the text so you can find the setting that's most comfortable for you. You move forward or backward through the pages by clicking the left arrow and right arrow buttons, and you can jump to a chapter name by choosing it in the drop-down list. A sample of such a window appears in Figure 5.7.

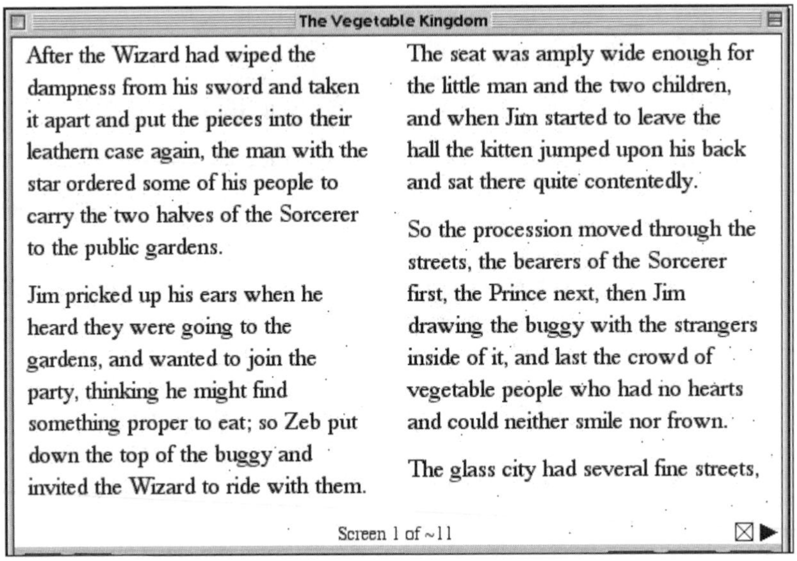

```
┌─────────────────────────────────────────────────────────────┐
│ ▢                    The Vegetable Kingdom                  ▤ │
├─────────────────────────────────────────────────────────────┤
```

After the Wizard had wiped the dampness from his sword and taken it apart and put the pieces into their leathern case again, the man with the star ordered some of his people to carry the two halves of the Sorcerer to the public gardens.

Jim pricked up his ears when he heard they were going to the gardens, and wanted to join the party, thinking he might find something proper to eat; so Zeb put down the top of the buggy and invited the Wizard to ride with them.

The seat was amply wide enough for the little man and the two children, and when Jim started to leave the hall the kitten jumped upon his back and sat there quite contentedly.

So the procession moved through the streets, the bearers of the Sorcerer first, the Prince next, then Jim drawing the buggy with the strangers inside of it, and last the crowd of vegetable people who had no hearts and could neither smile nor frown.

The glass city had several fine streets,

Screen 1 of ~11   ⊠ ▶

Figure 5.7: This online e-book is on the WordPop.com Web site.

When you read books using this system, you must be connected to the Internet the whole time you are reading. When you go to a new page, the text for that page is then downloaded. Because of this, you need to have your Internet connection on. This same site does let you download the entire book to your computer for offline viewing, which makes it somewhat more flexible than if it insisted on a persistent connection. The browser technology stays in use offline, however, so you still can't copy the text or save it outside the browser.

Connectionless

Another kind of DRM doesn't require a persistent connection to the Internet. In this type of system, typically the e-book is downloaded over the Internet when it's purchased, but then the user can hang up the modem and would never need to dial back in or connect to the Internet when reading the particular book. Of course, anyone who wanted to purchase more books would need to dial in or reconnect to the e-book site.

The common types of e-books that we've been describing so far in this book use this kind of DRM. These include the **Microsoft Reader** (http://www.microsoft.com/reader) and the PDF system used by Fatbrain's **MightyWords** (http://www.mightywords.com). Another company that uses this connectionless approach is Infinite Ink, which is a subsidiary of a company called InterTrust. You can find out about **Infinite Ink** at http://www.infiniteink.com. The parent company, **InterTrust Technologies Corp.**, can be found at http://www.intertrust.com.

Hardware Devices

Hardware devices have their own ways of protecting against copying that differ not only from the software methods but from those of other devices. The most common approach to protection is to give each individual device (not brand of device, but each *separate device*) its own secret number. You, the owner of the device, know half of the secret number. When you purchase a book for the device, you supply your half of the secret number. The Web site from which you're downloading the book will then encrypt the book specifically for your device using the half you supplied. After the book is downloaded to your device, the device can display it using the other half of the secret number, which is safely stored away inside the device. If you downloaded the e-book to your PC and gave it to somebody else with the same kind of e-book device, it won't work for their device.

Digital Rights Standards

At the time of this writing, there are still no industry-wide standards for digital rights. Why should there be any standards? Because the hope is that eventually all e-books can be displayed on any e-book device or any e-book software. But that means if the file can be displayed on any device, and if the file has some sort of copy protection attached to it, the device needs to know how to handle the copy protection.

Although there are not yet any industry-wide standards, there are groups and companies working on creating standards, hoping that they will take off. The following are some of the standards being worked on.

EBX and BISG

EBX is a standard originally created by **Glassbook** (http://www.glassbook.com, the maker of the Glassbook Reader, which was acquired by **Adobe**, http://www.adobe.com). Since then, the members of the EBX working group have moved the standard over to the domain of the **Book Industry Study Group**, or BISG (http://www.bisg.org). The BISG is a nonprofit organization devoted to analyzing and reporting on trends within the book industry.

EBX is a rather thorough specification. It tackles such issues as sharing books, borrowing books, and loaning books (when you loan a book, the recipient can see it on his or her computer and you can't see it on yours until you get it back), as well as the complete process of purchasing a book. The specification lays out in technical detail the entire process by which this all takes place; in general the information in the technical specification is more information than the e-book author or creator needs.

You can find information about EBX, as well as the entire specification, at the **EBX Working Group Site**, http://www.ebxwg.org.

Patented Fears—If you're interested in EBX, you should be aware of some of the concerns that have been brought up by many people within the e-book industry. The original specification stated that the technology included various patents owned by the creator of EBX, Glassbook. This has created great friction within the industry, because companies are hesitant to use a technology that might later turn out to require payment of royalties to the owners of the patent. During various conferences, the people from Glassbook have assured everyone that they would place the patents in the public domain (or something like that; it was not very clear). However, as it happens this is all likely to fade away now that Adobe owns Glassbook. Adobe owns both copyrights and patents on PDF technology and has made PDF an open standard, anyway, without requiring companies to pay royalties to Adobe. We can expect the same is likely to become true with EBX. However, you will want to check with Adobe on such matters before making a decision.

Open eBook

Originally, **Open eBook** or OEB (http://openebook.org) was simply a way of "marking up" text to tell the computer what's a header, what's italic print, what the title of the book is, and so on. While OEB is still all this, its standards group has long recognized the need for a digital rights management system. In mid-2000 the group began work on enhancing the standard to support digital rights. At the time of this writing, the Open eBook Forum has not yet released a standard for Digital Rights Management, and the official documents only state that they are working on it. Because of who the creators are, you can be assured that the Open eBook Digital Rights Management standard will have much industry acceptance, and most likely Microsoft will support it.

Standards Are Always Competing—Like so many other things in the computer industry, there are competing standards for digital rights management. In the world of publishing, it seems like it always comes down to Microsoft versus Adobe. Microsoft has become a hearty backer of Open eBook. Adobe has become a big supporter of EBX, which should be no surprise since EBX focuses primarily on protecting PDF documents. Besides, the company that originally created EBX, Glassbook, has been purchased by Adobe.

XrML

XrML, or Extensible Rights Management Language, was created by **ContentGuard** (http://www.contentguard.com), which was originally a part of Xerox. ContentGuard has developed XrML as a standard, and encourages others to use it royalty-free; however, those companies must license it from ContentGuard. (If you're interested in the details, see the **XrML** site at http://www.xrml.org for more information about licensing. Figure 5.8 gives you a glimpse of the offering.)

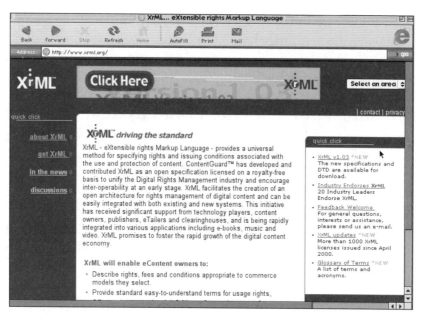

Figure 5.8: The XrML site provides a complete description of the Extensible Rights Management Language.

Other DRM Players

Other companies are working on digital rights management relating to the publishing field. These companies are, in general, pushing forward with their own products, not a standard.

One such company is **InterTrust** (http://www.intertrust.com), the parent company to Infinite Ink. Although InterTrust only recently acquired Infinite Ink, a small e-book software company, it has actually been around for some time laying the groundwork for digital rights management in other areas such as music. It has developed software that puts digital rights protection software on various devices such as Windows CE computers. It has also created a technology that ensures that a particular piece of media (that is, a single song or a single e-book) can be stored on a Zip disk and cannot be copied. Presently it is using this technology primarily for music, although it's conceivable that the company has plans to move this technology to the e-book arena.

Softlock (http://www.softlock.com) is another company that has been around for some time and has also laid much of the groundwork in digital rights management. Recently it has teamed up with another company, **Inceptor** (http://www.inceptor.com). Together the two companies have created a search engine that lets people search for so-called *premium content,* that is, content that is for-pay and is digitally protected from being copied. This includes e-books.

Although InterTrust and Softlock have pioneered much of the technology for digital rights management, they have not moved forward with much force in the e-book world. Even if they do, their technology is primarily working behind the scenes—you probably won't be buying it for yourself.

Selecting an E-Publisher and a DRM System

If you are an e-book author looking for a home for your book, you will want to know what DRM technology the various online publishing houses are using. Let's take a quick look at some things you'll want to know about copy protection before choosing an e-publisher.

This chapter gave you an overview of the DRM technology, and enough information to understand what the different DRM types do and don't do. Using that information, combined with your own copy protection desires, you should be able to decide whether any particular e-publisher provides the copy protection you want.

Here are some questions to ask when evaluating an e-publisher.

- Do you want or need copy protection?
- Does the publisher provide any form of copy protection?
- Does the publisher use a DRM created by another well-respected DRM company, or has the publisher rolled its own DRM software?
- Does the publisher require that consumers be logged on to the Internet at all times? Does this matter to you?
- Can the consumer select text in the book and copy it to the computer's Clipboard and then save the text?
- Can the consumer print books? How many copies?
- Can the consumer loan the book to people and if so can the consumer still see it while it's loaned out?
- Can the consumer download a free preview of the book?
- What other consumer rights are available?

Regarding the final point, recall the "Consumer Rights" list earlier in this chapter—is there anything else you want your readers to be able to do (or not do) with your e-book?

If you can't find the answer to these questions on the e-publisher's Web site, don't be afraid to ask, either through e-mail or in a phone call. Remember, the e-book is your content and you want to make sure that it's protected in the way that you want or need. The last thing you need is to see your e-book being copied all over the planet by seemingly honest people who don't even realize that it's copyrighted material and that they're obligated to pay for it.

Remember: It's the Law

The government of the United States has gotten into the digital copy protection issue. Congress passed a law in 1998, known as the Digital Millennium Copyright Act, making it illegal to circumvent the copy protection in any software that has such protection, such as e-book software and devices. Certainly, this won't stop hackers from doing so, but now there is a law on the books by which the government can prosecute such hackers. If you're interested in reviewing the actual law, you can find it by visiting the **Library of Congress** site at http://thomas.loc.gov/ and searching the bills for "Digital Millennium Copyright Act."

PART III
Getting Your E-Book Published and Sold

CHAPTER SIX

Checking Out the E-Publishers

You have many different models and options for getting your e-book published, from going with the traditional author–publisher relationship to producing and marketing the book on your own. And there are many roads in between. There's no single right choice for everyone. Some situations call for a hands-on approach, while others lend themselves to more traditional models. It all depends on what you have to offer, who wants it, and what you can do about it. But to help you decide how and where to publish your e-books, Part III provides details about the various players in the e-publishing world, including the publishers, the booksellers, and the various entities that support the publishing process.

This chapter focuses on e-publishers, those companies using the traditional "author sells, publisher buys and distributes" model found in print publishing. We've split the publishers into various groups, featuring the major players in each group. (You'll find a useful list of the companies in this field in Appendix A, "E-Publishers," where the entries are grouped by genre.) With these publishers, your experience will be similar to that of a traditional author–publisher relationship. You are *not* self-publishing—and, therefore, you usually cannot sell your own version of your book in competition with one of these e-publishers (they want you to refer your customers to them) or sell your book to more than one publisher at the same time. Of course, all this varies, depending on the publisher, as you'll see in the following pages. Chapter 7, "Assembling Your Own E-Publishing Venture," tells about the various companies and services you can use to help you with a do-it-yourself approach, including a list of the distributors and booksellers offering different combinations of services and payment for publishers. Should you decide to go it alone, Chapter 8, "On Your Own: Book Marketing Strategies," will tell you how to go about marketing your books online and getting them noticed.

E-Publishers and Distributors

In the world of electronic publishing, it can be difficult to distinguish a publisher from a distributor or bookstore. Although it's nearly impossible to put some of these companies into any category, we're going to define a *publisher* as an entity that does not focus on selling directly to the public. Instead, a publisher's primary objective is to distribute its books through various booksellers. We will exclude any e-publishers who do not acquire books directly from authors. (E-publishers who specialize in taking already-published books and turning them into e-books are covered in Chapter 7, "Assembling Your Own E-Publishing Venture.") Generally, e-publishers offer some variation of the traditional publishing contract for authors, which means that you'll be selling the rights to your work in exchange for royalties.

In the world of printed books, most publishing companies work with one or more *distributors,* middlemen who transfer your books from the publisher to the bookstore—and collect a small percentage for the task. Distributors have become a huge influence in the print publishing business. Although there are many small distributors in the world, generally offering books in a specific region or field, the unhappy fact is that a few major players control most of the flow. This has had the effect of limiting the types of books that get published. Why? Because there are fewer and fewer people choosing books. Acquisitions editors don't really choose books like they used to. They often present books to their marketing department and the marketing department then gets a general idea from the folks at the distributor as to whether they'd buy the book. If the book buyers at the distribution companies have a lackluster response to the book, then the publisher is likely to reject the manuscript. Well, it's not always like this and it's not always this direct, but the idea that there are fewer, larger companies controlling the channel of book distribution (both into and out of the stores) does have the effect of limiting the options. As an author, it's common to hear something like this from a publishing company: "Well, your manuscript got through the editorial review just fine, but the sales department didn't think they could sell it, so we're going to have to pass on your book at this time."

The Beauty of Specialization—While it's true that the big distributors control most of the channels, there are plenty of smaller, niche distributors who specialize in certain types or categories of books. For example, BookPeople at http://www.bookpeople.com specializes in distributing self-help and spiritual books to retail outlets on the West Coast of the United States.

With electronic publishing and distribution, there really isn't a channel of distribution. The function of moving books from the publisher to the bookseller falls either on the side of the publisher (selling directly to online booksellers) or the booksellers themselves (who purchase books from publishers, then sell direct to the public). Amazon.com may call itself "The world's biggest bookstore," but it is also one of the biggest book distributors—storing books in warehouses all over the world and sending them out (one by one) to customers. Amazon has such a large distribution system that companies in other industries, such as toy manufacturers, are working with it to distribute their products.

When it comes to e-books, the channel of distribution is the same as the sales channel. It's not uncommon to see books being sold directly from the author to the public—with nobody in between, not even a publisher. And most of the e-book publishers sell directly to the public, too. For an e-publisher, distributing e-books means getting them listed with the e-bookstores. The books go directly to the store with no need for a distribution company. And the major e-bookstores are easy to find. We've listed them in the next chapter in case you decide to bypass the e-publishers and go it on your own.

All that being said, it's important to note that the major book distributors in the print world are also getting into e-book distribution. This includes **Ingram** at http://www.ingrambookgroup.com/default.asp/ and **Baker & Taylor** at http://www.btol.com. The services these companies offer to e-publishers (since distribution of physical books is not a needed service) include making e-books available in proprietary formats, such as the one for the Microsoft Reader and Print On Demand book production and distribution—two things that many e-publishers cannot provide for themselves. For more information about e-book distribution, refer to Chapter 7, "Assembling Your E-Publishing Venture."

***Distributor Markup**—With no distributors in the middle of the transaction between publisher and bookstore, shouldn't e-books end up costing less than printed books? After all, there's no middleman taking a cut, right? Well, it's not clear yet what the typical pricing of e-books will end up being and whether e-books will be cheaper than their printed counterparts. In Chapter 9, "Publishing Economics 101," we talk about the pricing of e-books and how e-publishing economics work.*

A Brief History of E-Publishing

It's difficult to say where and when it all started. Before the days of the Internet and World Wide Web, a few early starters thought it would be a great idea to place book manuscripts on computer disks and distribute them like software products. For the most part, these electronic books (not quite e-books as we know them today) were simply word processor files saved onto disk. Few of them were really successful except perhaps electronic versions of the Bible—of which there were many. Later, when interactive CD-ROM technology caught on, electronic books became more like interactive experiences and less like books on paper. These interactive products required a significant amount of development and a writing approach different from typical book production.

For details about the interactive writing process, see *Writing for New Media* by Andrew Bonime and Ken C. Pohlmann (Wiley, 1997).

Around the same time, software companies began to realize that they could stop printing manuals and instead deliver their instructions as searchable help files. Users could access these help files while working with the program itself, making the information instantly available. And the help files offered the same information as paper manuals—including illustrations. The Microsoft Windows Help system inspired even more development of interactive help systems and electronic documents. Developers could take Microsoft Word documents (or other word processor files) and convert them into interactive help files, accessible through the Windows Help system. In addition to writers of computer instruction manuals, a few developers began to create reference material in this format.

Then came the Internet and, to make a long story short, HTML all but replaced the interactive help systems in Microsoft Windows, since it provided the same functionality (graphics, links, jumps, glossaries, interactive indexes, and so on) yet was completely independent of Windows. An HTML document could be used on any computer that could connect to the Internet. Electronic documents began to show up as Web pages and eventually as downloadable documents or even HTML documents delivered on disk. Although most people did not believe anyone would seriously want to read a book on their computer screen (and most people wouldn't), some pioneers set out to build publishing empires, creating and selling downloadable HTML documents. Many self-publishers also took advantage of this format to put their own material out into the world via the Internet. And even though there are now several more advanced e-book formats, you'll still see a goodly number of e-publishers using HTML to deliver their books.

Some problems with HTML as an e-book format include its lack of security and difficulty of formatting. Publishers are now replacing HTML with a number of other e-book languages that offer more sophistication (see Chapter 4, "The Production Process," for more about e-book formats). Although a common format would perhaps improve the availability of e-books and stabilize the market, it might also have the effect of limiting the options and stifling technology. It's yet to be seen how this will turn out.

Here Come the Conglomerates

Although they may be resistant to change, eventually, the big guys always join the action—especially when the action threatens to change their entire business operation. Many of the big multinational publishing companies are still not getting into e-book publishing seriously and the majority of those who are getting into it are doing little more than converting their printed books into e-books to make them available for the eventual e-book craze that threatens to hit the planet.

Two Early Birds

A few of the conglomerate publishers have started concentrated e-book efforts, opening separate e-book publishing divisions and publishing manuscripts as e-books *before* they make it into print. In the following pages, we discuss two of these early arrivals.

Random House

Random House (http://www.randomhouse.com/ and http://www.atrandom.com/) was one of the first big publishing conglomerates to enter the e-book market. The company acquires and publishes e-books in basically the same manner that it publishes printed books. Its e-books are available at all the major online bookstores as well as some traditional stores. Random House was the first of the major publishers to offer 50 percent e-book royalties for authors. In a press release circulated to the publishing community, it trumpeted its decision to "share its net revenues from e-books equally with its authors."

Before this, Random House was already one of the better-paying of the larger publishers for e-books, giving authors around 15 percent royalties on the e-book's *retail price*. After you figure for the difference between retail and wholesale (net revenues are based on wholesale price), you'll find that moving to a 50–50 split of net revenues doesn't make that big a difference over the old system. What makes it interesting and important is that it confirms the idea that e-book revenues should be shared equally with the author—just as third-party licenses are shared. For more information on all this contractual business, refer to Chapter 10, "Hot Button Issues in E-Book Publishing Contracts"

Because they work for a large publisher, the folks at Random House have an established promotions and marketing machine in place for their books. When it comes to e-books, however, we're not convinced that you'll get better marketing or distribution from Random House than you could get with any of the smaller publishers. Not that they couldn't offer something special. It's just that while the Random House family is quite large (including book clubs, international affiliates, and a lot of other ways to push books) it's not clear that the e-book program will get a significant amount of attention and cross-pollination with its more traditional brothers and sisters (cross-marketing between corporate divisions is one of the advantages the big publishing houses offer, although it's apt to be more theoretical than real for many books). But Random House is committed to the new electronic technologies and has been converting all its previously published books into electronic books. It has even created a special publishing imprint (division) just for publishing e-books, called **atRandom** (http://www.atrandom.com/).

Among the dozens of Random House publishing divisions and imprints in the United States are Ballantine Books, the Bantam Dell Publishing Group, the Crown Publishing Group, the Doubleday Broadway Publishing Group, the Knopf Publishing Group, Fodor's Travel Guides, Random House Children's Books, the Random House Trade Group, and the Random House Audio Publishing Group. Random House has affiliate companies in Canada, the United Kingdom, Germany, Spain, Australia, New Zealand, and South Africa. The company is a division of Bertelsmann AG, one of the world's biggest media conglomerates, which also owns huge music companies, magazine and newspaper publishers, direct-to-customer book and music clubs, print and media services, and e-commerce companies.

Recommendations

While we applaud Random House's e-book royalty policy, we can't really say that publishing with this company is any better than publishing with one of the smaller companies offering similar or better royalties. The possible advantages of publishing an e-book with Random House include their ability to get their e-books into many different formats, the status the company offers, and the chance of getting your book picked up by one of the other divisions. A smaller publisher will probably offer a more personal author–publisher relationship. Since Random House matches some of the best royalty deals in e-book publishing (there are some better deals, but a 50–50 split is pretty good), it can't hurt to submit your manuscript there along with the other places. If your book does well, it could end up in print and get into the Random House distribution system for printed books.

Summary

Random House and atRandom.com are substantial e-book players. While their systems are based in the traditional print publishing world, they offer top royalties and huge marketing potential. If you can get your e-book published here, then we suggest you go for it. The status and infrastructure offered can only help an author. But check out Chapter 10, "Hot Button Issues in E-Book Publishing Contracts," before signing their standard agreement so that you understand what you'll be getting into.

Rights purchased. All rights.

Distribution. Online retailers, traditional distributors, and the Random House Web site.

Marketing. Great marketing potential through the company's huge media muscles, but it's unclear whether e-books will get much of its people's attention.

Construction of book. Publisher handles all book production, including cover, internal design, and e-book conversion. Random House offers many e-book formats. It registers the ISBN and copyright for your work. It has a complete and traditional editing process.

Advances. Depends on the book and author.

Fee to publish. None.

Royalties. 50 percent of publisher's net.

Contract negotiable. Yes, particularly if you have an agent.

Simon & Schuster

Simon & Schuster's e-book division is called **iBooks** (http://www.simonsays.com/). Although iBooks is a small division of S&S, with its own publishing program, it is nonetheless a traditional publisher, with a traditional contract and publishing model. It publishes primarily online in e-book format, but also makes some books available in paperback. It specializes in instant book subjects, such as books about movies (called *entertainment trade books*), video games, and such. Its e-book royalties are not great, ranging from 4 percent of net revenues (for licensing deals) to 10 percent. S&S treats e-books just like normal books, giving the same royalty rates for both. The contract is exclusive and gives the company pretty much all rights.

***The Value of a Domain Name**—Notice that the Web site URL for Simon & Schuster's iBooks division is* http://www.simonsays.com, *which is the normal Simon & Schuster Web site. The company's iBooks division does not have its own URL—largely because an online bookstore (discussed in Chapter 7, "Assembling Your E-Publishing Venture") already owns the domain name ibooks.com. If you want to get in touch with the editors at iBooks (Simon & Schuster), you'll need to go through an agent, as they do not deal with authors directly. That's typical of the larger publishers.*

The iBooks imprint is basically a specialty publisher, using the speed of Internet e-book publishing to produce timely books on faddish subjects. It is way behind the typical e-book publisher and even far behind Random House when it comes to the quality of author royalties and e-book contracts.

Recommendations

Since iBooks is a specialty publisher, we can really only recommend it if you happen to have a book that fits its specialty. Even then, you'll be dealing with an old-school attitude and lower-than-average author deals. However, in its field, it has been known to sell a lot of books and some of the opportunities it offers have great potential. As with any of the big publishers, we recommend that you understand the basics of publishing contracts (see Chapter 10) before signing a deal.

Summary

iBooks is a small division of Simon & Schuster, specializing in entertainment trade books and other "instant book" subjects (topics that require instant publishing due to their faddish nature). It offers a fairly low royalty and requires all rights, just like any print publisher. Its books often appear as both e-books and paperbacks.

Rights purchased. All rights.

Distribution. Online retailers, traditional distributors, and the iBooks Web site.

Marketing. Good marketing through the S&S infrastructure and in the particular areas covered.

Construction of book. Publisher handles all book production, including cover, internal design, and e-book conversion. It offers many e-book formats and registers the ISBN and copyright for your work. It has a complete and traditional editing process.

Advances. Depends on the book and author.

Fee to publish. None.

Royalties. 4 percent to 10 percent of publisher's net.

Contract negotiable. Yes, particularly if you have an agent.

E-Publishing Services: The New Vanity Publishers

Publishing a book these days is sort of like buying a stereo. First, there are dozens of brands to choose from and each has countless options and features. You have to educate yourself on the various technologies out there, so you know what you're getting. More important, you have to decide what you really want and what you can live without, because it soon becomes clear that none of the brands offers everything. It's a matter of which package you prefer—that is, which set of features you like most. Next, you get to decide if you want to get all those features in a single, self-contained unit, or if you'd prefer to get separate components and assemble the thing yourself. Naturally, it's more difficult to work with separate components, but many people believe that's the only way to get the best quality in each piece of the system.

When publishing an e-book, you get to make the same decisions. Do you want Print On Demand capability along with the e-book? Do you want your book to be downloadable or readable online or both? What e-book format do you prefer? All of them, you say? Well, which ones can you live without? Do you want to get the entire experience packaged by one publisher for ease and efficiency—or would you rather work with separate entities and put together your own publishing system? Your answers to these questions depend on many factors. How much time and energy do you have? What are the income potentials with the different options? What companies do you trust? How much do you know about this process? For sure, the easiest solution is to get everything in one place. But is that the best solution for you? In the next few pages, we'll explore the all-in-one publishing services. These are companies that, more or less, handle everything for you, the author. As you'll see, the services they offer vary widely. What makes them publishing services (by our definition) is that the author generally pays *them* to get the book published. The publishing services do not invest anything (or not much) in the books—and consequently they accept all manuscripts presented from anyone who is willing to pay the fee.

What Do E-Publishing Services Do?

E-publishing services are sort of like publishers in that they take a manuscript and turn it into a book that can be sold to the public—whether in printed form or electronic. But publishing services are also quite different from traditional publishers in that they are really just providing a service for anyone willing to pay for it. The service includes taking a document and turning it into a book. But as you'll see, it's not always so simple. These companies differ greatly in the services they offer. So let's start by reviewing just what types of services might be needed to get a book published and who you might choose to fulfill each one:

***Your Own Publishing Process**—In Chapter 7, "Assembling Your E-Publishing Venture," we discuss each of these functions from the perspective of the self-publisher. You might choose not to use a packaged publishing service and instead choose separate companies to construct your own publishing program.*

Writing. This has always been the author's job and continues to be. However, it's interesting to note that we're seeing more and more publishers filling this role by using staff writers to create books. This is a common practice with publishers who have strong series or brands, such as the Dorling Kindersley picture books, HungryMind's Cliff's Notes, or Lonely Planet's travel guides, just to name a few. It's unlikely that any of these publishers are signing authors to royalty-based contracts for writing books in these series.

Editing. Rarely the author's job (it's tough to edit yourself well), editing has traditionally been in the publisher's purview. But more and more publishers hire outside editors to fulfill this function. And when it comes to e-publishers, many expect the authors to get this done. The fact is, it doesn't really matter who hires the editor as long as editing happens. And if publishers save money by having authors do this function, then authors should get better royalties in exchange.

Layout and design. The "look and feel" of the inside of the book is more important for some books than for others. Fiction books are generally not very "designed" on the inside, while nonfiction picture books, for example, require a lot of attention to graphical presentation. This has always been the publisher's concern with printed books, but e-book publishers differ in their approach. When internal design is important to a book, some e-publishers rely on the author's original files as a guide for layout, while others have their own standards for design. Here's a general rule: If you create your own e-book file using PDF or XML or any other format, then you are probably the one in charge of the layout.

File conversion for e-book. Getting a manuscript from a typical word processor document into an e-book format can be as complex or as simple as you like. Some publishers have proprietary formats that require their own conversion process, while others simply publish downloadable PDF or HTML files—a format that practically anyone can provide. If you publish your own book, then you need to think about what formats to use and how you're going to convert manuscripts. Part II, "Planning and Creating an E-Book," should help with this. If you end up going with an e-publisher, it's likely to have its own process for converting files into the formats it uses.

Security. Security is commonly referred to as Digital Rights Management (DRM)—a fancy phrase that means keeping people from copying or otherwise using your stuff without paying for it. Some e-book formats include DRM features while others do not. Some electronic publishers have their own schemes. Some authors are concerned about this and others are not. It's a complex issue. We discuss DRM in great detail in Chapter 5, "Digital Rights and Copy Protection."

Cover design. Most traditional publishers will never let go of controlling the outside appearance of their books. The fact is, people do judge books by their covers and publishers know this. Most authors are not good writers *and* good artists, so publishers do not trust them with the covers of their books. This is even true of e-publishers, although it's more common to see them accept authors' cover suggestions or even use an author's graphics.

The decreased importance of the cover is probably due to the fact that e-books do not usually appear in stores and are not purchased the same way as printed books. People do not browse them in the same fashion. Instead, people more often purchase e-books that they have heard about and decided they want. If the book has an ugly cover, somebody who's already interested will probably still buy it.

Print On Demand fulfillment. Even if you are committed to having a paperless society and plan on selling most of your e-books as electronic files, it's probably worth thinking about what you want to do for those people who want a printed copy of your book. Some e-publishing services have POD components while others do not. If you work with a publisher who deals only with e-books, then you want to be sure that you can and do hire out the POD component to someone else. (Some possible candidates appear in the next chapter.)

E-book order processing. Someone has to collect all that money. When a customer buys your e-book (usually online), who has the Web technology to collect money online with secure servers? Generally, that would be your publisher. But if there are components of the publishing process that you end up handling yourself, then you want to make sure the money collection task is done well. Most publishing services will have a solution, but in case you need something for your own Web site, some options are covered in Chapter 7, "Assembling Your E-Publishing Venture."

ISBN. The International Standard Book Number (ISBN) system is a way of keeping track of all books published (see the back of this book's title page for an example). If your book has an ISBN, then you can get it listed with various bookstores, distributors, and other services. Books without ISBNs are not really taken seriously. Usually, your publishing service will take care of getting a number for you, but if you choose to self-publish, then you'll have to handle this yourself. Details are covered in Chapter 11, "Business Issues for the Self E-Publisher."

Listing with online resellers. Some publishing services list their books with the various online bookstores and others only make their books available through their own Web sites. This chapter focuses on publishing services that list books with other resellers, while the following chapter talks about entities that sell directly to the public without using other online resellers.

Promotion and marketing. Not all electronic publishers are terrible at promoting books, but most of them are. Generally, the e-publishers who invest time and money in editing or author advances will also invest more in book marketing and publicity. That pretty much rules out most publishing services. Publishing services use a completely different publishing model. They invest little or nothing in acquiring and producing each book and rely on the author's efforts to get the book noticed. Some offer authors considerable assistance, but the responsibility ultimately falls on the author. But don't assume that the publishers who *don't* require fees for publishing your book are going to do much marketing and publicity either. These days, there's just no way around it—authors have to build their own brand and name recognition.

Selling subsidiary rights to the work. Traditional publishers almost always handle this for authors, but publishing services may or may not deal with subsidiary rights or licenses to your work. Even those who do want to represent the sub rights may not always handle them well. So if you're serious about getting your work translated into Spanish or converted into an audiotape, then you'll want to consider what to do about sub rights and how to share them with the publisher (or not share them, as the case may be). In the following pages, we'll try to indicate which publishers are successful at selling various sub rights, but it's a challenging area to follow.

Stay Current—For a more up-to-date report on e-publishers and what they are doing, refer to some of the Web resources in the following list. (And you'll find a more complete list of e-publishing resources in Appendix A: "E-Publishers.")

E-Publishing Opportunities Newsletter
http://www.myplanet.net/vanburen/

John Kremer's Book Marketing Update
http://www.bookmarket.com/

Jeff Cogswell's E-Publishing Update
http://www.geocities.com/jeffcogs

Electronic Publishing Connections by Jamie Engle
http://www.epublishingconnections.com/

eBooknet
http://www.ebooknet.com/

Fees and Compensation

E-publishing services are strange because on one hand they charge authors a fee for their services while on the other hand they pay authors a royalty on the sales of their books. It really just comes down to the fact that they don't want to risk any investment in their publications, so they make the authors pay for the setup and publishing costs. That means every sale earns a profit, which gets split in some way with the author. Usually the setup fee is minimal. It covers the cost of converting your file into their e-book format, producing the cover, getting an ISBN, and listing your book with the various bookstores or their own bookstore. E-publishing services usually are not in the business of making money on these fees (although some of them might not be doing too badly on author payments). Because there is no risk and no great investment, the services split proceeds generously with authors—often giving 50 percent royalties and sometimes even more. With this type of revenue model, it's easy to think of these e-publishers as mere services, taking a small commission for their troubles.

Publishers that take most of the money and give the author a small portion (as in traditional publishing) had better be offering something fabulous to the end result and to the marketability of the book in exchange for taking such a large portion of the pie, don't you think? Philosophically, it's much more satisfying to think of the creative process as the main component of a book and the publishing and production process as a service to the author. But most traditional publishers don't see it this way and feel that the publishing process adds as much (or more) to the end result as the writing itself. This is, of course, debatable. Some publishers do, indeed, add a great deal to the success of a book, while others do not. Mostly, traditional publishers have been able to take such a large percentage of the pie because it's extremely difficult to gain access to the channel (distributors and bookstores) for printed books. In the e-publishing world, authors are compensated relative to the contribution of the publisher. As you saw earlier in this chapter, even some of the big publishers such as **Random House** (http://www.randomhouse.com/) are beginning to change their perspective on this—paying authors more for e-books.

E-Publishing Services: The Players

There are a few major e-publishing services and several smaller ones out there. In the following pages, we'll provide an overview of the important players and give our recommendations as to how and when they might be used most effectively.

iUniverse

iUniverse at http://www.iuniverse.com/ is one of the larger of the new electronic publishers. This company has been through various changes in its short online lifetime but seems to be settling into a nice combination of offerings. It has two main functions: It offers publishing services for authors and business-to-business services for publishers and corporations. The Web site explains these functions pretty well, as Figure 6.1 shows.

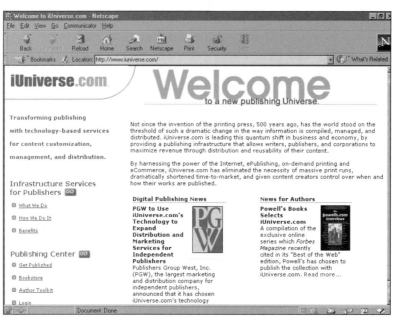

Figure 6.1: This iUniverse.com page explains its publishing services.

Most of its publishing services for authors are vanity-type services. That is, it will accept any book from any author, as long as the author pays the setup fee. The setup fees are generally reasonable, ranging from zero (for most out-of-print books) to around $300. The difference depends on the publishing service you choose (what iUniverse calls a Publishing Program).

It's unclear why one Publishing Program is more expensive than another, though we suspect that it's due to how marketable a book is (the more marketable, the lower the setup fee), but nothing on the site or in its documentation actually says this. iUniverse offers one service where the extra cost is easily explainable—it provides an editorial review of your book.

Although basically a vanity publisher, or publishing service, iUniverse will get your books listed at the online bookstores, such as Amazon.com and Borders.com. You will also have a listing with Ingram, the largest book distributor in the United States, which makes your book orderable by bookstores, although that will probably only happen if you get yourself into the bookstore and ask for it (or set up a book signing). Because of its relationship with **Barnes & Noble** at http://www.bn.com/ (essentially B&N owns iUniverse), you'll find some iUniverse titles at B&N stores and all of them in the B&N online bookstore. However, iUniverse also has its own bookstore and sells books directly to the public. In the past, this would have upset the resellers—not wanting the manufacturer to compete with them by selling direct—but these days, just about every publisher is selling some copies direct to consumers via a company-owned Web site. iUniverse is no exception, but you'll find that the iUniverse bookstore is not the primary feature of its Web site. It would just as soon have consumers purchase its books from bn.com or any of the other booksellers.

iUniverse makes a decent income selling books to the authors of those books—so you won't get many free copies or very good author discounts. So be it. Some books are so limited in their appeal that only friends of the author will end up buying them. The Family History Publishing Program at iUniverse is an example (which is why the setup fee is higher). You will, however, get good royalties on electronic and subsidiary rights (sale of licenses is discussed in Chapter 9, "Publishing Economics 101," and Chapter 10, "Hot Button Issues in E-Book Publishing Contracts"). iUniverse makes its e-books available in many different formats and you'll find them sold wherever fine e-books are sold. (That's another way of saying, "Who knows where e-books will be sold in the future?")

Printed books are made available (for example when a consumer finds and orders your book through Amazon.com) using Print On Demand technology—and these sales will pay you a whopping 20 percent of publisher's net receipts. Considering that it does almost nothing to get your books noticed (other than making them available) and that the author usually pays the setup costs, we feel that 20 percent is rather low. Some POD publishers offer much more, and a few will make your book available in POD at wholesale, if you feel like managing the POD sales process yourself. Of course, these companies offer a different set of benefits and services—so it's not like comparing apples to apples (if it were that simple, you probably wouldn't need this book).

Recommendations

iUniverse offers a great turnkey solution for authors. You get your book in various forms, including POD and several e-book formats, while getting listed at all the major online resellers. You can also order your book through bookstores for signings and such. It's great to have the physical book available as well as the e-book. The iUniverse staff does a good job on cover design, so you end up with a professional-looking publication. The downside is that you'll make a smaller royalty on the POD books than you might if you created a POD product yourself (as you can with **Digitz.net** at http://www.digitz.net/ or others discussed in the next chapter). But then you'd have to go through all the trouble to sell the thing on your own Web site. If you aren't up for doing all of these things yourself, iUniverse is a great solution. Don't count on selling a lot of copies just by virtue of the fact that your book exists online in all these locations. Sure, you'll sell a few, but you should count on doing some marketing and promotion to assist. iUniverse has some ideas to help you with this, and you can refer to Chapter 8, "On Your Own: Book Marketing Strategies," for even more. If you want to focus on writing and let someone else do the publishing, check out iUniverse. If you have the desire to self-publish several books or if you have an existing market for selling copies of your books, then you might find some other options a bit more profitable, if a bit more work.

Summary

iUniverse offers a variety of publishing services, from vanity publishing (author pays) to specialty publishing (specific genres) to corporate publishing services. It has a large focus on Print On Demand services and all its books are offered both as e-books and POD books. Its contract is exclusive, but gives authors some freedom to get out of it or change it to a nonexclusive deal. Royalties on its Print On Demand books are rather low, considering that it's doing next to nothing to market the books and that the author is paying the setup costs.

Rights purchased. Limited exclusive rights for print publishing, electronic publishing, and subsidiary licenses. Term of exclusivity is three years, but author may cancel agreement and turn it into a one-year nonexclusive deal.

Distribution. Like a print publisher, iUniverse makes books available to any retail bookseller, both through its distributor (Ingram) and directly. Your book will be available at Amazon.com and other online resellers, as well as listed in *Books In Print,* which makes it available for ordering by bookstores.

Marketing. iUniverse does not really contribute to the marketing of the books, except by listing them with the various online resellers. Assists authors in book marketing online.

Construction of book. Author sends file and iUniverse constructs the cover and body of the book (author can influence the cover if desired). Formats books in a proprietary XML format that it says allows it to port the book to all kinds of e-book readers and e-book formats. It registers ISBN. It does no editing, so you need to have this done yourself.

Advances. None.

Fee to publish. From zero to about $300, depending on the service you choose.

Royalties. 20 percent for print-on-demand. 50 percent for electronic sales. 50 percent for subsidiary licenses.

Contract negotiable. Not really. Somewhat negotiable in certain areas, such as technical books or corporate deals or for established authors. First-time authors with unknown books will probably find it difficult to negotiate its contract.

MightyWords

Originally an offspring of Fatbrain.com, **MightyWords** (http://www.mightywords.com) specializes in what it calls *e-Matter*. Although the definition of e-Matter is somewhat broad, you can think of it as electronic publications that are between 10 pages and 150 pages. MightyWords favors this range on the grounds that shorter documents will probably be read online as e-mail (usually free) while longer documents probably won't be read onscreen at all (at least until e-book devices become more popular). Documents between these sizes are special in that they can be easily read online yet they are large enough to warrant purchasing. Although MightyWords accepts documents of all sizes, its e-Matter niche makes it somewhat different from other online publishers or distributors. Of course, MightyWords is not turning away larger documents, especially considering the market acceptance to reading longer documents onscreen thanks to new e-book technology.

E-Matter pieces do not generally make it into wide distribution. Rather, they are available only from the MightyWords site. For this reason, MightyWords is a hybrid publisher and bookseller. MightyWords makes a big deal of getting people to its site to actually purchase e-Matter, and certain e-Matter subjects attract a variety of people needing short, concise treatments of certain subjects. (MightyWords is quite successful with its executive summaries of technical topics, for example.) When you get to the MightyWords site, the first thing you'll see is the bookstore, which makes it look more like a reseller than a publisher. The opening page at the MightyWords site is shown in Figure 6.2. But since it accepts any document (with a few exceptions) for which the owner pays the service fee, MightyWords qualifies as one of the publishing services you can use to get your book out into the world.

MightyWords is not what you'd call full service. It offers only electronic versions of its books, so if you want POD or other print versions, you'll have to take care of that somewhere else. Its contract gives it the right to sell subsidiary rights to your work, but it's not clear if it will make a big effort to sell licenses.

But don't forget that MightyWords is both a publisher and a reseller. It doesn't make its publications available through other online resellers, so you'll be limited to the MightyWords site for sales.

Like most publishing services, MightyWords does not help you with editing or proofing your work. If you send in a PDF file, it will keep your document

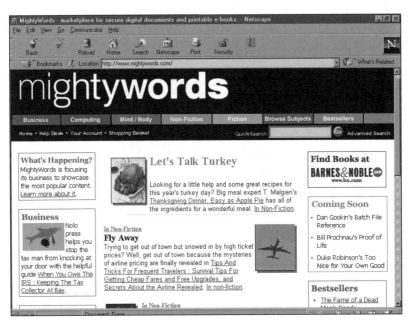

Figure 6.2: The MightyWords bookstore, showing the various book categories available.

formatting and layout, otherwise, it may make some layout changes. Its documents are all delivered in PDF with security controls to prevent copying. Unlike most publishing services, MightyWords does not charge you for setting up your document. You pay only a $1/month hosting fee to keep your document on the system. This is likely due to the fact that its people are not really doing much to set up your document. There is no POD version, so all they really do is convert your file to PDF format. The upside of this story is that this leaves you free to create a POD version of your book if you like. The MightyWords contract only transfers rights to electronic versions of your work, so you can create and sell other versions yourself.

Recommendations

The super-low hosting and setup fee, along with the great royalties and the ability to set the price of your publication, makes MightyWords a great choice for any author seeking a publishing service without marketing assistance. If most of your sales are made from your own efforts or communities, then you won't suffer too much from not having your e-book listed at Amazon.com or other online bookstores. On the other hand, you can always create your own POD version (or any other print version for that matter) and list at Amazon and Barnes & Noble yourself. This makes MightyWords a more profitable option than iUniverse for those willing to do some of the work themselves.

The fact that it only purchases electronic rights also makes it a good candidate for existing print publishers who want to make e-book versions available online. MightyWords basically acts like a third-party licensing partner, giving you a 50–50 royalty on e-book sales.

Summary

MightyWords specializes in e-Matter (pieces between 10 and 150 pages) but accepts documents of all lengths. You set the price of your document and reap 50 percent royalties on sales. It sells e-books only through its own site and purchases only electronic rights. It does some marketing of works on its own site and has a regular client base—particularly for the short executive summaries. So, depending on the subject of your work, you could find MightyWords a good publicity partner.

Rights purchased. Electronic rights.

Distribution. E-Matter is available only at the MightyWords site.

Marketing. None to speak of. Some author infrastructure to help with promotion.

Construction of book. Author sends file and MightyWords converts to PDF format. Authors can send PDF files to control formatting. MightyWords registers the ISBN for your work in electronic format. It does no editing, so you need to have this done yourself.

Advances. None (possible advances for technical pieces).

Fee to publish. $1/month management fee.

Royalties. 50 percent.

Contract negotiable. Not really. Somewhat negotiable in certain areas, such as technical books or corporate deals or for established authors.

Xlibris

Among the publishing services, Xlibris appears to be most oriented toward selling services to writers (as opposed to selling books to bookstores). For this reason, it is perhaps the most service-oriented of the publishing services, providing you with many options and support kits. Of course, everything has a price—with the exception of the basic publishing service, which it calls its *core service*. The core service gets your manuscript into e-book format and into the system for Print On Demand. It also gets you listed with the distributors and booksellers online. For added support, you can choose from one of the more complete service kits, which include various combinations of marketing material, design templates, and cover ideas. The services range from free (core service) to $1,200 for the Premium service kit, which lets you work directly with the design staff. It also sells marketing and promotions packages to help authors get the word out. It even offers a number of add-on services, including

- Editing
- Proofing
- Creating the index
- Registering the copyright
- Putting the file on CD-ROM
- Getting a Library of Congress number
- Entering data

Xlibris does not purchase rights to your work. That is, it is a completely nonexclusive publishing service. You are free to exit the agreement at any time and enter into other agreements with other companies. If you do this, you could end up with more than one version of your book available—perhaps even at different prices, depending on how (and with whom) you publish other editions. Xlibris will set the price of your book for print and e-book sales. Royalties are on the low side at 10 percent of cover price for POD books, although this is equivalent to the 20 percent of *net receipts* that iUniverse offers (refer to Chapter 10, "Hot Button Issues in E-Book Publishing Contracts," for more information about contracts and royalties and the difference between *net receipts* and *cover price*). Xlibris will pay you 25 percent of cover price if it sells the book directly to the public through its own bookstore, which gives you a slightly larger portion of the proceeds on direct sales made by Xlibris compared to the 10 percent when sold through other resellers. E-book royalties are 25 percent of list price (more or less equivalent to 50 percent of net receipts) for sales through other resellers and 50 percent for direct sales through their own site.

Recommendations

You really don't have much to lose by placing your book with Xlibris. The nonexclusivity of its contract makes its service a possible addition to any publishing program—unless you intend to sell exclusive rights to a different publisher, which could create a conflict. You can self-publish and sell your book at your own Web site while still placing it with Xlibris. The cost of its basic service is about the same as iUniverse when you include the "for pay" add-ons to make its services equivalent. You then have the option of spending even more money for its additional services and kits.

Summary

Xlibris is a true publishing service, offering many publishing programs and add-on services for the would-be author. Getting basic publishing service is relatively competitive. Xlibris offers the advantage of a completely nonexclusive contract, which lets you use its services as part of an overall publishing program that might include services from other companies. Royalties for e-books are standard at 50 percent while POD royalties are low at 10 percent of retail price.

Rights purchased. None. Nonexclusive contract.

Distribution. E-books and POD available at online resellers and Xlibris site.

Marketing. Various kits available (at additional cost) to help you with marketing.

Construction of book. Author chooses interior design and cover options. Some publishing packages include more design and cover options. E-Books are PDF files. Editing is an add-on option at extra fee to author.

Advances. None.

Fee to publish. Basic service is free. Additional services up to $1,200 and add-on options at various prices.

Royalties. 25 percent of list price on e-books and 10 percent of list price on POD. On sales made directly to the public from the Xlibris site, you'll get higher rates: 50 percent for e-books and 25 percent for POD.

Contract negotiable. No.

Category Publishers: The Small E-Publishers

More and more e-publishers are appearing on the scene every week. It's difficult to keep up with the stream of new entries. Most are small publishers specializing in particular genres or categories of books, such as romance or technical books. Many started out as self-publishers, authors who published their own e-books and now have opened their doors to other authors. Although the publishers themselves differ in their approach and the materials they acquire, their contracts and publishing programs are generally very similar. You'll find that they acquire either all rights to a book or specifically electronic rights. Most have term limits on their contracts, meaning that rights can revert to the author when the term is up, although some of the more traditional companies have unlimited terms. Royalties range from 20 percent of proceeds to 60 percent or even 70 percent. Most fall into the 35 percent to 50 percent range. All of these companies can get your e-books listed with the various e-bookstores and most have some sort of promotion and marketing program, although author-initiated publicity and marketing is always an important part of the process.

As you check out the various publishers, you'll probably want to find a publisher who specializes in the type of book you have (science fiction, romance, humor, or whatever). This is because it's easier for a publisher to market several books in the same genre than a few books across many different genres. A publisher who specializes will likely be better at marketing that particular type of book—though you'll still probably have to do your own marketing if you want your book to sell well.

Regarding e-book formats, you'll find some great differences. Some of the category publishers are still using HTML files, available as downloads from their own Web sites, while others are putting out e-books in several different formats that can be accessed and read on the different e-book readers. Usually it's best to have your book available for any type of reader, since that will make your work available to a wider audience. However, that's not *always* the case. A publisher who sells a lot of HTML downloads is going to be more desirable than a publisher who has all the e-book formats but sells very few books. After you identify some publisher candidates for your work, visit their Web sites and check out some of their other books to get a better feel for their publishing capacity.

Two Good Examples

In the following pages, we've provided some details about two of the more established category publishers. These will provide you with a good idea of how the smaller publishers work and what they offer. There are many others, as you'll see listed in Appendix A, "E-Publishers." Don't be afraid to contact as many as you like about your manuscript.

Join the Crowd—Don't let the number of small independent e-publishers discourage you from starting your own e-publishing venture if you're inclined to do so. In the print publishing world, there are literally thousands of small independent publishers putting out all kinds of books in all categories. There's still plenty of room in the e-publishing market for many new ventures.

DiskUs Publishing

DiskUs Publishing at http://www.diskuspublishing.com/ was one of the first of the small e-publishers and now has a healthy collection of books, publishing as many as five new books each month. The folks at DiskUs publish primarily fiction, including romance, science fiction, mystery, fantasy, western, and children's fiction. They make their books available as PDF files and publish them online as e-book downloads. They also support many of the e-book readers, including Nuvomedia, Librius, and even Palm Pilot. In addition, they put many of their books on CD-ROM, which come with full-color booklets inside. They put some books on audiotape, but they do not offer paperback or POD editions. They have decent author support, and offer 40 percent royalties on publisher's net receipts. They provide the ISBN for authors, but no copyright registration (see Chapter 10, "Hot Button Issues," for more details about copyright). They have an exclusive contract, but the term limit is only one year so you can renew after that or choose to go your own way. Authors can be involved in the layout and cover design of their books.

Recommendations

DiskUs Publishing is a great player in the arena of small e-publishers. It has a constantly growing list of books and has gained some recognition for high-quality publications. Staff work closely with authors during the production process and support author promotion after the book is published. They are aggressive in getting their books in all the different formats available. They are primarily a fiction house.

Summary

Rights purchased. All rights, with a one-year term.

Distribution. DiskUs gets books into all of the major online bookstores. It also provides downloads from its own site and has contracts with many of the e-book readers. DiskUs CD-ROM packages can be found in selected stores.

Marketing. DiskUs offers marketing and promotion assistance to authors in various forms, including support of author signings, bookmarks, and promotional gimmicks. It submits books to e-book competitions.

Construction of book. Author sends file and DiskUs constructs the book. Authors have input on cover and internal design and can even provide cover art if acceptable.

Advances. None.

Fee to publish. None.

Royalties. 40 percent of net receipts across the board.

Contract negotiable. Sure. You might particularly check for treatment print rights, since at the present time, the company doesn't offer printed books.

Sansip Publishing

Sansip Publishing at http://www.sansip.com is a generalist among small e-publishers. It publishes in just about any of the categories, including all types of fiction (romance, science fiction, fantasy), humor, and nonfiction (cookbooks, travel, informative). It offers 50 percent royalties and publishes books as downloads that can be read with the proprietary Sansip Reader software. Sansip books are available exclusively from the company's own site and e-book store. Sansip staff do not produce covers for their books, get ISBNs, or register the copyright. Nor do they do much editing. Their contract can be arranged to let authors handle print editions elsewhere, so you can work with a POD publisher to get your books available at other outlets. They require finished manuscripts before they are willing to consider a book.

Sansip is somewhere between a publishing service and a certified e-publisher. Its people acquire books much like a publishing service: You must have a completed book before talking to them, but once you do it's pretty easy to get accepted. Like a publishing service, they offer little or no manuscript preparation (editing, proofing, and so on). However, it is an e-publisher in that it does not require a publishing fee from authors and it does purchase exclusive e-book rights for the life of the work. Its e-books are available as downloads and it is seeking distribution through various e-book readers.

Recommendations

Sansip may be a good choice for authors having trouble getting published elsewhere or who are thinking of using a publishing service. Since Sansip leaves you free to publish a print or POD version of your book elsewhere, you can use it like a publishing service, but it demands no author fees for publishing.

Summary

Rights purchased. E-book rights for the life of the book.

Distribution. Sansip focuses on its own Web site for selling books, but does plan to make books available for various readers.

Marketing. Assists authors in self-promotion and offers online promotion of its own.

Construction of book. Author sends finished manuscript and publisher gets book online with a minimum of editing and layout. No covers are provided. No ISBN.

Advances. None.

Fee to publish. None.

Royalties. 50 percent of net receipts.

Contract negotiable. Some parts may be negotiable.

CHAPTER SEVEN

Assembling Your E-Publishing Venture

Okay, so you're thinking about joining the ranks of electronic publishing professionals and starting your own e-publishing program. Maybe you have written a number of books and would like to retain control of how they are published and perhaps profit more by publishing them yourself. Or perhaps you have an itch to play with Internet technology and online marketing. Perhaps you're interested in locating and publishing the works of others—perhaps in a special genre or literary category (that series of books about life on Mars could well find a healthy readership). Whatever your reasons, creating and running an e-publishing enterprise can be rewarding both creatively and financially. This chapter provides details about how to put together a publishing program using Internet services and technologies. In addition to the advice in this chapter, you'll probably enjoy hearing from those who have traveled before you. You'll find some of their accounts in Chapter 12, "Personal Success Stories."

Are You a Writer or an E-Publisher?

Before we get too far into the details of creating a personal e-publishing program or e-publishing company, we issue the following warning: If you want to spend most of your time writing, then think twice about self-publishing. As a self-publisher, you'll probably spend a great deal of your time planning and creating the e-publishing venture. You'll be formatting books, building a Web site, making deals with publishing services, and listing your books with online bookstores and then promoting them. If you want to do all of those things well, then you'll probably be spending a good deal of time doing them. That means you'll have a lot less time available for writing. Because of the considerable time and energy required to publish books, many writers feel it's worth sharing their proceeds with a company dedicated to these tasks.

Also consider this: When you go through all the effort of creating and marketing *one* book, you might as well do it for *several* books. What's the use of building a Web site with secure credit card transactions, for example, if you've only got one or two books to sell? Spreading all that effort and expense over dozens of books makes a lot more sense. The same goes for many of the components of publishing.

Of course, there are exceptions to this rule. For example, if you have a business with a following of some sort—a built-in readership or market through which you can sell your books, you might find it profitable to create an e-publishing program to augment that business. Suppose you are a successful yoga teacher with a number of students and a special method of instruction that's all your own. Your students have been begging you to publish your book so they can continue to study your techniques. Setting up a simple Web site and e-publishing venture would make a lot of sense for selling your works to your pupils. Likewise, many small businesses have special written materials that can be sold to their customers or employees. An online bookstore to accompany your existing Web site could be just the ticket. Or maybe you have a Web site that already has a good deal of traffic and a ton of content. Now you want to sell that content in the form of books to your existing visitors. A self-publishing venture to augment the site may well prove worthwhile.

Components of a Self-Publishing Program

The components of a self-publishing program can be boiled down to two things: making e-books and selling e-books. That was easy, wasn't it? Well, it's easy as long as you don't try to do either of these things all by yourself. The key to successful e-book publishing and distribution lies in the relationships you forge and the partners you choose. In the following pages, we'll provide information about third-party services available for the self-publisher, both for creating and selling e-books.

Some issues affect both the production and the distribution of your e-books. For instance, the e-book file format you decide to use will determine where and how you can sell your books. Many of the popular e-book readers use proprietary formats and, therefore, limit your sales to people who have the particular reader in question. If you choose a more "open" format, such as PDF, then your books won't be available on certain readers. Some e-publishers will try to publish for as many formats as possible, which can be a major effort. Many e-publishers offer six or seven different types of files for each e-book they publish. Now that's covering all the bases.

Actually, there is a third component of a successful e-book publishing program. That's the task of running the business itself. You can easily find plenty of resources for business management, so we won't be giving you general advice on building a business in this book. However, in Chapter 11, "Business Issues for the Self E-Publisher," we'll talk about some of the specific wrinkles you'll want to think about as you get set up.

Another thing we won't get too deeply into is the task of building a Web site to host your e-publishing venture. Many good books provide details about building and maintaining Web sites, such as *Poor Richard's Web Site,* by Peter Kent (Top Floor Publishing, Second Edition, 2000). We will, however, cover some things you might consider doing in your Web site that specifically relate to selling books.

Making E-Books

Making e-books is the subject of Part II of this book, "Planning and Creating an E-Book," so in this chapter, we summarize the process and the services that are available to help. We'll also help you put the process of creating an e-book into harmony with the process of selling an e-book, so you can make the best choices for your new venture.

When you think about how to create e-books, you might want to ask yourself a few basic questions. The answers to these questions will affect the decisions you make about the way you choose to construct your e-books.

What types of books will I publish? Some types of books are easier to create than others. Fiction, for example, generally does not include illustrations or fancy text design and will therefore be easier to format. Certain nonfiction genres will require some thought as to document layout and the treatment of illustrations. Cookbooks, for instance, generally require some attention to the display of the text—making the recipes easy to read—as well as photography. Some books may require color.

What formats will I support? Do you want to support every e-book format or concentrate on a specific format? Getting your books into Microsoft Reader format, for instance, may be all you want to do. Or perhaps you'd be happy just having well-designed PDF files.

How will I design the covers? Are you interested in fancy covers, or is a basic text display enough? Information-oriented books probably require less attention to the cover than romance novels. This is generally because people don't *need* to buy novels, but they may need the information in a nonfiction book. Novels need to seduce the consumer into buying the book. The cover is part of that seduction, to be sure.

Do I want to have Print On Demand editions? If you intend to offer your books in POD form, then you'll be needing a POD-compatible format. This is generally a PDF file. So if your manuscript has been created in

Microsoft Word, for instance, you'll need to convert it to PDF as well as any other e-book format you plan to offer.

Where will I sell my books? If you plan to enter the commercial marketplace and sell your e-books at all the major online retail outlets, then you need an e-book format that works with this system of distribution. If you plan to make your books available for one of the e-book readers, such as the Rocket eBook and its descendants (RCA and REB devices), then you'll have to look into options for converting to that format. If you have a built-in market through your own Web site, then you have more freedom to choose a format that works best for your customers. Refer to Chapter 4, "The Production Process," for more details about e-book formats and how to create them.

In the following pages, we provide a summary of the components required for constructing an e-book—from finding good e-book manuscripts to editing and preparing final drafts to getting documents into an e-book format. The idea is to give you a sense of the overall process involved, so that you can create your own e-publishing program using some of the ideas and resources provided here.

Content: Acquiring Intellectual Real Estate

If you intend to acquire content beyond the books you write yourself, then it's important to have a process for acquisitions. The first step is finding good material. Then, when you have a good prospect, you'll need to convince the author to let you publish it (or at the very least, give the author tools for getting you the manuscript in the manner you want to receive it).

Where to Acquire Books

Your next-door neighbor may be the next Henry Miller, but that's not something to count on. And although many e-publishers started out as self-publishers (authors publishing their own e-books), most of them end up opening their doors to outside authors to enhance their e-book offerings. If you are looking to acquire good books, there are a few primary resources to which you can turn. These include agents, rights brokers, and writers' communities.

Agents

Agents are in the business of representing writers. Generally, agents have sifted through hundreds of manuscripts to find a few good ones. So, in theory, dealing with agents will get you closer to the good stuff. Finding agents is not difficult. The primary resource is **The Literary Marketplace** (http://www.literarymarketplace.com/), known in the business as "LMP," which you should be able to find in book form at any good library, as well as online. This tome lists pretty much all the agents in the business. For a another online look, try **Writers.Net** at http://www.writers.net/, which includes a list of agents and their e-mail addresses.

When dealing with agents, remember that they are working for the author (and themselves). They generally get paid a portion of the author's earnings. If the author earns nothing, the agent earns nothing. For this reason, agents don't accept manuscripts that they don't feel are salable. It costs you, the publisher, nothing to work with an agent—except that the agent might negotiate a better deal for the author than the author would have negotiated alone. In exchange for this possible increase in your terms, you get to work with a professional who knows the publishing business and won't waste a lot of your time with crazy contract issues. If an author you're working with has an agent, then remember that it's not appropriate to negotiate financial terms with the author directly. That's the agent's job.

Rights Brokers

We discuss rights brokers in several parts of this book (including later in this chapter under "Selling E-Books"). They are useful both for selling various rights to your books and for finding and acquiring rights to various works by other people. You can browse through their listings to find material you might like to use—then place a bid for the rights you want to acquire (or contact the broker to deal directly). Figure 7.1 shows a typical listing and bid page at RightsWorld.

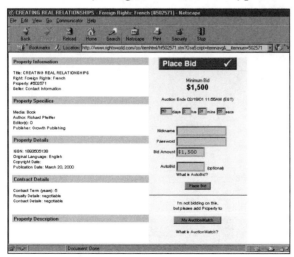

Following are some rights brokers. Rights brokers deal with publishers and agents to get rights listed on their sites. They also deal directly with authors. So you're likely to see a great mix of books.

RightsWorld
http://www.rightsworld.com/

RightsCenter
http://www.rightscenter.com/

SubRights
http://www.subrights.com/

Figure 7.1: RightsWorld bid page for acquiring rights to a work.

Writers' Communities

There are probably hundreds of writers' lists and online communities you could visit on the Internet. Finding some of them is as easy as going to one of the Internet search engines and searching for "writers." Still, here are a few good resources to get you started. Keep in mind that if you plan to specialize in a particular area, such as books about golf, then you might be better off avoiding the writers' lists and targeting the golf lists.

Writers.net at http://www.writers.net/ is a community of writers and publishing professionals. The community revolves around the listings available at the Writers.net Web site. When you get to the site, you'll be able to look through hundreds of author biographies in numerous categories to narrow down your search. Figure 7.2 shows some of these categories.

Writer's Digest at http://www.writersdigest.com/ is a long-standing writer's community that now has an active online component. The Web site lists resources for writers, and the company publishes an e-mail newsletter that provides tips, author interviews, and industry information.

E-Publishing Opportunities Newsletter. This is a shameless plug, since one of your friendly authors (that would be Chris) publishes this little journal. Now that we've acknowledged our predisposition, here's the info: This e-mail newsletter is a resource for authors interested in getting their books published

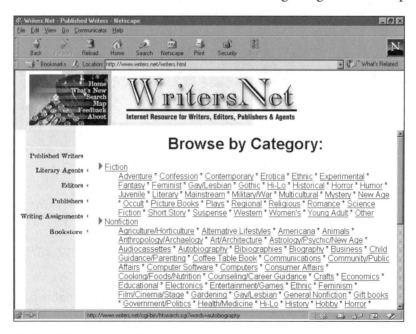

Figure 7.2: The Writers.net author categories.

online (as well as other online writing possibilities). It provides regular listings of projects being sought by e-publishers. You can check it out at http://www.myplanet.net/vanburen/.

Craig's List at http://www.craigslist.com/ started as a San Francisco area community for jobs and events. Now it has turned into a national resource for employment, events, and classified ads. The site provides hundreds of résumés and dozens of job categories—even a few categories for writing jobs. If there's something specific you're looking for, you might try posting an ad. Be warned: You'll probably be flooded with replies. Figure 7.3 shows a typical writing job listing at Craig's List.

Figure 7.3: A Craig's List writing opportunity.

How to Acquire Books

Now that you have an idea about the "where" and "why" of acquiring books, let's take a quick look at the "how." An e-book acquisitions program can start out small and personal. As you grow, you can add more components to help your authors deliver their masterpieces to you. All you need are some basic guidelines and business documents.

Submission Guidelines

You'll probably want to let authors know how they should submit their books to you. That's what submission guidelines are for. Most e-publishers post their guidelines online at their Web sites—so potential authors can just check out the information and submit their proposals without having to ask questions. Submission guidelines vary. Some publishers want to see a full proposal, including a summary of the book, a table of contents, information about competitive books, and some sample chapters. Other publishers want to see the finished manuscript—100 percent complete. It's really up to you how you screen your candidates, but we can assure you that as your e-publishing venture grows, you'll get more and more submissions to look through—most of them far from what you want to accept. Figure 7.4 shows an example of online submission guidelines for **DiskUs Publishing** (http://www.diskuspublishing.com/submission.htm).

Writer's Guidelines

Once you've accepted a manuscript, you might want to let the author know how to deliver it to you. The writer's guidelines, also called the author's guide, is

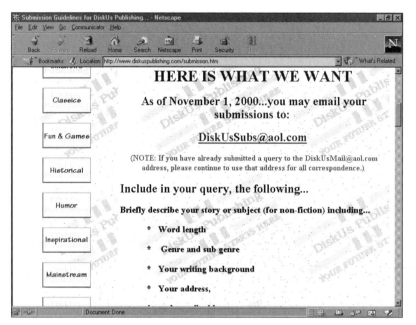

Figure 7.4: Online author submission guidelines.

where you can tell authors how to prepare their manuscripts for delivery. This is particularly useful for informational books. For example, the folks at Top Floor Publishing provided us with guidelines for creating the manuscript to this book. This included such things as how to reference and deliver illustrations, how to differentiate a first-level heading from a second-level heading, and how to format special elements like lists and tables.

Rejection Notice

It's always nice to be able to reject manuscripts personally, but as you get more and more submissions and have less and less time, you'll probably find it useful to create a rejection notice. We recommend being friendly but brief. The more information you give, the more you'll find authors resubmitting manuscripts to incorporate your suggestions. Here's a good sample that should do the trick:

> *Dear [author]:*
> *Thank you for submitting your book [title] for our review. Unfortunately, it is not something we feel fits our editorial plans at this time. Please feel free to submit other works to us in the future. Our submission guidelines can be found online at [location]. Best wishes with your project.*
> *Sincerely,*
> *[the publisher]*

Publishing Contract

The author contract is the next step in acquiring a book. Your contract should specify what rights you wish to acquire and how you will pay for them. It should also include items that protect both the author and the publisher should certain things occur. Details about publishing contracts are covered in Chapter 10, "Hot Button Issues in E-Book Publishing Contracts." You'll find a sample contract designed especially for startup e-publishers in Appendix C, "Sample Contracts."

Editing and Editors: Making Books Readable

We've talked about editing and editors several times in this book—usually with the advice that they are worth using and improve the quality of your books. Chapter 2, "What's an E-Book?", talks about the importance of editing in creating quality e-books and Chapter 9, "Publishing Economics 101," talks about how editing fits into the pre-production costs of book publishing. Here, we talk a little about what types of editors you might work with, how to work with them, and where to find them.

Acquisitions Editor

The acquisitions editor is responsible for finding and acquiring good manuscripts, usually as an employee of a publisher. Generally, they don't do this in a vacuum. After acquisitions editors find possible manuscripts, they usually present them to the rest of the team for a collective review. If the manuscript is desired, then the acquisitions editor negotiates the contract with the author or agent to acquire the book. Most likely, you won't need acquisitions editors in the early stages of your e-publishing venture. It will be your responsibility to locate good books to publish (or to write them). We offered a few ideas earlier in this chapter, under "The Content: Acquiring Intellectual Real Estate."

Production Editor

The production editor is responsible for taking the book from manuscript to "bound book" (or in the case of e-books "from manuscript to downloadable file"). While they don't perform all the functions in the process themselves, production editors oversee and are responsible for them all—passing the manuscript from service to service to get the entire production process done. As with the acquisitions editor, it's most likely that you'll be performing the functions of the production editor—finding and working with the various components of the process as described in this chapter. If, like some publishers, all you end up doing is converting an author's manuscript into PDF or some other e-book format and putting it up on your Web site to sell, then your production process will be simple and quick. But if you include other components in the process, such as editing the manuscript, adding Print On Demand, or designing a cover, then you'll have a few additional steps to accomplish. But the production of an e-book is not brain surgery and you should find it a relatively easy process.

Once the book is finished and ready for public consumption, you're ready for the second half of this chapter, which will help you take it from there—getting your book into the online stores and distribution services. The next chapter will complete the story by giving you some ideas for promoting and publicizing your books and authors.

Copyeditor

In the case of a small e-publishing venture, quality often comes down to the copyeditor. As you saw above, the acquisitions and production editors will probably end up being *you*. But working with a good copyeditor is an important part of the production process. Here we'll give you a quick overview of the things a good copyeditor will do for your book, followed by a couple of online organizations that will help you locate copyeditors for hire.

Generally a copyeditor will make several passes at a manuscript to get everything in order. Each pass focuses on a particular thing. That's because for any given pass at the manuscript, it's more effective to limit the types of issues for which you're searching. As the book is reviewed, rewritten, and edited again, the basic types of edits are repeated to be sure new problems have not been introduced. Figure 7.5 shows how these edits may be stacked up to get a manuscript perfect. The final two tasks (format edit and proofing) are usually performed by a different person from the copyeditor, as a fresh pair of eyes is important in these two edits.

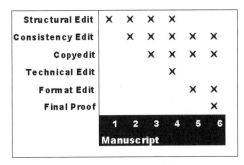

Figure 7.5: Various types of edits are performed and repeated to get a manuscript perfect.

Structural Edit

The structural edit is the first edit done to the manuscript, since it checks the foundation of the book. (The structural edit is sometimes done not by the copyeditor but by the production editor, since it involves core issues with the book.) Problem areas usually go back to the author for fixing. During a structural edit, the editor will check for things like these:

- Headings and subheadings are consistent in presentation.
- Headings do not skip levels.
- Material is presented in logical flow.
- Material covers all of the goals set for the book.
- Book contains all components (front matter, appendices, and index if applicable).
- Table of Contents matches headings in book.
- Cross-references are correct and referenced sections exist.
- If applicable, all chapters have introduction and conclusion or other established items.
- Material that needs further explanation is identified for author.
- Material that receives too much attention is identified for author.

Consistency and Style Edit

During a consistency edit, the editor checks to make sure material is presented in the same way throughout the book. This includes things like these:

- Presentation of illustrations and tables is consistent.
- Presentation of captions is consistent.
- Cross-references are presented consistently.
- Special words or phrases are consistent (such as ebook versus e-book).
- Point of view is consistent throughout (author does not switch from "We" to "I" or suddenly start—or stop—addressing the reader as "you" halfway through the book).
- Events occur in proper time sequence (the car crash happened yesterday ...how can he be driving the same car again today?).
- Character traits are consistent (blue eyes remain blue unless changing is part of the story).

Copyedit

Also called a "language edit," the copyedit checks for problems with the use of language. This includes spelling, grammar—all of the following things:

- Grammar is correct—or at least appropriate to the situation.
- Spelling is correct.

- Writing is clear and concise.
- Punctuation is correct and consistent.
- Repetitious words or phrases are removed.
- Capitalization is correct and consistent.

Technical or Factual Edit

Most books contain factual information. Even fictional works usually have references to factual information in this world. Manuscripts that are mostly technical information, such as computer books or instruction manuals, may even require a separate technical editor who is knowledgeable in the particular field. During a typical technical or factual edit, these things are checked:

- External references (references to other books or material) are correct and exist.
- Technical information is correct.
- Historical references are accurate.
- Geographical references are accurate.
- Proper names are spelled correctly.
- Footnotes are presented correctly and contain proper references.
- Potential legal problems are identified.

Format Edit

When the book goes into page layout and formatting, it's important to check for formatting problems. As mentioned earlier, it's important to use a different person for the format edit—someone who is not already familiar with the content of the manuscript is much likelier to see things that need to be dealt with at this stage. A format edit covers the following things:

- Pages are presented consistently (for example, the page numbers are in the same location on each page).
- Widow and orphan lines are identified.
- Headings are not separated from following paragraphs.
- Running headers and footers are consistent.
- Fonts are correct and consistent.
- Tables and other specially formatted material are correct.

Final Proofreading

The final proofreading step makes sure last-minute changes did not introduce new problems. Again, this task should be performed by a person not already familiar with the manuscript. While almost anything can be brought up in a final proofing, at this stage, the focus is on the following types of things:

- Typos in text are identified.
- Missing punctuation is identified.
- Formatting problems are identified.
- Anything else needing attention is identified.

Where to Find an Editor

Now that you know what to expect from an editor, try one of the following resources for locating a good editor for your books. Payment for editing varies. Traditionally, contract copyeditors are paid by the 250-word manuscript page (anywhere from $5 to $20 per page, depending on the complexity of the manuscript). Proofreaders usually get less—about $2 to $4 per page. It's not uncommon to hire editors on a project or hourly basis. These organizations can give you more information.

Bay Area Editors' Forum
http://www.editorsforum.org/

List Foundation
http://www.listfoundation.com/

Freelance Help
http://www.freelancehelp.com/

Freelance Online
http://www.freelanceonline.com/

BookZone Pro
http://www.bookzonepro.com/sources/

Getting Into E-Book Format

Getting your e-book manuscript into an e-book format can be as easy or as difficult as you want to make it. Converting Microsoft Word files into PDF files, for example, is not a huge problem. If you want to add a PDF-compatible copy protection scheme, then it gets slightly more difficult. Getting files into XML or Open eBook format is not trivial. But the difficulty of conversion should not sway you from targeting certain e-book formats. Your choice of e-book formats is as much a marketing decision as a development decision. So here we've compiled a few resources you can use to give you a hand with document conversion. Note that there are two ways to get your books into the various formats: You can convert the documents yourself using software and other tools, or you can hire a third-party service to do it for you. Since this chapter is about assembling a publishing program, we're going to focus on the services you can hire. For more information about how to format your own books, refer to Chapter 4, "The Production Process."

What we're hearing from e-publishers is that the two most popular and asked-for formats are the Adobe Reader's PDF files and Microsoft Reader's .lit files. Rocket .rb files are a distant third. If you can handle the top two formats, you'll probably be covering the majority of your potential readers. Adding HTML to the mix is simple.

One Publisher's Method—*I convert our books to various formats myself. I just don't trust anyone else to do it. I begin with Microsoft Word documents (.doc files) and convert to Rich Text Format (.rtf files), PDF, and ASCII text (.txt files) from there. I use Microsoft Front Page to convert .rtf files to HTML, but I do a lot of tweaking. I use the HTML file to convert to RocketBook's .rb files, using the free conversion program from the Rocket Library, and to Microsoft Reader .lit files, using the professional version of the* **Reader Works** *software at* http://www.overdrive.com/readerworks/. —*David Dyer,* **Renaissance E Books** (http://www.renebooks.com/)

Adobe

If you want your books in PDF format, you'll probably be working with Adobe software. That's because Adobe owns the rights to the PDF format specifications and has not yet made them public. You can purchase the Adobe Acrobat software to convert your files into PDF format, or you can use the low-cost Adobe conversion service at the **Adobe** Web site (http://www.createpdf.adobe.com/). For start-up e-publishing ventures, it's a great option. Simply log onto the site and upload one of your files as a free test. If you like the results, you can sign up for the conversion service.

Texterity

Texterity at http://www.texterity.com/artstech/textcafe/ provides a service for converting your original documents into various e-book formats, including Open eBook (HTML), Microsoft Reader, and Rocket eBook. The service is semiautomatic. You select the file types you want and upload your files directly to the Web site. You'll get an online quote before the conversion is done. The resulting files are yours to do with as you please. You can make the book available to download from your home page, or send it along to the various online resellers.

Lightning Source

Lightning Source at http://www.lightningsource.com/publisher.html is a publishing service designed to help publishers get their books into various digital formats—as well as Print On Demand. It also handles fulfillment to booksellers and distributors. It can get your book converted to just about any e-book format, including the Microsoft Reader, Adobe PDF, and the Glassbook Reader formats. Lightning Source uses a DRM system for protecting its books. All books handled by Lightning Source are distributed by Ingram Books and are available to booksellers. Publishers receive payment at wholesale price for each sale (approximately 45 percent of list price). Keep in mind that Lightning Source only takes books from established publishers who have more than a few books to offer. Listing your book with Lightning Source means that you'll be entering into a distribution agreement.

BookZone

BookZone at http://www.bookzone.com/ offers conversion into PDF, MS Reader, Glassbook, and other formats. The BookZone staff do custom work, too, including covers. They have many other services for small e-publishers, including online e-commerce solutions for electronic content and distribution. It's worth checking out their site and offerings.

Books and Their Covers

We're not about to tell you how to design covers for your e-books or where to find a good graphic artist. That's a bit out of the range of this book. But we do want to mention a few things about e-book covers and packaging.

First, while e-books do not appear on store shelves luring the casual shopper with their stunning cover designs, e-book covers do often appear on Web sites and e-book retail stores. So having a professional-looking cover design might be something to consider. But professional does not have to mean expensive or complex. Consider the simple examples in Figure 7.6.

Figure 7.6: Simple and effective book covers.

Print On Demand

Making e-books available in Print On Demand format is becoming extremely popular and common among e-publishers. Many people will want a printed version of your book, even if they have already downloaded and read an electronic version. POD versions tend to cost a bit more than normal printed books, but it's usually worth making them available for those customers who are willing to pay for the physical product. The following pages list a few Print On Demand services you can use to augment your publishing program. Since this chapter is focused on being your own publisher, we do not include POD publishers who want rights to your books, such as iUniverse. These are covered in Chapter 6, "Checking Out the E-Publishers."

Digitz.net

Digitz.net (http://www.digitz.net) is a POD service specifically targeted to small e-publishers and corporations. It offers conversion of your digital files into a POD-compatible format and archives your books for printing as you send in orders. Its staff ship to the customer, then bill you for the wholesale price of the book. You can maintain control of the sale and collect the money from the sale at your own site, or pass that task on to Digitz, too. It calls itself a "plug and play" service, since it's an add-on to your existing publishing program. The wholesale prices it charges are not cheap. An average 200-page book will cost you in the neighborhood of $6.50 per copy. Although it's expensive, we recommend Digitz because of its plug-and-play nature—especially if you want to remain in control of the sales process. And you can use the service for one book or a dozen books; it has no quantity requirements.

Lightning Source

Lightning Source (http://www.lightningsource.com/) is the POD division of Ingram distribution, the largest book distributor in the United States. It got into POD early and now dominates the market, working with most of the large publishers. To work with Lightning Source, you need to have more than a few books. Its people don't want to deal with small publishers or self-publishers, referring them to one of the many POD services, such as iUniverse. These services, of course, use Lightning Source as their source for POD fulfillment—so Lightning Source gets its share one way or the other. Working directly with Lightning Source will get you distributed into the online bookstores (and any other bookstore for that matter), since Lightning Source also supplies the resellers.

Because it is one of the sources of POD, having the actual equipment in its huge facilities, Lightning Source is among the least expensive of the POD services. But you will most likely not be working with the company directly until you have a publishing house operating in full swing with plenty of new titles being released every year. Because of this, many POD resellers (companies who are basically reselling the Lightning Source service) offer services to small publishers. By combining many smaller publishers, these services have the quantity necessary to work with Lightning Source.

Replica Books

Replica Books (http://www.replicabooks.com/) is a division of Baker & Taylor, one of the largest book distributors. As such, it acts much like Lightning Source, getting your books into POD format and then fulfilling them to resellers. You get paid a wholesale rate for the books. The company specializes in out-of-print titles and in helping publishers keep their books from going out of print.

Contracts and Business Issues

An important component of your publishing program involves the contract you use for your authors. It's important to know how to acquire the right to publish someone else's material. There is a lot to know about contracts, so we've dedicated an entire chapter to it. Chapter 10, "Hot Button Issues in E-Book Publishing Contracts," will give you a general idea of the issues to consider when dealing with contracts. Appendix C, "Sample Contracts," provides some example publishing contracts.

As an e-publisher, there are a few things you'll need to do from the business side of things. You'll need to decide if you're going to register the copyrights to your books and whether you want ISBNs. (You'll need ISBNs to get into Amazon.com and the other big booksellers online.) Other issues to consider include protecting yourself legally from certain potential problems and setting up royalty tracking systems. A royalty tracking system will not only help you pay your authors for their books, it will also show you some important information about your publishing program—from a numbers standpoint. Refer to Chapter 11, "Business Issues for the Self E-Publisher," for more information about these issues.

Selling E-Books

When the Internet first started to gain popularity, many people thought that it would diminish the need for huge marketing and advertising efforts to sell products. You could put up a Web site and anyone could find you out there in cyberspace. True equality and open economy. People could buy things based on the quality of the item, instead of on advertising. A small mom-and-pop operation had as much capacity and existence online as a huge corporation. After all, the instant experts argued, it's as easy for a consumer to get to momandpop.com as to pepsi.com.

But in the years to follow, we began to see that getting the consumer's attention is not so easy. Although distribution is more of a level playing field online, the task of getting noticed is as difficult online as it is anywhere else—if not more difficult. That brings us back to selling. But since a lot of folks think *sell* is just another four-letter word and mentally shut down rather than think about it, let's break it down into its two major components:

Distribution. Known as getting *into* the channel, e-book distribution is the task of getting your books to the various online booksellers and distributors. Distribution is all about relationships and partnerships. Many e-publishers report that the majority of their books are purchased directly from their Web sites—more than 75 percent in the case of DiskUs Publishing. Others say that sales from online booksellers are increasing. Hard Shell Word Factory reports that nearly half its sales are coming from outlets such as Amazon.com and Barnes & Noble's Rocket Editions.

Publicity. Known as getting *through* the channel, publicity is the major power behind selling books *out* of the stores and into the hands of the customer. Book publicity is definitely more of an art than a science. Each book has its own publicity potential and the publicity "package" you create for one book may be different from another book's package.

The remainder of this chapter will focus on getting into the channel (distribution), while the following chapter focuses on getting your books through the channel using publicity.

Priced to Sell—Pricing for your e-book depends on your genre. An e-book about a computer programming topic may go for as high as $50, while fiction is usually somewhere between $2.50 and $15 and averages around $7. Keep in mind that you want a convenient price that isn't going to make people gag when they see it. Remember, Stephen King sold his first e-book for $2 and change, although it was only 33 pages. Shorter works naturally cost less. **Dreams Unlimited** (http://www.dreams-unlimited.com/), for example, offers e-novelettes for as little as $2 and some publishers give away books for free—counting on advertising revenue to make up the difference. Refer to Chapter 9, "Publishing Economics 101," for a few more thoughts about e-book pricing.

The Distributors

Distributors and booksellers (discussed in the next section) are often difficult to distinguish online. Many booksellers act like distributors and distributors sometimes sell books to the public. If you work with a distributor, you may not be selling directly to some of the big online booksellers, because the distributors will do that for you. Generally, getting to the big distributors is difficult for small e-publishers with few books to sell. Distributors prefer to work with established publishers. You can get your books to the distributors through one of the publishing services described in the preceding chapter, or through the Print On Demand services of Replica Books and Lightning Source.

E-Bookstores

As a small e-publisher, you'll most likely be working directly with many of the online bookstores—getting your books listed in their online catalogs and databases. Many of the online bookstores that sell printed books to their customers now also sell e-books as downloads. Most of these online stores have programs that make it relatively easy for publishers to list their books. Almost all of them require that your books have ISBNs, so you'll want to refer to Chapter 4, "The Production Process," and Chapter 11, "Business Issues for the E-Publisher," for more information about getting ISBNs. Once you have a series of ISBNs, you can assign numbers to your books and begin listing with Amazon.com and the others. In the case of Amazon.com, you'll find several programs for small publishers to get their books listed. You can join their Advantage program, list titles in the "standard" way, or list multiple titles at once. You simply use the **Publisher's Guide**, located at http://www.amazon.com/publishers/.

CyberRead (http://www.cyberread.com/), an e-book specialty store, will place your PDF file on its secure server. Along with the book information and ISBN, the site also displays author photos and book excerpts. It has a distribution agreement that publishers are required to sign—although it is really a bookstore (yet another confusion in the online e-book market).

Barnes & Noble (http://www.bn.com/) makes it a bit difficult for small e-publishers to gain access to its system. Its people primarily work with distributors or refer smaller publishers to their affiliated company, iUniverse, for distribution. As a result, their publisher relations could use a bit of upgrading. Still, they are one of the big booksellers and should not be overlooked.

The following is a list of online bookstores you can approach with your books. This is by no means a comprehensive list, but it should get you started. For a more complete list, you can refer to any of the major search engines online and search for "books." You can also check the lists at **BookZone** (http://www.bookzone.com/) and **BookWire** (http://www.bookwire.com/). Your friendly authors have also put a list together at **E-Publishing Opportunities** (http://www.myplanet.net/vanburen/).

Amazon.com
http://www.amazon.com/publishers/

Barnes & Noble
http://www.bn.com/

Borders
http://www.borders.com/

iBooks
http://www.ibooks.com/

CyberRead
http://www.cyberread.com/

Amazon.com and E-Commerce—*"People don't want to be automated; they want to have what they do automated. It's a lesson those enamored with technology tend to forget between breakthroughs. Amazon isn't about ordering books online. To the customer, Amazon.com is about easily getting books. That kind of fulfillment promise requires physical facilities, which is why Amazon has built eight customer service centers and twelve distribution centers worldwide, totaling more than five million square feet of warehouse and distribution space. For a so-called pure Internet play, that's a lot of bricks and mortar, not to mention wood pulp."*
—*Frank Catalano, Industry Analyst, From an essay in the* Puget Sound Business Journal

---

eBookAd
http://www.eBookAd.com/

bookstore.com
http://www.bookstore.com/

booksamillion.com
http://www.booksamillion.com/

commonreader.com
http://www.commonreader.com/

A1Books.com
http://www.a1books.com/

Textbooks.com
http://www.textbooks.com/

BookZone
http://www.bookzone.com/

Your Company Web Site

It probably goes without saying that you'll want to sell your e-books through your own company Web site. If you already have a site that has a bit of traffic, it should be easy to add a bookstore section. If you are starting from scratch, then you'll need to educate yourself on the many details about building and running a successful site. Here, we'd like to offer a few tips for making your online bookstore a bit more successful.

Get shopping cart technology. Adding a shopping cart e-commerce function to your Web site is not a simple task. Thankfully, there are services that can handle this for you. Your shoppers will thank you by buying more books. Two companies that offer shopping cart services for e-books are: **BookZone**, http://www.bookzone.com/ and **MultiCards**, http://www.multicards.com/.

Sell books by their covers. Take the time to design attractive covers for your books. A beautiful cover will, in fact, help sell a book—especially a novel. You can find a list of book cover designers online at the BookZone site.

Offer samples. One of the aversions people have to buying e-books is that they cannot always sample the material. The joy of flipping the pages to get a feel for the book is just not present. Instead, you can offer free samples online. You can post an excerpt in HTML on your site, or use one of the more sophisticated services, such as **Real Read** at http://www.realread.com/.

Serve your audience. You're not going to be able to offer the same kind of service that Amazon.com offers. So it's best if you focus on serving your particular audience. These are people who have already seen or read your e-books or know your Web site in some other way. Turn them into a community. Start a discussion group. Send them a newsletter. Give them something for free. Do whatever you can to turn them into a family.

Selling Rights to Other Publishers

As an e-publisher you want to take advantage of all opportunities for selling your books. Naturally, you won't have the ability to do everything possible with your books. For example, most publishers don't perform their own foreign translations to sell books in other countries. To take full advantage of a book's potential, you will probably be working with other publishers in partnership. You, as the original publisher, license certain rights (such as French language rights) to another publisher in exchange for a royalty. These are known as subsidiary rights—rights that are not exploited by the original publisher. You pass a portion of that royalty on to the author and keep a portion (usually 50–50).

Keep in mind that to license subsidiary rights to a book, you must first own the rights. Hence, your publishing contract with the author is an important part of this process. If you purchase only electronic rights, for example, then you can't sell print rights to anyone (and can't print books yourself). If you don't specify that you are purchasing rights in all languages, then you can't market the French rights to your books. Refer to Chapter 11, "Business Issues for the Self E-Publisher," for more information about rights and licenses for small e-publishers.

Finding Publishers to License Rights

The task of finding publishers who might be interested in translating your books or purchasing other subsidiary rights to your books is not trivial. You'll need to form relationships with foreign publishers or agents to market translation rights. If your books have other subsidiary rights potentials, then you'll have other relationships. For example, if your books contain artwork that can be resold as posters or postcards, then you might form relationships with publishers who specialize in these things. Finding all the various players who might be part of your subsidiary rights program will take some time. Following are a few places to start your search.

Foreign Agents

Most foreign rights deals are made through foreign agents. (No, these foreign agents are not undercover spies—they're literary agents specializing in buying foreign rights and bringing books into a particular country.) When you consider that there are several publishers for each language you want to target, you'll realize that selling direct to foreign publishers is a huge effort. It's much easier to deal with a single agent in Japan, for example, than with dozens of Japanese publishers. Finding foreign agents is not really too difficult. You can try looking them up in the *Literary Market Place,* which is available in most good public libraries or online at the **Literary Market Place** site, http://www.literarymarketplace.com/. Also most foreign agents attend the big book trade shows.

Book Shows

Selling of subsidiary rights is a huge part of the program at the major book trade shows and most of the big players are present to buy and sell rights to books. Keep in mind that these are traditional book shows, so most participants are dealing with printed books. Best if you bring a POD version of your book to display—since e-books are not yet widely traded at these shows.

The biggest domestic show for publishers is Book Expo America (BEA), which is usually held around February each year. Many domestic and foreign agents attend to deal with rights. You can make appointments to discuss deals at the show. The same is true of the biggest international book show, called the Frankfurt Book Fair. This is held, of all places, in Frankfurt, Germany, every year. Frankfurt is *the* place to sell foreign rights, although most small publishers find it a bit expensive to attend. As an alternative, you can talk to the folks at **Publishers Marketing Association** (http://www.pma-online.org/) about representing your e-books at the Frankfurt Book Fair. You can also check out the Publishers Marketing Association's Foreign Rights Fair online at the same site. Other international shows can be located at the **Book Expo America** site at http://www.bookexpoamerica.com/industry/indlink.asp or the **BookZone Pro** site at http://www.bookzonepro.com/resources/.

Frankfurt Book Fair
http://www.frankfurt-book-fair.com/

Book Expo America
http://www.bookexpoamerica.com/

Foreign Rights Fair
http://www.pma-online.org/

E-Book Communities

If you find it a bit difficult or costly to schedule a trip to Germany, try some online connections. You can open discussions with various publishers through these online e-book and e-publishing communities. For more resources like them, refer to Appendix B, "Resources."

EBookNet
http://www.ebooknet.com/

Publishers Marketing Association
http://www.pma-online.org/

BookZone Pro
http://www.bookzonepro.com/

Electronic Publishing Connections
http://www.epublishingconnections.com/

Ind-e-pubs Online Community
Subscribe by sending an e-mail message to Ind-e-pubs-subscribe@egroups.com

Inkspot Electronic Publishing Resources
http://www.inkspot.com/epublish/

Online Rights Brokers

If you've decided to make a go of publishing your own e-book and sell all the various rights yourself, then you should consider listing your book with one of the online rights brokers—they're just as useful here as on the selling end (discussed earlier in this chapter), or maybe more so. Without a doubt, there will be certain rights that you don't really know how to exploit. You may have great connections in France for a French translation of your e-book. Perhaps you even have friends who want to create an online, interactive course from your work. Maybe you've contacted **Bookface** at http://www.bookface.com/ and have an advertising-based version of your book available, too. That's great. Now you can list your book with one of the online rights brokers and see if you can get some interest in the other rights. Maybe someone in Japan would like to translate your book....

Online rights brokers are services that list literary works, along with the rights that are available for the work. Customers can search through the database of properties (books) and bid on certain rights for certain works. Here are a few rights brokers:

Rights World
http://www.rightsworld.com/

RightsCenter
http://www.rightscenter.com/

SubRights
http://www.subrights.com/

CHAPTER EIGHT

On Your Own: Book Marketing Strategies

In the preceding chapter we discussed ways and means for getting your e-books into the sales channel—into the bookstores and distributors. But getting into the channel is only the first part of e-book publishing success. You also want to get your books back out of the channel—in the direction of the consumer's hands. This is known as getting your e-books *through* the channel and it's done primarily by creating desire for your e-books. This is a process with two components: First, you must create books that people want to read—high-quality, well-written books about popular subjects. Second, you must let people know about your books. There may be millions of people thirsting for the information in your book, but if they don't know it exists, you won't sell a lot of copies. This chapter takes a stroll down the path of creating desire for your e-books—both by choosing subjects and topics that people want and by getting the word out about your books. Although choosing subject matter for your books may depend more on your expertise than on unlimited choice, this chapter nevertheless provides a look at the topics that are doing well in the e-book world. To help you get the word out about your e-books, this chapter also explains some basic publicity tactics, such as the use of bestseller lists, review copies, e-mail promotion, and more.

For Love or Money: What Sells and Why

The first step in creating books that people want to read is to know what books people are already buying. In the print book market, we know that romance novels account for almost 50 percent of mass market fiction sales. Not surprisingly, the types of books that seem to do well in e-publishing are romance, horror, and science fiction—and a large percentage of e-publishers offer these types of titles. Just take a look at our e-publisher listing in Appendix A and you'll see just how many e-publishers are in the romance business.

While traditional romances do okay, several publishers have found particular success with romances that cross genres, such as science fiction romances or romantic suspense. As a result, many e-publishers are seeking good manuscripts in that fall into these various romance categories, called *subgenres*. Other types of fiction such as mystery, horror, science fiction, and fantasy are also quite popular—although several e-publishers have noted that they see fewer high-quality manuscripts in these areas.

Traditional print publishers have many reasons to refuse a particular fiction manuscript, the most important of which is that the author has no existing reputation. Also, the book may be too long or too short, or have the wrong kind of protagonist, the wrong setting, or any number of other elements that don't fit into the norm of today's print publishing world. Electronic publishing allows publishers to take more chances with books and experiment with fresh, exciting new voices and approaches. Of course, whether you're creating a work of fiction for print or for the online market, you still need to have a tight, well-written story line and interesting characters.

The nonfiction realm also offers plenty of opportunities and perhaps even more money to be made than with e-fiction. Because nonfiction e-books can let the reader jump around the text as though using an online help system, e-books are ideal for instructional material. And because e-books can be produced more quickly than printed books, they are also ideal for delivering information that changes quickly. All this spells success for books about technical or scientific topics, such as computer programming. As you might expect, technical and computer topics make for some of the better-selling e-books. In fact, a huge number of Web sites are dedicated to presenting technical information and instruction. Dozens of online courseware companies are selling virtual classes via the Internet—some for as much as $500 per student. One of the most successful of these companies is **DigitalThink** at http://www.digitalthink.com/, which is now a public company with many Fortune 500 clients. Its people specialize in selling online courses in programming and computer science for their corporate customers. Granted, their courses are much more interactive than a typical e-book, but other online computer courseware companies offer products that very much resemble e-books—and some companies offer e-books along with their online courses. Figure 8.1 shows an online course offering by eHandsOn.

People who want up-to-the-minute information about technical topics can and will find it online and, if it's good, they'll tell all their associates about it. What's more, they're usually willing to pay a bit more for this type of information—since it usually affects their job and income-producing capabilities. And finally, since a huge number of people who use the Internet are also computer savvy (perhaps that's a foregone conclusion and perhaps not), it

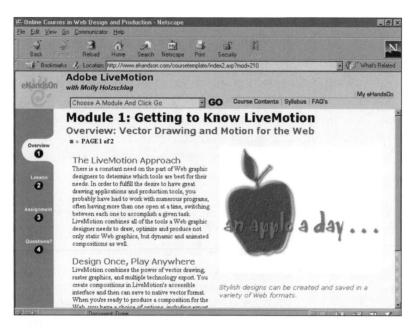

Figure 8.1: Get in motion—take an online computer course.

makes sense that marketing e-books over the Internet means that you'll be marketing to a group with computer skills and interests. So it's no surprise that technical books are probably the biggest print book market for online bookstores. Strangely, there are few computer e-book publishers specializing in electronic computer books. But we'll soon be seeing most of the paper-based computer book publishers offering e-book versions of their books. Already at the time we're writing this book, both MightyWords and iUniverse have specific publishing programs for technical works and have even been known to pay advances for them. Meanwhile, many of the large, established computer book publishers (such as HungryMinds and Osborne/McGraw-Hill) are not offering their authors competitive royalties for e-book sales. So there is a big opportunity for computer and technical e-book publishers who offer normal e-book royalties (that's 35 to 50 percent of publisher's receipts) for their authors.

Other nonfiction topics can be successful as e-books, especially anything instructional in nature, such as cookbooks, travel guides, home electronics guides, and home improvement guides. People love to learn new things, and e-books make learning accessible. Indeed, many educational institutions are joining the frenzy, fearing that the Internet will soon make them obsolete. Most colleges and universities now offer electronic courses—delivered online over the Internet. Most of these courses include electronic documents that are (or could be) published as e-books. Without a doubt, online learning is an exploding market. Just about any good instructional e-book could be turned into an online course with interactive components. Several software packages are available for doing just that. If you want to exploit the online course rights to your e-books, check into some of these possible conversion services. **eHandsOn** (http://www.ehandson.com/), for example, has course production, hosting, and delivery services for publishers.

Finally, we should add that business-related topics are finding happy homes as e-books. Like the people who buy and use technical e-books, executives and businesspeople are usually willing to pay well for information they need—information important to their jobs. MightyWords has capitalized on this tendency to develop a thriving business selling short executive briefings on all sorts of topics. These briefings range from 20 to 40 pages and are targeted at managers. A well-written briefing can be quite valuable to an executive who needs to make a decision or prepare a presentation to the board. This executive can find a related document on the Internet and download it in minutes, which can save a lot of hassle and often a lot of money. Generally with business publications, the more technical and specific the better. Any number of books talk about how to motivate employees or be a better manager. But its much harder to find a clear explanation of why a company might want to switch from a Windows computing environment to a Linux environment, or a summary of the political and economic climate in Argentina designed for companies thinking of expanding in South America. Now that's valuable stuff!

We're not saying that to be successful you have to create e-books in these categories. What's more important is that you are good at what you publish. Quality will always be noticed (eventually). But knowing what sells is important when designing a publishing program.

Book Publicity in a Nutshell

When people think of book publicity, many think of authors traveling the country to bookstores and of cafés with lines of people waiting to get their copies of a book signed and shake the author's hand. But book tours are only a small part of a book's publicity campaign—and an ever-shrinking part at that. Tours are becoming a thing of the past due to the high cost of travel and the low margins in book publishing.

So just how *do* publishers get their books noticed? Most publishers have on-staff publicists to handle the various components of a publicity program. Some publishers use outside publicists for certain books that they feel warrant a more robust campaign. Here are some of the things publicists do:

News Releases. The first line of fire for getting the word out on a new product is the news release. A news release is an announcement that goes out to all interested parties (usually Internet, print, and broadcast media) who might be able to mention your book. Writing a news release requires a touch of the artist. A good news release will follow a traditional structure while calling attention to itself at the same time. A news release should not be more than two pages long—the shorter the better. A sample is shown in Figure 8.2.

Complimentary Copies. You should expect to send out numerous complimentary copies of your e-book. Send freebies to any and all possible reviewers, people related to the book or its topic, contacts at bookstores, magazines, and Web sites, and any other VIPs that you think could help you in any way. It's not uncommon for publishers to send hundreds of complimentary copies to the press and other useful friends. Plus, publishers will often give away copies of books to consumers—just to get momentum started and word of mouth going for the book. It's best to reserve consumer promotional copies for special events, however. For example, if you were to write a cookbook about traditional Portuguese cuisine, you might work with a travel Web site to provide a number of free copies for their customers interested in Portugal.

Cross-Marketing. As long as you're sending out free copies and news releases, you might as well make note of some important Web sites that you might work with in an exchange type of situation. The example of providing free copies of a Portuguese cookbook to customers of a travel Web site is a good one. There might be many different types of cross-promotions you can create with other sites. The folks at HungryMinds, for example, created a promotional e-book by combining sections from several of their popular "Dummies" books into a special sample edition. They got together with Microsoft Corporation to deliver this promotional book for free with numerous Microsoft Reader devices. They've done similar deals with Kodak and other large companies. Creativity and contacts are the main ingredients in these types of cross-marketing deals.

Author Signings and Appearances. Author appearances are still useful for promoting books. However, in the world of e-books, it's best to limit your author tour to online events. Many online bookstores offer author presentations for their customers—where people can chat with the author. For nonfiction authors, expert presentations can be a way to get the word out. For example, if you wrote a book about gem-cutting techniques, then you might make an expert presentation at one of the many gem shows around the country—or find out about the most popular online gem events. If you are determined to sign books, then make sure you have POD copies of your book available for these appearances.

Figure 8.2: A successful news release—doesn't it make you want to stretch a bit?

For Immediate Release   Publicity Contact: Maureen Watts
                                                    (415) 826-9488
                                                    wattsmo@earthlink.net

Three million flexible bodies can't be wrong!

STRETCHING

20th Anniversary Revised Edition
Bob Anderson
Illustrated by Jean Anderson

"A bible of the stretching gospel."   **—The Washington Post**

Can one of the world's most popular fitness books get even better? It can! *Stretching* by Bob Anderson has been completely revised—with all new drawings, 25 new stretching routines, and updated stretching information throughout. The new *Stretching* is out just in time for the beloved book's 20th anniversary.

With three million copies sold, *Stretching* is an international bestseller in 19 languages. Favored for its sensible, simple approach and clear black and white illustrations, *Stretching* has helped people of all ages, sizes, and levels of fitness increase their flexibility and stay in shape.

Stretching keeps muscles flexible and ready for movement, improves performance, and prevents injuries. It's not only good for you, it feels good too. In *Stretching*, Bob Anderson explains how to stretch and provides a guide that can help anyone begin a lifelong program of physical fitness. The book has over 1,000 clear drawings and more than 250? stretches, including stretching routines for 54 sports and activities. Here's what's new in this first revision of *Stretching* in twenty years:

- 1,000 new drawings by Jean Anderson—with men and women in clothing appropriate to their sport or activity
- Eleven new everyday routines, including stretches for: kids, travelers, lower back tension, and gardening
- Fourteen new sports routines, including: mountain biking, rock climbing, snowboarding, bowling, and inline skating
- New hand, wrist, and forearm stretches for people with carpal tunnel syndrome
- Modified stretches based on research and feedback from athletes and readers
- Streamline versions of each routine for people in a hurry
- A new section on "PNF" stretching—a new technique for increased flexibility

— more —

What hasn't changed in *Stretching* are the basic principles of staying flexible and fit for a lifetime. Also, Bob's methods of slow, steady stretching — paying close attention to how the stretch *feels*—remain the same. The book still reflects the idea that stretching is the simplest of all fitness activities, one that can be done throughout the day—and for a lifetime.

Why do people need *Stretching* more than ever? Sedentary lifestyle? Participating in sports? Going to the gym? More time spent in front of a computer? An aging population? No matter what kind of shape you're in or what kind of activity you do, stretching both relieves stress and gets you ready for action.

Bob Anderson's book has remained a favorite over the past two decades, proving that no matter what kind of activity people engage in, *Stretching* never goes out of style.

About the Author and Illustrator

Bob Anderson is the world's most popular stretching authority. For over 25 years, he has taught millions of people his simple approach to stretching. In addition to *Stretching*, he is the author of *Stretching At Your Computer or Desk*, the software Stretchware, and co-author of *Getting In Shape*. Through his travels, lectures, and workshops, he's kept in constant touch with people in all degrees of physical condition. These days Bob spends most of his workout time on a mountain bike and running in the mountains above his house in Colorado.

Jean Anderson was photographer, illustrator, typesetter, and editor of the fist home-made edition of *Stretching*. She developed a system of shooting photos of Bob doing the stretches, then making clear ink drawings of each stretch. Jean has illustrated all of Bob's other books. These days she oversees Stretching Inc.'s mail-order business and hikes, cycles, and plays tennis to stay in shape.

"We hope you like this new book, and that it helps you remain limber and in good health for the rest of your life!" –Bob and Jean Anderson

Stretching: 20th Anniversary Revised Edition
Bob Anderson, illustrated by Jean Anderson
$14.95 quality paperback
8 1/2 x 11, 224 pages, ISBN 0-936070-22-6

Published by Shelter Publications, Inc., Bolinas, CA
415-868-0280, email: shelter@shelterpub.com
www.shelterpub.com
Distributed to the trade by Publishers Group West 1-800-788-3123

Collateral Material. Although advertising is usually not a valuable investment for books, collateral materials can often pay off. These materials consist of post card flyers showing the book's cover (you'll find a lot of free post card advertising services if you look for them), bookmarks that you can give away in stores or with other books, and even posters. Online collateral materials could include free excerpts, companion Web pages, or free screen savers related to the book.

The world of online publicity is growing and there are new opportunities all the time. The rest of this chapter will give you some specific ideas and contacts that you can use to get the word out on your books—over the Internet.

The Prized Publicity Database—It's not difficult to figure out that the quality and number of your publicity contacts is what makes or breaks a publicity campaign. For this reason, publicists hoard and treasure their contact databases. As you grow your publicity program, be sure to maintain your contact database and collect as many different publicity sources as you can.

Publicity Services

If you want to outsource your promotion and publicity tasks, there are online services that can help. You can also augment your own publicity campaign with some of these services. Check out the list of resources at **BookZone Pro** (http://www.bookzonepro.com/) for more publicity services you can hire.

Copywriter.com (http://www.copywriter.com/) is an online business resource center. Its staff offer creative services for copy-intensive Web sites, free Internet marketing reports, and a direct e-mail list source that gives you literally thousands of places to advertise via e-mail without spamming.

Foxcontent.com (http://www.foxcontent.com/) is a site that helps you promote your work over the Web. Its people can plan a marketing campaign with you, do research on the Internet, publicize your book to evaluated sites (including requesting space for excerpts or links), create the files necessary for the excerpt, announce the book's Web page to all major search engines, and provide you with a site listing. Foxcontent charges for these services.

Bookpromotion (http://www.bookpromotion.com/) offers resources and marketing services for authors and self-publishers. Besides promotion on its lists, services also include Web site creation and hosting, search engine registration, news release writing and submissions, affinity linking, newsgroup postings, e-mail newsletter advertising, targeted e-mail campaigns, and chat tour scheduling. Most packages that Bookpromotion sells include a Web site for the author's book, search engine registration, and a news release service. This runs about $500. This is the typical package that authors purchase, but cost really boils down to what services the author requests.

The Power of E-Mail

Perhaps your most powerful tool for publicity over the Internet is e-mail. Unlike a Web site that people may or may not visit, e-mail is proactive. It gets delivered directly to the recipient's in-box. Just about everyone you want to reach out there has an e-mail address. Without a doubt, e-mail is the glue holding the Internet together. Well-written, unobtrusive e-mail messages can be a powerful way to boost your sales via the Internet. Here are some ideas for how you can use e-mail to promote your books without offending anyone.

> **E-Mail Announcements.** You can create various types of announcements for various types of recipients. Create a standard news release for people in the media. Create a casual announcement for your existing customers and a more flashy announcement for prospective customers.
>
> **E-Mail Signatures.** The recipient of every piece of mail you send is a potential book buyer. Be sure to include a one-line announcement and Web site address in every message. Many mail programs have an automatic signature line function. E-mail signatures should be no more than four lines.
>
> **E-Mail Newsletters.** Round up the list of addresses of fans who have sent mail to you and send them a newsy letter reminding them about each of your upcoming book releases. To collect these addresses, you should have a Web site with plenty of opportunities for people to sign up for your newsletter. You might also consider a separate site for each book—or at least a separate page at your main site. Be sure to cross-reference the Web site address with the book. Every copy of the e-book should list the Web site and e-mail contact information of the publisher and even the author.

For more information about using e-mail to promote your products on the Internet, refer to *Poor Richard's Internet Marketing and Promotions* by Peter Kent and Tara Calishain. For more information about creating online newsletters, check out *Poor Richard's E-Mail Publishing* by Chris Pirillo. For information about creating an effective Web site, try *Poor Richard's Web Site* (second edition) by Peter Kent. As you can tell by the titles, all these books come from Top Floor Publishing.

Online Communities and Groups

Readers who enjoy the same types of books usually congregate on online communities where similar topics are discussed. For example, if you love reading biographies, you might spend time on the **Biography Channel** Web site (http://www.biography.com/). As an online marketer, you'll need to focus on these kinds of niche communities to build a following for your book.

Subscribe to and contribute to e-mail discussion lists in your subject area or genre. Writers' lists are both common and popular; they can generate huge numbers of messages each day, so check them out carefully and keep your subscriptions to the ones that really interest you (and are likely to be interested in you). If you publish books written by other authors, encourage them to subscribe and participate in discussion lists and online communities, too. Besides e-mail discussion lists, online communities include newsgroups and message boards.

Don't Spam—Spam e-mail is junk e-mail. Nobody likes it and that's the truth. We honestly don't know why some people use spamming as a tool for making sales. Worse still are the messages that try to trick you into reading them—messages with subject lines such as "Oh, and one more thing..." or "Answer to your question." Perhaps these tricks work for certain types of things and certain types of people. But if you're serious about creating an online business, spamming will only serve to create more bad will than sales. Spam e-mail usually does not include an e-mail return address (where you can send nasty replies to get back at the sender for spamming you). Instead, it usually tries to get you to make a telephone call. This type of e-mail characteristically advertises alternative health products, real estate, home loans, network marketing schemes, and many other things that most people would not purchase from a stranger over the Internet. Spam e-mail is generally unsolicited by the recipient and employs tricks for getting people to open and read it. E-mail advertising, on the other hand, is sent to people who have a genuine interest in the topic or have subscribed to a mailing list service or have otherwise requested the information. It always includes a return address and usually tells the recipient where and how the sender got the address information, so it's easy to get off an unwelcome list.

Some sites with specific categories, where you can join online discussions, include **About.com** (http://www.about.com/), which plays host to over 700 sites and lists, and **TalkCity.com** (http://www.talkcity.com/), where you can create your own folders within a book discussion area and start talking about your own book. Another possibility is **eGroups** (http://www.egroups.com/), which has a huge listing of online chats and newsletters that you can receive. At eGroups, you can also start your own discussion list, as they offer a subscriber management service. Chat moderators are always willing to have authors in for a visit to answer questions from the regular attendees. Not only do you get to visit with fans for a night but most moderators have their own mailing lists to introduce the guest each week.

Another way to find an audience is through newsgroups, e-mail discussions, book clubs, and e-zines, to name a few. You need to find the specific chats and newsletters that your audience reads and get your book listed and talked about there. Tossing a few free copies around couldn't hurt. **Deja.com** (http://www.deja.com/) is a site that lists newsgroups for every subject imaginable. They help consumers decide what products to purchase and where to buy them. The Arts & Entertainment section includes books on 24 subjects.

Most of the discussion-oriented groups are free—there's no charge to join and they welcome anyone who expresses an interest, but they do have restrictions on advertising and self-promotion. To work with such groups, you need to participate. It's usually considered okay to mention your stuff in a short signature line attached to the e-mail you send to the group—but the e-mail itself should be relevant to the current discussion; launching epistles of self-praise is out of bounds.

You might consider sponsoring your own discussion group about your book or related topics. The **eGroups** site (http://www.egroups.com/), in addition to listing online discussion groups you can join, also has tools for hosting your own group. You may also want to check out *Poor Richard's Building Online Communities* by John Levine and Margy Levine Young (Top Floor Publishing, 2000).

Another good research tool is **Tile.net** (http://www.tile.net/). The site provides a list of e-mail discussions, Usenet newsgroups, FTP sites, computer product vendors, and Internet and Web design companies.

Book Reviews

Reviews broadcast your work and can provide valuable publicity—more valuable than advertising. Sites that include reviews matching your target audience act like a continual promotional tool for you. To find review sites, you can use the **Literary Marketplace**, located at http://www.literarymarketplace.com/, **BookZone** http://www.bookzone.com/, and **BookWire**, http://www.bookwire.com/. They have lists of book review syndicates and book review sites that you can contact. Here are several of the main book review sites online:

Amazon.com
http://www.amazon.com/

Barnes & Noble
http://www.bn.com/

Book Reporter
http://www.bookreporter.com/

BookWire
http://www.bookwire.com/

Electronic Review of Computer Books
http://www.ercb.com/

Smart Books (Books About the Internet)
http://www.smartbooks.com/

Also note that most major newspapers and magazines have separate online book reviews, like the one you'll find at the **Atlantic Monthly** site, http://www.atlanticmonthly.com/.

Send your book, news release, and pitch letter to a book club. Book clubs are discussed later in this chapter.

Best-Seller Lists

Best-seller lists come in all shapes and sizes. Most of them do not include lists for e-book best-sellers as we write. But keep an eye on things, as some of these lists may just start reporting on e-books. The most renowned list is the one put out by the *New York Times*. If you meander into Barnes & Noble, Borders, or even your local library, they may have a copy of this best-seller list posted for customer reference. Another popular list is produced by *USA Today,* which publishes a weekly tally based on a computer analysis of retail book sales nationwide. And *Publisher's Weekly* has several best-seller lists and may soon be offering one for e-books.

With the onset of the Internet, Amazon.com has created a Hot 100, and so has Barnes & Noble. Both are updated hourly! Everything you could want is online now, all your favorite best-seller lists, and even the ordering. Here are some Web sites for best-seller lists:

Amazon
http://www.amazon.com/exec/obidos/subst/lists/best/best.html

Barnes & Noble
http://www.barnesandnoble.com/bestsellers/

Oprah Winfrey
http://oprah.com/obc/pastbooks/obc_pb_main.html

Publisher's Weekly
http://www.publishersweekly.com/bestsellersindex.asp

USA Today
http://www.usatoday.com/life/enter/books/leb1.htm

New York Times
http://www.nytimes.com/books/yr/mo/day/bsp/

EBook Connections
http://www.ebookconnections.com/bestsellers/b_home.htm

Book Awards

There are a few e-book awards to consider. Listing your e-book with one of these awards programs could win you prize money and even promotional goodies. Most winners get plenty of media attention—better than any publicity effort you could do on your own.

The Independent e-Book Awards has several categories for e-books, including fiction, nonfiction, short books, children's books, and books that include special electronic elements such as hypertext. The awards are open to authors and e-publishers and books do not have to have ISBNs to be accepted. The cost is $25 for each entry. Refer to the **Eligibility Requirements** for complete details (http://www.e-book-awards.com/eligibilty/requirements.html). The **Independent e-Book Awards** main page is located at http://www.e-book-awards.com/, and you can also find links there to more information.

Another e-book–specific awards event is the Frankfurt e-Book Awards. This happens in conjunction with the Frankfurt Book Fair. Winners of this e-book award usually get plenty of international media attention. For more information, refer to the **Frankfurt Book Fair** Web site at http://www.frankfurtbookfair.com/.

For a list of other book awards events, check out the **BookWire** list of awards at http://www.bookwire.com/index/Book-Awards.html or the list at **BookZone** (http://www.bookzone.com/).

Book Clubs

Book clubs can be a great way for you to market your book. Book clubs usually sell books to their members (at a reduced price) and also review books and discuss them. The problem is, you have to find a club that is interested in the types of books you have to offer. Many book clubs exist online. Participants read books on their own and then send their comments to a central Web location. Here are a few to look over:

A and E
http://www.aande.com/bookclub/

Women.com
http://women.com/clubs/book.html

Book Chatter
http://www.bookchatter.tierranet.com/

Book Group
http://members.tripod.com/~bookgroup/

Book Lovers
http://mindmills.net/booklovers/index.shtml

RPMDP
http://books.rpmdp.com/

Net Language
http://www.net-language.com/readingclub/

Free Reads

Publishers have been giving away excerpts and samples of their books for quite some time. It's a tried-and-true method of publicity. If people like the sample, they'll buy and read the rest of the book. The first and easiest way to get samples distributed is to put them on your own Web site as free downloads or excerpts that can be read onscreen.

You can offer the entire book for free online and earn advertising revenue by using the ad placement services of **Advertising.com** (http://www.advertising.com/). You can select ads that go into your document and earn revenue each time a customer clicks the ad from your e-book.

Another outfit called **RealRead** (http://www.realread.com/) has created a service to e-publishers that lets you post samples from your books onto the RealRead site. Then you can add a link to your online bookstore that lets the customer read those samples from your book. The samples are actually located on the RealRead site, but the customer has the experience of reading samples on your site. It's slightly more sophisticated than putting an HTML sample on your own site—but it's basically the same thing.

Finally, it's worth mentioning that some self-published e-book authors are making their entire e-books available for free without advertisements. How do they make any money? They charge for the print or Print On Demand version. The theory is that people who love the book will still want a printed copy even if they have already read it electronically. This could very well prove to be true (at least until e-book devices evolve to the point where they actually rival printed books). Such a strategy could prove successful in attracting customers to your Web site, even if you only have one or two free e-books there. People love free stuff! Refer to Chapter 3, "New Ways of Publishing," to read about LifeWeb's free e-book approach.

PART IV
E-Book Business Issues

CHAPTER NINE

Publishing Economics 101

Before you decide to publish your own e-book, it's useful to know a thing or two about the financial end of the business. How much does it cost to create an e-book? And if you end up creating a printed version, what's that going to run? Even if you decide to work with an established publisher or one of the many new e-publishers making a name for itself, it's useful to have some background in publishing economics so you can avoid getting into bad deals. Why do publishing contracts have certain language and how do you estimate the publisher's costs in producing your book? This chapter will help you make sense of all this and prepare you for your own e-publishing venture should you decide to take that step.

A little background in print publishing can only help, so this chapter will make a lot of comparisons between traditional (print) publishing and electronic publishing. Although much is yet to be defined and the technology is bound to keep improving and changing, one thing is for certain: The new world of electronic publishing is forcing us to change how we look at books, book contracts, book distribution, the writing process—in fact, just about every aspect of publishing. You're going to see a consistent message throughout this book: Electronic publishing economics are different from print publishing economics and these differences should be (and often are) reflected in the kinds of partnerships (publishing deals) authors can make. In the next chapter we'll get into some detail about how e-book deals differ from traditional deals and what issues you should look for when making a deal, from a contractual point of view. For now, here's a run-through on some of the main economic differences between print publishing and e-publishing.

Pre-production Costs (Quality Usually Costs More)

It's usually more expensive to do a good job than to do a poor job. With e-books, this is certainly true—especially in the pre-production stage. Originally, the job of turning a rough manuscript into a polished piece of literature fell to the publisher and its editors. In the electronic publishing world, we have many different publishing models. In some cases, the e-publisher edits and produces the e-book; in other cases, editing is the author's responsibility, which means that the e-book may or may not be edited. And then there's the fact that some editors are better than others. It's one thing to give a manuscript a quick pass to catch spelling and grammar errors. It's another thing completely to *edit* the manuscript. A professional editor will usually take several passes at a manuscript to check for different types of things each time. Here's a brief idea of the types of things a good editor might do for a manuscript:

- **Structural edit.** Before you get too far, it's a good idea to check the outline and basic structure of the book for proper form. For example, a formal outline should always have more than one heading at each level and you should never skip levels. If you refer to another part of the book, it's important to make sure that part actually exists—or you'll have some frustrated readers on your hands.

- **Consistency and style edit.** If you refer to an illustration as "Figure One" in one place, you should not refer to another illustration as "Fig 1-3" or "in the following figure." Consistency also affects page numbering, cross-references, use of capitalization, and much more. For example, in this book, we use e-book instead of eBook—and you will not find a single occurrence of the latter except where it's somebody's trademark. With works of fiction, an editor will check for continuity in the manuscript—making sure the hero's eyes don't change color half-way through the book, for instance. It's a good idea to give the manuscript one more run-through to catch this type of error.

- **Copyedit.** This is what most people think of when they think of editing: correcting spelling and grammatical errors and generally cleaning up the language. This one is a must. It's also the hardest to do for your own writing. You already know what something is supposed to mean (you wrote it, after all), and often won't notice if the words don't actually communicate that meaning.

- **Technical or factual edit.** If your book involves technical information, historical references, or other types of facts, it's important to check them for accuracy. In some cases, it's important to get legal advice if a book contains information that might offend readers or infringe on someone's rights, libel someone, or otherwise get you into trouble. See Chapter 11, "Business Issues for the Self E-Publisher," for more information about legal issues involved in being your own e-publisher.

Format edit. Once the book is designed and formatted, it's important to check the final pages for problems such as widow and orphan lines, separating an illustration from its caption, and so on. Many e-book formats use the same basic page layout structure as a normal book, so these problems can still come up.

Final proof. Now you can do one final run-through to make sure your corrections did not introduce more problems and to look for missing punctuation and leftover typos. Now you're ready to get into the book's production.

Editorial Insight—For more information on editing, you might check out the Bay Area Editors' Forum at http://www.editorsforum.org. *They have some good information about the kinds of work involved in editing a manuscript. It also includes contact information for editors you can hire.*

Naturally, getting these edits done requires time and money. Remember the old adage "an attorney who represents himself has a fool for a client?" Well, this also applies to editing. In other words, it's almost impossible to do a decent job of editing your own work. To put out a high-quality book that people can easily read, you need a professional touch. If your e-publisher does not provide it, then you're working with more of a distribution service and, hopefully, you're getting a bigger piece of the pie in exchange for the costs you incur in pre-production. Of course, you can always put out an unedited book and hope for the best. But one of the problems in the e-publishing world is the amount of really bad material that's out there. Those of us who appreciate good books would prefer that you don't add to the pile.

Good Editing Seal of Approval

The phenomenon of badly written e-books is really becoming an issue. E-books are getting a reputation for being books that nobody would waste the paper to print. As an author, you don't want your well-written, professionally edited work of art lumped together with a bunch of schlock. If the publisher or distributor you're looking at using has a reputation for publishing any old piece of junk, then you probably don't want to be one of the few jewels in the rough. Chances are, customers won't keep coming back to read more. At some point, it might even be common to see some kind of stamp of approval that you can put on your e-book, showing that it was professionally edited. If you're thinking of creating your own e-book publishing enterprise, you might consider advertising the fact that your books are professionally edited (assuming, of course, that they are). For more information on editing and editing services, refer to Chapter 7, "Assembling Your E-Publishing Venture."

Production Costs (Pulp Fiction With Less Pulp)

The obvious thing about electronic publishing is that it does not involve a physical product. Electronic publishing is pure information exchange with no dead trees. This has a huge impact on the publishing world, since publishing economics have always revolved around the printing process. Let's take a closer look at how the cost of putting ink on paper affects the cost of producing books and, consequently, the author's compensation. Afterward, we'll see how e-books and Print On Demand differ from traditional methods and how that affects authors and self-publishers. That takes us directly into contemplating just how much an e-book should cost.

Starting Up the Presses

When the price of paper goes up, the price of books goes up. And as with most physical products that are mass produced, the more books you create at one time, the cheaper they are per unit. That's because there are several fixed costs associated with print publishing. Not only the fixed costs of pre-production, as discussed in the preceding section of this chapter, but also fixed set-up costs required for printing. One way to look at it is that the first book off the press costs $5,000 and the next 5,000 books only cost one dollar each. Well, that's not exactly how it works, but it's not a bad way to look at it. Because of the high cost of starting up the presses, publishers generally don't print fewer than 3,000 copies of a book. A minimum first run is in the range of 5,000 copies, depending on the book. It's just not economically practical to print fewer than this, because the cost per book is too high. At some point, publishers have to decide if it's worth reprinting certain books—books that sell slowly. To help make it feasible to keep slow-sellers in print, publishers have added clauses like the following to their author contracts:

> *On all sales of copies of reprint editions of the Work undertaken by the Publisher more than 12 months after publication for which the total press run is fewer than 2,500 copies, the Publisher shall pay a royalty equivalent to half the rates specified above.*

Basically, this is saying that the publisher and the author will share the expense of printing so few copies. The author will share by getting a reduced royalty and the publisher by making less profit per book. After all, this is a partnership between the author and publisher. Now, with Print On Demand technology, this type of clause is becoming a thing of the past, since publishers can print one or two copies of a book for only slightly more cost per book than traditional publishing. More on this in a moment.

Name Recognition—*In recent years, print publishers have grown cautious about what they publish. An author needs not only a great concept and a well-written, well-thought-out manuscript but also a well-known name to help attract attention to the book. Without the fame, publishers hesitate to take a chance on a book. But think about it...an author who already has an audience and market through speaking engagements, TV or radio presence, or other efforts is contributing a great deal to the sales of the book. Given the decline of the independent bookstore and the rise of the superstore, publishers have become more like middlemen between the author and the distributor—merely providing access into the distribution channel (the superstore) and looking for the author's name to get books into the hands of the consumer.*

So...if an author is responsible for a large percentage of the sales of the book in addition to the execution of the book itself, then that author should get a larger percentage of the receipts. Print publishers are reluctant to give up their old business models. In the e-book market, however, where publishers are either services for authors or distributor-publisher crossbreeds, authors can look for partnerships that compensate them for their contributions to the success of the book.

Let's look at the opposite extreme. Suppose a book becomes a best-seller. Everyone is thrilled. The publisher can print tens of thousands of copies and get the price per book down and profit per book up. Thankfully, literary agents have forced publishers to share the reward with the author in these situations. As a result, most print publishing deals give authors higher royalties when a book sells more copies. Here's an example of a royalty clause in a publishing contract:

> *Royalties from sales of the completed Work in the United States: 10 percent of the net dollar receipts on the first 15,000 copies sold; 12 percent of the net dollar receipts on sales of from 15,001 to 25,000 copies; and 15 percent of the net dollar receipts on all copies sold beyond 25,000.*

Royalties go up as volume goes up. Why? Simply because of the economics of printing and the fact that publishing agreements have attempted to compensate authors for these printing benefits—just as they have compensated publishers for excessive costs, such as that of keeping a book in print when it's not selling well. But don't assume that this is because publishers are so generous or fair. No, it's generally the literary agents who have forced publishers into sharing the wealth with their authors. When there's an economic benefit to the publisher, agents have made publishers share that benefit. One of the potential problems with the world of e-publishing is that authors are going direct to publishers and distributors without the benefit of representation. Many of them are agreeing to things that do not reflect a fair division of proceeds, which is making it harder for others to negotiate compensation that accurately reflects the contribution of the author. The job of an agent (assuming you get a good one) is to help you negotiate a good deal. In fact, the better deal often makes up for the commission you pay. If you have a publishing contract in hand ready to sign, you can probably just consult an agent for some quick advice. For more information and advice on publishing contracts, check out some of the resources listed in Appendix A.

Enter E-Books

Compared to the cost of printing books, the costs associated with publishing e-books are relatively small and, given the continuing evolution of computer technology, will likely be even smaller in the future. (See Part II, "Planning and Creating an E-Book," for more information about the technology involved in creating an e-book.) After the pre-production costs mentioned in the first section of this chapter, producing copies of an e-book costs almost nothing. And these costs do not typically change when quantities go up. The per-book cost of producing one e-book is about the same as it is for producing a thousand. In fact, e-books are not really even "produced." In some cases, an e-book is simply downloaded from one computer to another—which constitutes a copy. If a hundred people download your book, then you've produced a hundred copies. In other cases, e-books are read, or accessed, online—each access constituting one copy. (Remember, we're talking about production costs here, not the costs associated with selling the book, such as discounts or premiums paid to others. We'll cover those issues in the next section of this chapter.)

A Likely Outcome—The e-publishing world is still pretty much finding itself. When the dust settles, it's likely that the results will look like other types of businesses on the Internet—a handful of sites dominating the field while dozens of others play second and third string. Just about anybody can create a Web site, but not many people can make a site popular and well visited. So it's likely that you'll see a few e-book publishers dominating the field with hundreds of others publishing niche e-books. Small e-book publishers will probably still be able get their books listed at Amazon.com and other big reseller sites. But getting their books noticed and publicized (and therefore sold) is quite another story. See Chapter 8, "On Your Own: Book Marketing Strategies," for more information about reaching potential customers.

Getting a book from an electronic document such as a Microsoft Word file into a readable e-book format such as a PDF file is not a complex problem these days. Sure, there are some costs—you need to buy software for conversion and layout, for example—but there is no *production,* so the economics of production are nonexistent. Eventually (or all the better...now), publishing deals are going to have to reflect this change in publishing economy. How? By giving the authors a larger royalty than they would normally get on printed books and, perhaps, by removing adjustments that reflect the world of printed books—such as the stepped royalty rate (mentioned in the "Starting Up the Presses" section earlier in this chapter) and the reduced royalty for high discounts (more on this subject in the "After an E-Book Is Published" section later in this chapter).

Enter Print On Demand

Print On Demand technology makes it cost about the same per book whether you're printing one copy or one thousand. However, it's important to note that the cost per book for POD is slightly higher than it is for a normal press run, as discussed in the "Starting Up the Presses" section earlier in this chapter. For this reason, POD is particularly useful for books that sell relatively few copies. To be fair to publishers, the royalty for POD books should probably be lower than the royalty for normal printed copies—but not as low as half, as in the sample low-volume royalty clause we quoted under "Starting Up the Presses."

What Is the Price of an E-Book?

Generally, the price of a product is greatly influenced by the cost of producing that product. If it costs one dollar to create a widget, then the factory sells that widget for about two dollars, essentially making 100 percent on the deal. Well, that's not always true. Sometimes pricing is based on pure greed. In the music business, for example, record producers promised a reduction in music prices when the world changed from vinyl records to digital CDs in the early 1980s, because CDs are much cheaper to produce than the old vinyl records. But did costs ever go down? On the contrary, they went up. Why? Because music producers have a lock on their industry—just as book publishers have had. When there are only a limited number of ways a consumer can find a product, then you're probably going to see a cartel controlling the business. The activities of the cartel are likely to restrict the variety of materials available to the public as well as the compensation paid to the suppliers—in the case of the publishing industry, that means a restriction in what is likely to be accepted and published as well as in royalties to the authors.

But then came the Internet, along with digital music formats such as MP3 and music exchange software such as Napster. People began exchanging music for free over the Internet. This opened the eyes of the music publishers and even many recording artists. While there are some key differences between the music publishing business and the book publishing business, one message that can be drawn from this is that excessive overpricing will, at some point, be balanced out—if only by excessive bootlegging. Through the Internet and technology, people will find ways to get around overpaying for information. People know that it only costs about one dollar to produce a music CD—from the disk to the liner notes inside. So why do we have to pay around $16 for a new CD? Where is all the money going? Certainly not to the artists.

With books, it's the same basic story. How can an e-book cost about the same as a printed book when there's practically no cost of production? At this point, publishers are pricing e-books around the same as printed books. Where does the money go? Certainly a larger percentage *should* end up in the author's hands—and the consumer should also get a break.

Amazon.com—the highest-volume bookseller on the Internet—has a new department that makes e-books available to the public. Amazon has demanded a 55 percent discount from publishers to get books listed on its e-book pages. Given that there are no shelving costs and few returns, we feel this is rather high. But as the largest bookseller in the business, Amazon.com can dictate prices and discounts for e-books.

It's still too early to tell exactly what will happen with e-book pricing and author compensation. The publishing cartels will fight as hard as they can to keep their profits as high as possible—even increase them. But one thing is for certain: If we leave the decision to the publishers, most of the money will go to *them* and we'll all be overpaying for e-books.

As an e-book author and publisher, you'll need to think about what to charge for the reading experience you're offering. Keep in mind that the most popular Web sites and e-mail newsletters are...hold your breath...absolutely *free!* That means they are supported by advertising revenue. Advertising-based e-books are not necessarily right for every situation, but the economic model is a good one.

Some e-book publishers, which act more like distribution services, let the author determine the price of the final book. Print On Demand publishers, for instance, sometimes charge a small fee to the author for making the POD book available. This covers the publishers' setup costs. Then, the publisher will deduct the per-book cost of production and split the rest of the revenue in some way with the author—generally giving the author a hefty share. The point is, the author determines what the selling price will be and the publisher has a *no-risk* situation. Check out this example as you contemplate what to charge your readers:

Let's say you have the ability to create a PDF file from your original manuscript (now that you've read this book, perhaps you really *do*). So you choose to list your book with a POD service that charges *nothing* for setup, such as **Digitz.net** at http://www.digitz.net, since you've already done most of the setup yourself. You price the book at $15 and you pay Digitz.net, let's say, $4 wholesale per book. Your net income per book is $11 when you sell copies from your own efforts. If your costs for editing and setting up the book came to something like $1,000, then you'd have to sell less than 100 copies through your own efforts to break even. If you sold 1,000 copies, you'd make a clear profit of over $9,900.

And that's POD. If you sell the e-book experience online or as a download, then your cost per book is virtually nothing. Of course, the difficulty here is *how* you will sell 1,000 copies of your e-book—that is, where you'll list your e-book and how you'll get people interested in reading it. For information and advice on this, refer to Chapter 8, "On Your Own: Book Marketing Strategies."

If your book had gone the traditional publishing route, the numbers would look worse. Here's how. Let's say the publisher sells your book for $20 per copy. Your royalty is something like 10 percent of the publisher's "net receipts," which is the wholesale price minus some other items. To make it simple, let's say you're getting 10 percent of $9 per book, or 90 cents per book. If your publisher sells 1,000 copies, you'd make less than $1,000. To bring you around the same $9,900 you would make through the self-publishing model, your publisher would have to sell more than 10,000 copies. Now, many publishers would argue that their unparalleled marketing and publicity efforts will result in ten times the sales that you'd get on your own. In some cases, this may be true. The decision to work with an existing publisher or go it on your own is not an easy one.

How Printing Has Affected Publishing

In the past, publishers have always been burdened with the high initial outlay of cash required to print books. This cost has influenced a great many things in the publishing process and in publishing deals. Here are some of the cost areas publishers have to cover:

Acquisitions. Because of the high cost of printing, publishers have always been picky about what they accept. After all, they're making a huge investment in the work and they want to be as sure as possible that it will pay off. With electronic publishing, publishers can acquire just about anything. (Of course, acquiring a lot of garbage can only hurt a publisher's reputation in the long run. What we're really after here is a bit of balance.)

Accounting. Print publishers make payments to authors on a semiannual basis. That is, they calculate sales and royalty payments twice per year. (Some publishers these days pay quarterly and a few of the older publishers pay once per year.) As an author, you have to wait six months for each royalty statement. Since a book has to earn back the advance before you get additional royalties (the advance is, after all, a kind of loan on future earnings), the first statement is usually minimal. That means authors usually wait one full year before they see any royalties, assuming the book sells enough to earn royalties. Part of the reason for this accounting structure is that the publisher wants to be able to account for book returns *before* paying authors. Six months gives publishers some time to see how many books will be coming back from the stores. With electronic publishing, returns are minimal or nonexistent, so publishers *should* be able to provide monthly accounting statements for authors.

Royalty structure. The amount of royalties paid generally increases with the number of copies sold—which is a direct reflection of printing economics.

Promotion budget. In the past, just about every book would receive a certain amount of promotion beyond just making the book available through the publisher's catalog. Because the investment in the book (largely printing and author advance) was relatively high, publishers would invest in the book's success by putting a few dollars into publicity, even sending the author around the country for speaking engagements and book signings. Today, author tours are quickly becoming a thing of the past (or a thing reserved for high-profile books).

The editing process. The cost of printing and production makes it unwise to publish a printed book that is not well edited, so the paper publishers have traditionally invested significant sums in editing and proofreading. By contrast, e-books are so easy to produce that many e-book publishers are not taking the extra time and money to provide good editing. There is a mentality of quantity rather than quality.

Book pricing. Naturally the cost of production (printing, binding, and so on) affects the selling price of a book. When costs of paper, ink, and shipping go up, you'll find a relative increase in the cost of printed books. While there are costs associated with e-book publishing—particularly publishing on the "closed" systems, such as the Microsoft Reader—e-book production costs are lower than printed book costs.

After an E-Book Is Published (Distribution Costs)

Once your e-book is done and available for worldwide distribution and mass consumption, there are a few things to consider about the economics of distribution. At this point, we'll only talk in general terms. The specifics of distribution agreements are covered in Part III, "*Getting Your E-Book Published and Sold*," and there are many different possibilities available. Also, this area is a moving target and the world of online book distribution is a messy, complex thing. But it's worth taking a stab at it.

With printed books, distribution involves shipping large numbers of books (we all hope) to a central location (or several key locations), storing them, and then, at some future point, moving copies to retail outlets in small numbers for public enjoyment. Because we're talking about moving physical objects around, we're looking at outlays for shipping and storage. (And books are not light, as you find out each time you move to a new home and have to pack up your library—dealing with books is often the worst part of the experience. They're just as awkward to deal with as a day-to-day business.) Large distributors have made a science of maintaining cost-effective distribution centers and shipping mechanisms that can handle the flow of thousands of books from hundreds of publishers for only a small percentage of the price tag. Distributors get anywhere from 3 percent to 10 percent of the pie for performing this function.

Then there's the idea of wholesale discounts, so that the bookstores can make a living. Generally, retail outlets like to make a 100 percent markup on their merchandise, and books are no exception. So a book that sells for $20 probably shipped to the distributor at a discount of about 55 percent—that is, the publisher sells the $20 book for $9.50. The distributor takes 5 percent and that leaves 50 percent for the bookstore—or 100 percent markup (We made the math simple, but this is pretty close).

Of course, with e-books, there's no shipping or storage. So what kind of discount should a distributor get? A lot of publisher-distributors are offering authors 50 percent royalties, which basically translates to a 50 percent discount. That's normal, since e-books are often sold directly from the distributor to the consumer. But each e-publisher differs. Many traditional publishers offer normal royalties for e-books, while specialized e-publishers such as Fatbrain offer deals much more commensurate with the virtual world (a world without shipping and storage). However, booksellers such as Amazon.com are asking for discounts in the 55 percent range—which gives them a discount equivalent to a distributor discount. In other words in the case of Amazon.com, the bookstore has become the distributor. You've heard it before in this book, but we'll say it again just because we like hearing it: E-books are less expensive to produce than printed books and therefore royalties for authors should be higher (and, possibly, prices for the e-books should be lower).

Just How Deep *Is* That Discount?

At times, publishers offer a customer a special discount rate. This occurs when a chain such as Wal-Mart buys thousands of copies of a single title to sell through its various outlets. A single large purchase like this often gets made at a special discount, referred to as a *deep discount*. Deep discounts also apply to special sales opportunities, such as when a publisher sells a large number of copies of a single book to a corporation or other organization. Instead of the normal 55 percent discount that distributors get, this special sale is made at, perhaps, 59 percent or 60 percent discount. Because publishers claim that their profits are diminished by this type of sale, they usually reduce the author's royalties in an effort to share the pain. Here's an example of a contract clause to show you what we mean:

> *On sales of books at a discount of more than 50 percent, the applicable royalty rate will be reduced by .5 percent for every 1 percent the discount exceeds 50 percent. The minimum royalty rate will not fall below 5 percent of Net Revenues on domestic book sales. For example, at a discount of 51 percent, a royalty of 10 percent will be reduced to 9.5 percent and at a discount of 52 percent, the royalty will be reduced to 9 percent.*

But in many cases, it's not really in the author's best interest to even have a book at Wal-Mart because the profit per book is so low and such discounting often ends up diminishing the value of the book or flooding the market. So why do it? Well, the author usually does not have a choice. From the publisher's perspective, one reason for making special sales is that it saves money in printing. When a publisher can add, say, 5,000 extra copies to its existing print run of, say, 10,000 copies, then the per-copy cost of those original 10,000 copies goes down. The publisher can afford to make literally zero profit on the deep discount transaction, because it ends up making the money back in the higher margins the normally discounted books bring in due to the lower cost per book. This usually does not benefit the author one little bit, other than that authors get a big ego boost out of seeing their books stacked up on pallets at the discount stores.

Without the economics of paper printing, there is no reason for deep discounts in the e-publishing world. The cost to produce a single book is the same per book as the cost for 10,000. The cost to distribute that single book is the same as for 10,000. The moral of the story: Authors should not see a reduction in royalties for discounting of e-books.

You Bought It, You Read It

The book business is often referred to as a consignment business. That's because bookstores, the retail arm of the business, have the liberty (the *unrestricted privilege* even) of returning books to their publishers or distributors for a full refund. Imagine if this were true of the clothing business. You'd hardly ever see the kinds of blow-out sales you see now. Stores would not have to think about the kinds of styles and fashions they carry, because anything that did not sell would just go back to the manufacturer. Well, that's exactly what bookstores do—return what does not sell. In essence, books are sitting in bookstores on consignment. It's hard to believe this hasn't changed in recent years, but it hasn't. The publishing business is one of the last remaining fully returnable businesses in our culture.

Here again, because of the economics of printing, it actually works out to be more profitable for publishers to overprint books and flood the market as much as possible, getting a percentage of books back from the stores as returns. In fact, some publishing economists believe that if a publisher is not getting 15 percent to 35 percent returns, then it is not printing enough and probably missing the opportunity to sell more books. It's amazing. The cost of printing an extra 3,000 books, when you're already planning to print, say, 10,000, is really quite small. If you can get those extra 3,000 books *into* the channel (distributors and bookstores), then it's usually worth printing them—*even if 2,000 of them come back*. Again, the cost per book goes down when you print more books. So the publisher only has to cover the cost of the extra 3,000 books (which can probably be done by selling only a few hundred copies)—it will still make more money due to the improved margins on the original 10,000 books.

But this returns business is often way out of hand—especially now that the small, independent bookstore (which used to really benefit from the ability to return books) is all but extinct. Now the gigantic book superstores and bookstore chains—such as Barnes & Noble, Waldenbooks, and Borders—use the ability to return books as a way to play with the accounts. They'll often "pay" for a shipment of new books by simply returning older books for credit, thus not having any cash go out the door. Here's the point—and it's important to remember if you're planning to publish an e-book: Consumers do not really return all that many books. It's the bookstores and publishers that take advantage of this policy.

Happily, the e-book business is different, because the distribution channel is different. As an e-book publisher and author, you can offer a money-back guarantee to your readers without much fear. Your readers will probably not take advantage of your offer in great numbers. Returns directly from consumers are said to be about 1 percent to 2 percent, while print publishers expect around 20 percent returns and often see returns as high as 35 percent. Not only is the e-book channel different and often more direct from publisher to consumer, there's also nothing to flood the channel with. You can't exactly store thousands of e-books on a computer somewhere. It doesn't work that way. So the whole idea of returns is out the window. What does this mean? Well, it probably means that e-book prices should be (and will be) lower than printed book prices, while publisher profits on e-books are higher. It also means that author royalties should be higher. (Have we beat that drum enough times now?)

Expenses (Selling Costs)

We talked about marketing and selling e-books in Part III, "*Getting Your E-Book Published and Sold*," so here we'll only add that there are costs associated with selling books. And generally, it's more profitable to market ten books than it is to market one book. It's also important to remember that word of mouth is the most important form of publicity for e-books—and that can only be generated by producing a great book that people really need or really want. The best ways to market and publicize an e-book are those things that add to the community of your readership—which results in more word of mouth.

We don't recommend that you spend money to advertise a book online. Instead, spend a few hours talking online in a newsgroup about the topic of your book. People who are impressed by you will be interested in reading your book. That's how it works. Chapter 8, "On Your Own: Book Marketing Strategies," talks more about how to market and publicize your e-books.

CHAPTER TEN

Hot Button Issues in E-Book Publishing Contracts

The preceding chapter gave you some background on how the economics of publishing affect (or should affect) the compensation authors get for their work. It's important to have a grasp of these matters so that you can negotiate fairly over publishing rights. In this chapter, we'll get down and dirty with the publishing contract. We'll look at specific clauses and explore how electronic publishing contracts may or may not be different from traditional contracts. This is by no means a complete treatise on publishing contracts. Instead, we're going to focus on certain issues that are of concern in e-book deals.

Protecting Your Rights: The Standard Publishing Contract

Okay, so what issues do you want to look for in an e-book publishing contract? Or, more important, what issues do you need to understand to protect your electronic rights (or any rights for that matter), especially in traditional publishing contracts or the myriad variations of electronic, print, and media publishing deals? From a contract standpoint, it's best not to think of your deal as an e-book publishing deal. It's a *publishing* deal, plain and simple. That author-friendly, cutting-edge, break-all-the-rules electronic publisher that you find so attractive today could easily become the e-book prep division of a multinational publishing conglomerate tomorrow. And everything changes. Many e-publishers are in the process of defining themselves. As you saw in Chapter 2, "What's an E-Book?" and Chapter 3, "New Ways of Publishing," some e-publishers have Print On Demand facilities and are thus both electronic and print publishers. Others are just interested in electronic sales and distribution. Still others make a living from turning printed books into online products.

One scenario that we've seen involves a small, electronic courseware publisher that offers incredible deals and opportunities to authors. It gives small advances but huge royalties in order to attract authors to create online course materials for its customers. After all, its owners know, they need to do something to balance out the fact that they have no track record for selling courses online. At this stage of its life, the publisher can't really show authors a history of best-selling titles that will make them rich. An author might end up writing a course for these guys and not sell a single unit. And when advances are low, that's a big risk. They can't afford to pay cash to authors for their work, so they adopt a "share the risk, share the reward" model and offer authors an abundant royalty split. So far so good.

After a few years, this small courseware publisher is the leading online source for technology-related courses. It's gone through a dozen acquisitions managers and even more developmental editors. Anyone who was there in the old days when royalties were the order of the day is long gone. Today, it's a public company and needs to watch margins. That means...are you ready?...no more royalties to authors. The publisher has replaced all the old royalty-based courses with new courses done by work-for-hire writers. It pays cash up front now, and that attracts a lot of authors who need quick returns on their work. It's become a content factory. That means that it owns outright all the material that it uses. Its staff can do anything they want with the material, including republish it in other formats or media without compensation to the original author. The authors who helped get the company where it is today are part of its past and their courses are also long gone. To add insult to injury, the new acquisitions director calls the old authors and asks if they'd like to write another course for work-for-hire rates. Ouch!

Money Is Money—*Hey! We're not saying that it's always a bad idea to do work-for-hire writing for a company. Actually, it can often be a good deal if the up-front or hourly pay is decent. Better to get $10,000 in cash for your material and let the publisher have the work than, say, a $2,000 advance on royalties that never pay out. It's a guessing game, to be sure. And writers who have a thing about retaining their rights often end up schlepping cheeseburgers at the local diner to make extra income. Knowing the value of a piece of intellectual property is not a science, it's more of an art.*

Here's another true story: Another computer courseware publisher has a growing business of selling books that go with its courses. Customers might pay for a course about how to create Web pages with HTML, for instance. As required reading for the course, they must purchase the course guide—a printed book that accompanies the course. Good idea, right? Well, it's a good idea for everyone but the author of the book. Here's how it works: The publisher hires an author to write the course book for a normal royalty, let's say 12 percent. So far so good. It also buys the electronic rights to the book and creates the online course from material in the book. The author is not involved in this process— it's something the publisher does to exploit electronic rights to the book.

Problem is, this publisher offers a measly 2 percent of the receipts from the course as royalty to the author. This is way, way under normal market value—even given that the publisher is doing all the work to turn the book into a course and even given that each course also includes a book sale, adding the book's royalty to the 2 percent course royalty. The point is that this royalty rate is way below industry standards. A more common (and fair) number would be half the normal royalty rate (or 6 percent in this example), since this publisher is creating and marketing the courses by itself. Were it to license the course rights to another publisher, the common market arrangement would be to split the licensing fee in half with the author (or at least 70 percent for the publisher and 30 percent for the author, depending on the situation). Clearly this publisher has a great deal going. And the authors may not realize that this situation favors the publisher to an extreme.

How do you know what's fair and what's not? Well, let's get right down to it. The following pages offer an overview of the issues to consider in publishing contracts and, particularly, how they relate to e-publishing and e-book deals.

Grant of Rights

The essence of a publishing agreement is this: You own the rights to the work you created (or will create) and you are granting to the publisher some or all of the rights to that work in exchange for money. This is how content creators (that's *language artists* if you don't mind) and businesspeople get along. That means that if you don't specifically say you're selling something, it's still yours.

Other Types of Contracts

Not all e-book contracts involve a grant of rights. Some e-publishers have adopted publishing models that are more like distribution agreements. In these models, the author takes on the role of publisher. Still other models are a cross between traditional publishing agreements and distribution agreements. Many nonexclusive e-book deals fall into this category. You might be granting rights but also retaining them at the same time. We'll talk more about these different types of contracts in the next chapter. Sample contracts appear in the appendices. There are some basic assumptions in a standard "author sells, publisher buys" publishing agreement.

- The publisher has the ability to create, market, and distribute a product based on the author's work.
- The author's ability to create, market, and distribute such a product is inferior to the publisher's—or the author's time is more valuable spent writing than marketing and selling.

- The publisher is going to profit from using the author's material and the author, in turn, will profit when the publisher profits.
- The author and publisher are both risking something in this partnership: The author has invested a considerable amount of time and often money to create the book. The publisher will be investing a considerable amount of money to create and market the book.

Of course, some of the basic assumptions in the preceding list are complete fabrications in the real world and even more so in the world of e-publishing. If a book does not sell well, authors invariably blame the publisher for not knowing enough about creating and selling books. Authors usually consider their work priceless and beyond reproach; if a book does not sell, it's generally the publisher's poor marketing or publicity, or "that ugly cover design." In the past, there has been some logic to this author-centered perspective. After all, if a publisher has gone through the process of selecting a manuscript for publication, then that manuscript must have some value over the hundreds (or thousands) of others that were not chosen. In e-book publishing, however, the standards for acquiring a written work are often lower than those in print publishing. Okay, sometimes they're downright nonexistent. That's because with e-book publishing, the publishers are not putting out all that money to print, store, and ship physical books. They don't have to be so picky about what they acquire. They have a "throw a lot of spaghetti at the wall and see what sticks" approach.

So in most cases, if a book does not sell well, it's because the market did not respond to it. Or in other words, people didn't want the thing. It's really difficult for authors to accept this, but it's usually the case. Having a book in the stores does not guarantee sales. Having a book listed at Amazon.com does not guarantee sales. What sells books is, in most cases, the same thing that sells cars or carpets: customer satisfaction. Customer satisfaction leads to word-of-mouth sales and customer loyalty (coming back for more). In the world of e-publishing, this is even more true, since books often don't even appear on counter tops at the local book-and-coffee emporium for those impulse purchases. It's all about word of mouth.

In the world of e-publishing, publishers do not necessarily use professional editors who know how to refine a rough manuscript into a tight piece of prose. Sometimes, they're just publishing services with absolutely no criteria for selecting and producing books. (See Chapter 6, "Checking Out the E-Publishers," for more information about publishing services). And authors now have the ability to design and publish their own books. Hopefully, they know a thing or two about the English language (or whichever language they are using) and how to construct a sentence. But, as we all know, that's not always the case, either.

Sounds like the basis of a great partnership. The author will write it, the publisher will create and sell it, and we'll all get rich—yippee! But wait. Just how capable *is* the publisher of creating and selling your work? Maybe its people are great at publishing e-books, but don't know a thing about getting your book translated and published abroad. If you don't notice that little problem, you're apt to find yourself at a writer's convention where your friends are proudly displaying the Portuguese and Croatian editions of their work, while you sit quietly with your English language e-book on a CD-ROM. How could you have known? Or how about the opposite extreme, in which the publisher is really just a service for shipping books to the public. The author has to do all the work to create, produce, and market the book. Of course, in exchange for this, the author gets a terrific royalty rate. But if the author has no way of selling Portuguese language rights, or turning the e-book into an interactive experience, then these things are not going to happen.

This is what the grant of rights is all about. There are many rights associated with a creative work and most publishers cannot possibly take advantage of (*exploit,* in publishing terminology) them all. Some publishing contracts will list all the different rights and indicate which ones are being transferred from the author to the publisher. Others will just indicate that the publisher wants every right in existence or ever to come into existence in the future. A few e-publishers will state that the author is transferring electronic rights, but even that isn't as specific as it sounds. In any event, it's important to know the various types of rights you might be dealing with, so that you can decide which ones you might be able to exploit yourself. This is the key to choosing the right e-book publisher for you. Knowing what you can and can't accomplish yourself is the first step to determining what you need in a publisher.

Following is a summary of the many different rights associated with a written work.

English-Language Print Publishing

English-language printing is the main issue on most print publishing contracts. This right lets the publisher create a printed book, in English, and sell it anywhere it can. Sometimes this is called *Domestic Print* rights. At any rate, English-language editions of U.S. books often find themselves being shipped to Canada. This is called *foreign sales of the domestic edition.* Generally, publishers in the United States will not ship domestic editions to the U.K. or Australia; they will either publish a local English-language edition using a local office in

London or Sydney or license the right to print a local English-language edition to a publisher in those countries. That's generally a lot cheaper than shipping a ton of books overseas.

Several e-book publishers offer Print On Demand (POD) services to their customers. Essentially, this means that they are selling printed versions of the book. These publishers will, of course, want to have the English-language print publishing rights to an e-book. Without these rights, they cannot create a POD version of an e-book. As discussed in Chapter 9, "Publishing Economics 101," POD economics is slightly different from traditional publishing economics, and author royalties may reflect this.

Foreign Language

Usually, all foreign language editions are glommed together in one clause, giving the publisher the right to produce or license in any foreign language. Most publishers will sell a license to a foreign publisher, which then translates and sells the book in its own country, paying a royalty to your domestic publisher. Any publisher with a decent marketing arm will be able to exploit these foreign language rights fairly well. So unless you know you can sell the Ukrainian rights faster than the publisher can, or you have a special publishing contact in Afghanistan, you're probably better off letting the publisher have foreign rights—unless you have an agent who can handle the foreign rights for you. If you get the chance, it's usually better to let the agent deal with the foreign rights rather than sell them to the publisher as part of the basic deal. Here's why: Traditionally, a publisher will split income from foreign sales with the author 50–50 (you certainly won't get better than this). So, let's say your publisher sells a Japanese edition of your book for $1,000. Generally, there is a 10 percent foreign agent fee to take off the top. You should end up with around $450 as the author. Now let's say you withhold Japanese rights and let your agent sell them for you. Your agent will probably take the usual 15 percent commission, plus another 10 percent for the foreign agent. That's 25 percent off the top, leaving you with 75 percent of the $1,000, or $750. Considerably more than the $450 you would have gotten from the publisher. Not bad, eh?

Hardcover and Softcover

Publishers used to separate hardcover and softcover editions more than they do now. Many books don't even make it to hardcover anymore. And your e-book may never get either type of cover. At any rate, if your contract includes print rights, it probably includes hard- and softcover rights. Best-selling authors can sometimes find advantages in giving one publisher hardcover rights and a different publisher softcover rights, but it's unusual.

Some e-publishers are beginning to define electronic forms of binding. That is, they are translating the term "binding" to mean the medium by which the electronic file is delivered. Here are some of the choices:

- Internet (online)
- E-book (electronic file)
- CD-ROM
- Print On Demand

This is a good trend, as it attempts to deal with the various ways in which an electronic book can be created and distributed. From a contractual point of view, the more detail the better.

Dramatization and Motion Picture

This is the dream of all novelists: to have their story turned into a screenplay or script. If a publisher has dramatization rights, it can sell your book to a movie producer who can turn it into a script. All this can happen without consulting you. But, hey, if it happens at all, most of us would be thrilled! Most movies that come from novels come from best-selling novels, so you probably don't have to be too preoccupied with this issue if you're publishing an e-book.

Adaptation, Abridgment, and Anthology

Adaptation rights are quite important in online or electronic works. That's because it's easy to adapt a book in electronic format—especially when the adaptation is also an electronic work. For example, a large publisher of computer books is making a practice of chopping up some of its better-selling books and making the pieces available in an online database, where readers can search for answers to their computer problems. That's great. As an author, you want your material in as many formats and places as possible. That means more sales and more royalties. Uh, you are getting royalties on adaptations, aren't you?

Some publishers make their agreements simple and use the word "adaptation" to mean any version of the book that is substantially changed from the original. This would include foreign translations, revisions, dramatizations, electronic conversions (moving from one format to another—see e-book formats in Chapter 4, "The Production Process," for details) and many other rights that would otherwise be listed individually.

The point is that adaptations are becoming more and more common with electronic publishing, so this is an important item to pay attention to. We'll talk about many different types of adaptations in the following pages, so you'll be well prepared.

Audio

Audio rights (unsurprisingly) cover the conversion of a work into audio format. Some publishers make a decent side income on audiotapes of their books. Some books lend themselves to audio and others do not. Keep this in mind: Most books never make it into audio due to the cost of producing cassette tapes. Also, the market for audio books is just not big enough for most publishers to exploit. One publisher we know, who sells a lot of audio books, expects about one-tenth the number of audiotape sales as book sales. Now, in the coming age of Internet multimedia technology, this could change. Imagine programs that could literally "read" your book "live" for anyone who would rather listen to it than read it. An e-book reader might have a button on the side that says Listen. You push the button, put the e-book down, and listen to the computer as it reads to you. Publishers who do *not* have audio rights in this scenario will be a bit angry. Or the entire definition of audio rights will be up for discussion and reinterpretation. The point is, with electronic publishing, everything is changing. Till now, audio rights have always meant cassette tapes; in the near future, the term could mean something completely different. And the author compensation should change as a result. Why? Because future audio options will probably have completely different economics from the chore of creating and selling a cassette tape. More specifically, royalties on audio rights are generally lower than normal book royalties, due to the cost of producing the cassette tape. But in the future, when we begin seeing programs that can "read" your written words, why should an author get lower royalties for these sales? The publisher is doing virtually nothing to create the audio version of the book.

Here's what we suggest to both authors and publishers: Start breaking down the various types of electronic rights that are possible so that these contracts can effectively deal with all the variations (more about this under the heading "Electronic" later in this chapter).

Commercial and Merchandise

Commercial rights involve the ability to create products from the material in a book. With works of fiction, this typically means creating action figures or stuffed animals from the characters in a book. Some nonfiction books contain artwork that can be turned into postcards, posters, or other merchandise. Many books don't have merchandise opportunities and such rights are not important. If you think you are sitting on top of the next Pet Rock or Pokemon craze, then think about retaining merchandise rights. Unless your publisher has a thriving sideline business selling stuffed animals and calendars, you should not get much argument on this point.

First Serial and Second Serial

Serial rights refer to the ability to distribute a book in a series of smaller pieces or articles. Sometimes this means turning a novel into a series of stories—usually sold to magazines. In the world of the Internet, serial rights can be quite important. Many e-books can be broken up into pieces and sold online as articles. Technically, this could be defined as a serial right. If your publisher owns these rights, then you don't. Of course, if you have an opportunity to sell chapters of your book to a popular Web site, your e-book publisher will probably be thrilled. But if you did all the work creating this opportunity, why should the publisher get a large percentage of your payment for this usage? Indeed it shouldn't. If your publisher does not actively market serial versions of books, then you should think about retaining serial rights—or at least making the author–publisher split of such sales more commensurate with reality. In some cases, we've seen contracts specify two rates—one rate applies if the publisher sells the rights and another rate applies if the author sells the rights. Now that's cooperation.

Electronic

Now we're at the heart of the issue. Whether you're looking at a standard publishing contract or something more focused on e-books, you'll need to consider a few things about the electronic rights you're granting to the publisher. Most contracts just list electronic rights as a single item. But as the virtual world expands, we find that electronic rights include a number of possible uses of a piece of work.

Many traditional publishers are new to the game of e-books and electronic versions of a work. Some just figure on licensing e-book and other electronic rights to one or more of the various publishers specializing in electronic media. In such cases, electronic rights may be handled as any other license (such as the license for a foreign language edition). But more and more publishers are adopting e-book programs to augment their publishing program. Some are even selling their own e-books online—sometimes through their own Web sites and often through several electronic book distributors, such as **Books24x7.com** at http://www.books24x7.com/. In the preceding chapter, we explored the difference in economics between print and electronic publishing and saw that e-books often warrant a higher royalty than print publications. We also saw how a publisher might have its own definition of an e-book, depending on the financial advantages of this definition. But just what types of electronic products can be made from a manuscript? The following sections give you a quick review.

E-Book

The definition of an e-book is discussed in detail in Part I of this book, "Electronic Publishing Overview." Suffice it to say at this point that an e-book is a book-length literary work that can be read on a computer or other type of electronic device. While e-book formats can require some conversion of the document from a word processor file to one of the e-book formats, nevertheless, creating an e-book does not involve adding significant new content. That is to say that the *experience* that the customer has when reading the e-book is not significantly different from reading the printed book. The e-book technology that may be embedded in the file is invisible to the customer once the reading experience has started. As noted earlier, e-book rights are generally not considered licenses—even if handled by a third party. That is, if your publisher lets a different company create and sell an e-book version of your book, your publisher will probably consider that to be a normal book sale and *not* the sale of a license. Bottom line: You will get normal royalties on e-book sales from a traditional publisher unless your contract specifically indicates a different percentage for e-books. If a publishing contract breaks down the different types of electronic rights, then it should be easy to negotiate a fair rate for e-book sales. If the contract lumps all electronic rights into one paragraph (like most contracts do), then do your best to get e-book rights separated from the rest. We're seeing royalties on e-books ranging from 10 percent to 60 percent—even 80 percent in some publishing models. The point is, e-books warrant higher royalties than printed books and higher royalties than interactive electronic products. We also find that some publishers have no problem giving a slightly higher royalty for e-book sales while other publishers are adamantly opposed to it.

Interactive Multimedia or Interactive Courseware

Unlike a straight e-book, an interactive version of a book involves some alteration, addition, or enhancement of the content. This can be as little as a few embedded links throughout the document or as much as a full-blown multimedia experience with sound and live motion graphics. It gets a little tricky here, because some of the more advanced e-book formats provide some linking throughout a document—for example, you can usually click a heading in the table of contents to jump to the appropriate section of the book. But this type of simple linking does not significantly alter the reading experience. However, if a book were to have links throughout that take the customer to additional information in other documents, books, or Web sites, then it's beginning to offer a different reading experience. Now we're talking interactive.

Why make this distinction? Because, here again, the economics of creating these different types of reading experiences are different—and those differences should be reflected in the publishing contract and consequently in the author's compensation. Simply put, it's more expensive to create an interactive experience from an author's straight prose than it is to create an e-book from the same work. Hence, it's reasonable to expect a reduction in royalties for such versions. We've seen royalties from 2 percent to 50 percent on such interactive uses of a work. Sometimes a publisher will simply cut the normal print-edition royalty in half for these types of electronic uses.

Database Storage

Something we're beginning to see quite often in the world of instructional nonfiction is the online or electronic database adaptation (also called a *knowledgebase*). A piece of work gets chopped up and entered into a database along with tens of thousands of other pieces from other authors and the whole thing is provided online to the public—sometimes for a fee and sometimes for free (that is, supported by advertising). Some of the material in a knowledgebase may come from existing books, while other material may have been written specifically for the database. Most knowledgebases look more like online help systems than like databases. You simply locate the topic you want information about, sometimes by typing keywords or questions, and you arrive at a page or two of information—usually with plenty of advertisements and links to more information. The Internet itself is a kind of giant knowledgebase—fully searchable through the various search engines, such as **Yahoo!** at http://www.Yahoo.com/ or **AltaVista** at http://www.AltaVista.com/.

Figure 10.1 shows the online database options at the **Facts On File** Web site (http://www.factsonfile.com/). This publisher has many online databases available, through subscription, created from its printed books.

How authors get compensated for their contributions to these databases varies significantly. The trend is to recruit writers to create material for the database on a work-for-hire basis. The publisher then owns the material and does not pay another cent to the authors. This is much easier for the publisher, since it minimizes the accounting effort. The publisher does not have to track the usage of each author's contribution. Sometimes publishers will offer a flat fee to repurpose material from an original source (a book or e-book). This is very much like the work-for-hire scenario with one important difference. Since the material came from an existing publication, the author might want to make sure that the permission granted to use the material in a database does not allow the publisher to repurpose again from the database without compensation to the

Figure 10.1: The Facts On File online databases.

author. In other words, you want to sell rights for *single use* in the database in exchange for the fee. If you sign a work-for-hire transfer of your material for the database, then an unscrupulous publisher could pull your material back out of the database and assemble it into another book—without payment to you.

The idea of tracking usage of database material is quickly becoming unrealistic. Nobody seems to like the idea of collecting micro-payments for looking at a paragraph of information. Likewise, the publishers don't want to track micro-royalties for their authors—each time a person accesses your paragraph, you get .025 cents, and so on. Most likely, you will be offered a flat fee for database usage. Some publishers are simply calculating the percentage that an author's work contributes to the database and then pay that percentage of your royalties on the income from the database. For example, if your work comprises 1 percent of the database and your normal royalty is 10 percent on printed books, you would get 1 percent of 10 percent, or .1 percent on the net receipts from the database. If proceeds from the database are $50,000 for a royalty period, then you'd get .1 percent of $50,000, or $50.

In some cases, where it isn't clear how much an author's material will contribute to the success of the online database, we've seen publishers purchase rights for a certain amount of time. After the time is up, the contract can be renewed, renegotiated, or terminated. So if your treatise on sixteenth-century music turns out to be the most popular thing on the database, you would have the option of renegotiating your deal to improve your terms. This works to the publisher's benefit, too. If a piece of material is just not getting any hits, then the publisher doesn't have to renew the contract—and it's invested less money up front, because time-limited purchases demand much lower fees than a full buyout of the material.

Custom Publishing

Custom publishing is similar to knowledgebase publishing. In custom publishing, a customer can construct a book from any number of other books. ("I'll take two chapters of *American History 101,* three chapters of *World Religions in a Heartbeat,* and an appendix of *Astrology Made Easy,* to go please.") Custom publishing rights are generally part of adaptation rights, but they can also be handled in a Combined Editions clause. In any case, the contract should compensate the author based on the percentage of material used in the final product. For example, if a chapter from your book contributes 25 percent to a custom publication, then you should get 25 percent of the normal royalty rate. Of course, there are many ways to handle this scenario. Publishers will often seek an easy way out—offering a single fee for use of your material in other publications. If you think your material stands a good chance of being used in this manner, then a proportional percentage is the way to go.

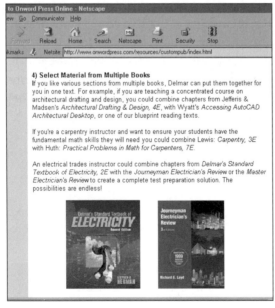

Figure 10.2: The OnWord Press custom publishing page.

Figure 10.2 shows the custom publishing program at **OnWord Press** (http://www.onwordpress.com/resources/custompub/), where you can combine material from a whole library of instructional books.

Advertising Revenue Editions

Here's a can of worms. Advertising editions are editions of a work given away for free, in exchange for advertising revenue. Companies like **Bookface**, http://www.bookface.com specialize in creating these ad-based versions of books. Publishers will sometimes consider these to be promotional—and therefore, non-royalty-earning—editions. But in fact, we've seen some authors earn considerable income from advertising-based e-books, so this is not something to cast aside casually. Currently, there are few e-book contracts (much less traditional publishing contracts) that deal effectively with this situation. What's fair is that the authors should get their normal royalty rate on the advertising income earned on the book. Whether a customer pays $5 to buy an e-book or pays nothing because advertisers are paying $5 per "hit" should not matter. Royalties should be paid on the income the publisher earns on the book.

But advertising versions of e-books are often sold as licenses. That is, publishers do not create their own ad-based versions of books, but sell the rights to other publishers who specialize in such things. In these cases, the income on such versions should be split with the author as a license. All the better for the author.

So What Rights Do I Transfer to the Publisher?

Now that you know what all these rights are, how do you determine which ones are best transferred to the publisher and which are best left in your capable hands? Common advice is that you should transfer to the publisher only those rights that the publisher has the ability to exploit. But these days, that's getting very difficult to determine. After all, you give a publisher the right to print copies of your book, but most publishers don't actually do their own printing. They use professional printers for that. And just because a publisher does not have offices in Spain does not mean that it can't get a Spanish copy made of your book. More and more, publishers are farming out pieces of the publishing process. When you get right down to it, many publishers don't even have editors on staff any more. It's all virtual. And in the e-book world, it's becoming even more so. In many cases, publishers just want to have access to all the rights they can. Here's an example of a typical Grant of Rights clause:

2. Publication Rights. The Author hereby grants and assigns to Publisher, its successors, and assigns, during the full term of copyright in each country where protected and any extension and renewal thereof, the exclusive license to:

a) Produce, sell, or license the Work to others, including, without limitation, the rights to reproduce the Work in any form by any mechanical, electronic, or other means now known or hereafter invented.

b) Publish, by itself or with others, republish, and distribute and sell any and all editions of said work, in whole or in part, throughout the world.

Notice that the publisher can exploit rights through its own efforts or through the sale of licenses to third parties. Here's the deal: Most publishers will want access to (or control of) any and all rights possible, as you can see in the charming phrase "in any form...now known or hereafter invented." That about covers everything, doesn't it? Publishers do this because they just might be able to license certain rights to another publisher and profit from them. More and more, publishers are not willing to publish your book if they can't get *all* the rights listed in the quote. This is especially true in the world of nonfiction. In many cases, publishers know in advance that they can sell certain rights. Most substantial publishers, for example, have connections with foreign publishers and license foreign language editions almost automatically. Because of this, many publishers include foreign sales in their financial projections for a given book and as a result, cannot purchase a book unless they also get foreign rights. Here's the Catch-22:

You want your publisher to exploit all the rights it can. You don't care if it's through direct efforts or through licenses. In theory, when the publisher profits, you profit as the author.

You want to hang onto rights that the publisher is not likely to exploit. If the publisher is not going to do anything with dramatization rights, then maybe you will. Better to have the rights in your hands than in somebody else's.

If a publisher does not have certain rights to your work, it won't exploit them. If you don't give a publisher the French-language rights to your book, it's unlikely that the publisher will call you up one day and say, "We have a great offer on the table for the French rights to your book. Will you consider selling them to us now?" More likely, your book won't even make it onto the table when the publisher displays books to the French publishing community.

Now here's an example from the publisher's perspective: A small e-publisher was contracting with authors to write material for use on the Internet in the form of short presentations on a given topic. Since this publisher was only interested in electronic rights for Internet presentations, the contract only transferred online electronic rights from the author. Later, the publisher entered into a deal with a large traditional publisher to print a series of books to accompany the online material. Since the e-publisher did not have rights to print editions of the works, it had to create new material under new contracts to fulfill many of the projects with the larger publisher—a lot of unnecessary wheel-spinning. In some cases, it was able to go back to the authors and explain that there was a new market for print versions of the material and that it would be in the authors' interest to assign those rights to the publisher at this time. Since the publisher was rather small, it was not a difficult task. Had the publisher been large, with hundreds of titles, the task of getting the print rights after the fact would have been extremely difficult and costly.

One way out of this Catch-22 is to limit the *term* of a publisher's control of certain rights. In other words, the publisher has a time limit in which to exploit the rights. If the publisher does not create or license a foreign language edition in, say, three years, then the foreign language rights revert to the author. The author can then exploit them or sell them to someone else. If you have an agent, then your agent might be able to find a buyer for certain uses of your material. Or you can even try one of the online rights services and put some of the rights up for sale—see "Online Rights Brokers" later in this chapter.

Another way out of this Catch-22 is to share the ability to sell licenses. If the publisher sells the license, proceeds are split one way; if the author sells the license, proceeds are split another way. Most publishers don't like this because they don't want authors interfering with their sales efforts (and possibly conflicting with their efforts). Most likely, only small publishers will be open to this idea.

Remember that the publisher you choose will often determine what rights you sell. Or perhaps this will work the other way around: The rights you choose to sell may influence the publisher you decide to use. In any case, some publishers will be flexible in negotiating rights and others will not. There are many things to consider when choosing a publisher for your e-book. Sometimes it's necessary to give up certain rights in exchange for other advantages a publisher might offer. For a more in-depth discussion of how to choose a publisher that's right for you, refer to Chapter 6, "Checking Out the E-Publishers."

Online Rights Brokers—If you've decided to make a go of publishing your own e-book and peddling all the various rights yourself, then you should consider listing your book with one of the online rights brokers. Online rights brokers are services that list literary works, along with the rights that are available for the work. Customers can search through the database of properties (books) and bid on certain rights for certain works. For details about rights brokers, refer to Chapter 7, "Assembling Your E-Publishing Venture."

The Truth About Copyright (All Rights Reserved)

Copyright ownership is an often-misunderstood concept. Many people think that you don't own the rights to a work unless you have registered the copyright. That's not actually true. More correctly, copyright is a symbolic representation of the ownership of an intellectual property. Here's how it works in real life: When you write something, you own the rights to it—simply by virtue of the fact that you created it. You created it so it's yours. Now, if someone steals your work and publishes it behind your back, and then claims that you were the one who stole the original work, well, you'll need some way to prove that you really created it first. That's where the copyright comes in. Copyright is the *registration* of ownership of a work. It's an official proof of ownership. It's kind of like having theft insurance for your work. While it's beneficial to authors, to some degree, it was really invented for publishers—to protect their investments. (See the accompanying note, "A Brief History of Copyright.")

Most authors do not take the time and expense to register the copyright of their work. You especially don't need to do this if you already have a buyer for your work—such as when you're writing on contract. The publisher generally has the facility to register copyright for the author, and in the past, publishers would often register the copyright of a book in the name of the author. However, more and more, publishers are registering copyright in the name of the publisher, and putting such provisions in their contracts—as in this example:

11. COPYRIGHT

a.   The copyright in the Work will be in the name of Publisher or its designee. The Author hereby assigns all rights in and to the copyright to the Publisher. The Author further acknowledges that the Publisher shall retain in perpetuity the sole and exclusive right to print, publish, distribute, sell, advertise, promote, and/or license the sale of the Work, or any derivative works based thereon, throughout the world in all languages. The Author shall execute such other assignments and instruments as Publisher may from time to time deem necessary or desirable to evidence, establish, maintain, and protect the aforementioned copyright and all such other rights, title, and interest in or to all such material.

b.   The Author hereby appoints the Publisher to be her/his attorney-in-fact to execute and file any and all documents necessary to record in the U.S. Copyright Office or elsewhere the assignment of exclusive rights made to the Publisher hereunder. Each party hereto shall, upon request of the other, execute such documents as may be reasonably necessary to confirm the rights of the other party in respect of the Work or to carry out the intention of this Agreement.

Copyrighting the work in the name of the publisher is common when you enter into work-for-hire agreements, where the publisher is paying a flat fee for your work—and wants to own the work outright. In royalty contracts, this is less common, but can be found when a publisher is essentially asking for all rights to the work, now known or ever to be invented (see "Grant of Rights" earlier in this chapter). In such cases, transferring the copyright is just a formality—since the publisher is already being granted every right in and to the work. Bottom line: If you're okay with granting the publisher all rights to your work, then you probably don't need to bicker over who owns the copyright. It will do you little good to own the copyright on a work in which all rights have been granted to another party. However, if you retain certain rights to a work—such as when you sell electronic rights to an online publisher but retain the print rights—then you should think twice about signing over the copyright to the work.

A Brief History of Copyright—Copyright law has been evolving since the creation of the printing press. In his day, Shakespeare never saw any money from printed copies of his works. He was paid from theater revenues or by British noblemen who acted as patrons for specific plays. Very early copyright law, if you can call it that, was created to increase government revenues and was not intended to protect publishers or authors. The British government handed out royal patents to certain authors and printers giving them exclusive right to publish material. The London Stationers had a huge monopoly throughout England and Ireland under this system.

In 1710 the Statute of Anne was introduced (the first step toward what we know as copyright today). The act was introduced to protect the consumer and the author. It gave authors copyright for 21 years, after which others could reproduce the work (which helped establish a public domain). Since the Statute of Anne, copyright has evolved to further protect authors' rights, allow unpublished material to be copyrighted, include fair use, broaden the scope of categories, and other such protections.

—Margot Maley, Literary Agent, Waterside Productions, Inc.

Out of Print

An out-of-print e-book? Now there's an oxymoron. How can an e-book go out of print when it was never in print to begin with? Print On Demand technology allows a publisher to create a printed version of a book whenever one (and we mean *one*) is needed. So these days you only need to print books when you sell them. It's possible to say that a book is *always* in print. Whichever way you look at it, the definition of being "in print" is no longer what it used to be.

In the old days (say, in the late 1990s), a book would be considered Out of Print (OP) when the publisher no longer listed the book in its catalog. In essence, this meant that a book was OP when the publisher stopped selling it. Usually that happened when inventory ran out and the publisher did not think sales were strong enough to reprint the book. At this point, all rights usually reverted to the author. The contract term was over and the author and publisher would go their separate ways. (There are some details to this, but they're not important for now.)

But with Print On Demand technology, much less totally electronic books, it hardly matters how many copies a publisher sells because it isn't keeping *any* printed copies in inventory. It costs a publisher virtually nothing to keep an e-book in inventory. After all, inventory is just a computer file. Need a printed copy? Just send the file to the POD printer and the book is "back in print." So sales are pretty much never too small to keep an e-book in print. This is good and bad. Good because a publisher will always have a book available, even if it sells just one or two copies per year. Indeed, Print On Demand has created a revival of many OP books—books that are worthwhile and should be available to the public but that did not sell enough in hard copy to warrant printing again (and storing in a warehouse somewhere). Moreover, traditional publishers can move a book from normal "in print" status to "print on demand" status and, while sales may be slow, continue to make the book available.

But the never-ending life of an e-book has a downside, too. While publishers may be able to endlessly make books available to the public, this means that they also endlessly retain the rights to those books. If a book never goes out of print, then the rights never revert to the author. There may be a point at which it's in the author's best interest to take the book elsewhere, revise it, or just sell it direct—from a personal Web site or other efforts. What if, in fact, those two or three sales per year are generally sales the author creates from self-promotion, such as speaking engagements? Shouldn't the author get more of the revenue at this point? The publisher in this scenario has become a fulfillment service rather than an active part of the book's success. The author might be better off with a different publishing arrangement—one in which the author does most of the work and the publisher just fills orders. In these arrangements, the author gets a much bigger piece of the pie.

Here's a good rule of thumb: If more than 50 percent of the sales of your book are coming from your own marketing and promotional efforts, then you should strongly consider using a nonexclusive fulfillment service rather than a traditional publisher. If the publisher's efforts are not contributing to the sales of the book, then you may be better off without a publisher, meaning that you are your own publisher. You have all the information you need in this book to be your own publisher, fulfill books through e-book distribution and POD, and even sell licenses (subsidiary rights) to other parties for creating other products from your original material.

But what if you've already sold the rights to a traditional publisher? You may be stuck. But it doesn't hurt to ask the publisher for the rights back, just in case. If the publisher has a robust POD business, however, it may not be anxious to return those rights. So, if you are going with a standard publishing agreement (and there are many reasons to do so), then pay attention to the Out of Print clause. Here's a typical one:

18. Reversion of Rights

a) The Work shall be deemed "In Print" so long as the Work in any edition or version, form, or medium is distributed or made available for sale from Publisher's inventory, or from the inventory of a distributor's or licensee's warehouse, or from Publisher's Internet server or the Internet Server of a distributor or licensee, or by any other means of distribution or sales activity used by Publisher.

b) Publisher will keep the Work In Print as long as demand justifies. In the event that Publisher, at its sole discretion, determines that it is no longer in its best interest to continue to sell or market the Work, it will declare the book "Out of Print" and so notify Author by registered mail. At such point, rights in and to the work shall revert to Author. Author may then purchase any remaining inventory and film for the Work. Any such offer to grant back to you a specific right shall not alter or diminish any other rights granted to us herein and any other rights shall remain in full force and effect.

This clause basically says that the work will stay in print as long as the publisher feels like keeping it in print. Indeed, if the work is available from the publisher's Internet server, it will be considered in print. That just about makes it impossible for the author to demand rights back at any point. At times this may be quite fair, such as when the publisher has made a considerable contribution to the value of the work. In some cases, the publisher's "brand," graphic elements, or editorial treatment add as much to the book as the author's original writing. (The stronger the publisher's brand, the less likely the publisher is to offer any royalties to its authors. Publishers with strong book brands generally purchase material outright for use in their books or pay small royalties.)

Of course, authors can become brands too—see *Poor Richard's Branding Yourself Online* by Bob Baker, Top Floor Publishing, 2001.

But if you're not working with a strong publisher brand, then it's in your best interest to make sure there's an "out" in the Out of Print clause. Here's a way to modify the clause to take into account the never-ending life of an e-book:

18. Reversion of Rights

The Work shall be deemed "In Print" so long as the Work in any edition or version, form, or medium, is distributed or made available for sale from

*Publisher's inventory, or from the inventory of a distributor's or licensee's warehouse, or from Publisher's Internet server or the Internet Server of a distributor or licensee, or by any other means of distribution or sales activity used by Publisher. **The foregoing notwithstanding, the Author may declare the Work "Out of Print" if the Work sells fewer than 100 copies in any form or by any means within any twelve-month period.***

In this revised clause, the author has the right to declare the book Out of Print if sales drop under a certain minimum. The book does not automatically go OP at this point, rather the author has the *option* of declaring the book OP. The number of 100 copies is not a bad choice, but you might want to think about what is best for your particular case. The higher the number, the more control you have.

There may be other ways to approach this issue. Ideally, the author and publisher could come to a mutual agreement regarding the life of the book. In any event, if you are granting rights to a publisher, you should be sure that there is a life span to those rights. The Out of Print clause is the place to establish this.

Non Compete (or How to Kill Your Career)

If you are dealing with works of fiction, you can probably skip this section. Non-Compete clauses generally apply only to nonfiction. If you sell a book to a publisher, it makes sense that the publisher will not want you to create or assist in the creation of a similar, competitive book for someone else. That would not be fair to the publisher. Generally, the definition of a competitive work is somewhere in this neighborhood:

A competitive work is any work of substantially similar subject matter, scope, and target audience that would harm or injure sales of the Work.

Seems straightforward enough, doesn't it? Well let's add e-books to this picture. Suppose you write *Astrology Made Easy* and sell all electronic and print rights to your publisher, who puts out an e-book and POD version of your work. Now on weekends, you teach classes on astrology and one day, somebody offers you a chance to create an interactive astrology class online. You jump at the chance and, without using any of your material from the book (that would be plagiarism—of yourself) you create a course for the Internet. Meanwhile, your original publisher has been wrapping up a deal with an Internet courseware company who has just licensed the rights to all the publisher's books for creating online courses from them. Your book soon gets turned into a course. Suddenly, you have two Internet courses with your name on them. Oops!

Is this a violation of the Non-Compete clause? Perhaps—it's certainly going to get a long, hard look. And if you weren't careful to sell *only* the online courseware rights to the second publisher, you could even end up with two e-books about the same subject, because the second publisher may turn around and morph the course into an e-book. All the more reason to be clear on what rights you're assigning a publisher—especially if you make your living writing and teaching about a particular topic. You don't want to put yourself out of business with a restrictive contract.

Another possible problem relates back to the eternal life of an e-book. Consider this: Your publishing contract is effective for the life of the e-book. That means your non-compete agreement is effective for the life of the e-book. Suppose your *Astrology Made Easy* e-book has declined in sales and now only sells a few copies per month. You are approached by another publisher to write the astrology book in their new series of books. Your new *Astrology for Total Losers* is directly competitive with your old, worn-out *Astrology Made Easy*. Technically, you would need permission from your publisher to write the new book. Even though your first book is essentially dead, it's still available in electronic form. That means it's technically not dead at all (remember, e-books never die). You are still bound by the contract of the first book.

The moral of these stories is...consider the Non-Compete clause in concert with the Out of Print and Grant of Rights clauses. The idea is to put limits into these clauses—time limits or quantity limits. You might want to add a similar type of "escape" to the Non-Compete clause that we discussed for the Out of Print clause. For example, if your book sells fewer than 500 copies in one year, the Non-Compete clause is no longer effective. In my opinion, any publisher who does not understand this issue or work with you on a solution is not worth dealing with.

Literary Agents (or the Contract Watchdog)

Some people say that the Internet removes the middleman from many negotiations and transactions. Indeed, many products are sold directly to consumers, without distributors in between. But in the case of literary agents (a type of middleman), it's most likely that you'll see an increased presence. But the role of agent is likely to change in the e-publishing world. In the print publishing world, agents provide two basic services. First, they provide access to the publishing community by getting your manuscript in front of the right people (it's all about who you know). Since agents work with these publishers and editors every day, it's probable that they'll know more people in the right places than any author would. When an author is busy writing, it's often not practical to be establishing contact with publishers and building relationships.

The second thing an agent does is negotiate the contract for the author. Besides working on the financial end of the contract, agents protect authors from signing away rights unnecessarily and from accepting hidden traps in publishing deals. And some publishing contracts are nasty, to be sure.

Since the publishing process is becoming more and more virtual, and access to e-publishers and publishing services is not as difficult as it is with print publishing, the agent of the old world will likely transform into a kind of electronic rights broker. The e-rights broker would be a kind of author's advocate, helping with all the steps of a publishing or self-publishing venture. For example, an agent who is electronically sophisticated (that is, able to tell an e-book from an emu) can . . .

- List your book with rights brokers
- Sell foreign or other international rights directly
- Help you contract for advertising editions of your book
- Present your e-book to other types of publishers
- Set up a Print On Demand situation for you
- Help set up publicity and marketing for the book

Chapter 7, "Assembling Your E-Publishing Venture," discusses the various components involved in self-publishing and talks about how an agent may or may not fit into the picture. Chapter 7 also contains a listing of agents and rights brokers you can consult about your venture.

Further Reading

Here are some further resources to check out if you're serious about publishing contracts or publishing economics. Also, we have included some sample contracts in the back of this book. They make interesting reading. Really!

The **Library of Congress Copyright Office** site at http://lcweb.loc.gov/copyright/ contains everything you need to know about copyright, including some easy-to-understand explanations of the basics.

The **National Writers Union** at http://www.nwu.org/ has a lot of information about publishers, contracts, and generally accepted publishing standards.

The **Publishing Law Center** at http://www.publaw.com/legal.html/ has many articles and publications dealing with contracts.

Chapter Eleven

Business Issues for the Self E-Publisher

M any young publishing companies are the ventures of authors like you who decided to go out and start their own businesses, often out of frustration with the bigger publishers. Coming to publishing from an author's perspective provides a lot of useful understanding and empathy for the author's plight—but it could be a somewhat limited perspective when it comes to the business side of publishing.

No matter how much greener the grass looks there, working on the publisher's side of the fence will certainly still be work. As a publisher you need to know how to prepare contracts that help protect your interests but at the same time don't infringe on the rights of your authors. You must understand copyright laws and what it means to own a copyright—and take precautions to ensure that your authors don't violate copyright laws, which could get you in trouble.

As a publisher, you must also know your obligations in paying out royalties, how to calculate them, and what a reasonable author royalty statement looks like. As much as people probably don't like to admit it, being a good publisher is mostly being a good businessperson. In this chapter we cover these issues, to help you run your publishing business as well as possible.

Copyright Issues

One of the most important things to understand as an e-publisher is copyright. After all, the business of publishing is, in fact, the business of working with intellectual property rights. Without rights and copyrights, the world of publishing would be very different. One of the main issues of copyright is the protection of intellectual property—protection from other publishers' copying and distributing your property without paying you.

As mentioned earlier in this part of the book, copyright did not exist in the days of Shakespeare and authors did not receive a penny for copies of their work distributed to others. Today the issue of copyright and protection of rights could be said to have gone overboard in the opposite direction. But in the case of literary works, the world of copyright is generally a good thing, protecting both authors and publishers from opportunists wishing to profit from the creativity of others.

With e-books, the idea of copyright goes beyond legal and philosophical matters and gets right down to the ability to copy a book. Most people wouldn't take the time or spend the money to illegally copy a 250-page printed book at their local copy shop. It's just not practical. With music, it has always been a question of sound quality. Although you can make cassette tapes of all your CDs and even distribute those tapes to others, everyone knows that the quality of the tape is much lower than that of the original CD. Even if you use Digital Audio Tape to copy your CDs, you still have disadvantages due to the medium of tape. While the MP3 revolution has brought up many copyright issues relating to the music business, most people agree that MP3 files are not of the same quality as CDs. With e-books it's a different story. Every copy of an e-book is identical to the first. And the quality does not change from generation to generation. It's perfectly feasible for someone to copy an e-book and distribute it in competition with the original publisher. This scares the living daylights out of established publishers.

Some publishers are not concerned with copy protection issues. Some feel that the market will dictate what sells and what does not. In the UNIX and Linux world, where the popular Linux operating system is absolutely free and available for anyone to copy and distribute, companies have made plenty of money selling customized versions of the Linux system along with user support and instructions to attract the consumer. What these companies have found is that people will still pay money to get the software and related support, even though the software itself is free. Some e-book publishers feel the e-book market can benefit from the same tactic; they offer their books for free with an open copyright, also known as a *shareware distribution model*. Others distribute copyrighted material, but refrain from using copy protection in their files, putting the consumer on the honor system in regard to making copies of the book.

Earlier in this book, in Chapter 4, "The Production Process," and Chapter 5, "Digital Rights and Copy Protection," we talked about many of the issues involved with copy protection and related technologies. In the following pages, we want to focus on a more practical side of the copyright issue: What exactly can you copy legally and what are you not allowed to copy? We'll then give you some advice on what to do if someone violates your copyright.

Cans and Can'ts of Reuse

All publishers need a basic foundation in the dos and don'ts of reusing written material—at the very least, to explain to authors what they can and can't do.

Further, you might believe one of your copyrights has been violated and need to know what is an actual violation and what's not. Here, we offer an informal foundation of the things you can and can't do with other people's material. If you are in any doubt as to the legality of a reuse issue, we suggest you consult a copyright specialist. You can find some online at the locations suggested under "More Copyright Information" later in this section. Here are some basic things to consider:

As an author, you cannot reuse your own material. Material from books that you've sold to a publisher is not yours any longer. If you've sold all rights to your work to a publisher in exchange for a royalty (which usually is true), then you don't have the right to use that material again—even though you wrote it. One of the most common copyright violations authors make is that they use their old material again in other publications—after it was already sold to a publisher. If you write frequently about a particular topic, you need to be sure that each of your works is unique and written from scratch.

As a publisher, you want to be confident that your authors' material is free of copyright violations. You cannot always catch author plagiarism problems, so it's important to hold the author responsible for copyright violations. This is usually done with a clause in the publishing agreement. This clause, usually called "Author Warrants," specifies that the work is unique and original and does not violate any copyright or use any material in the public domain (without the author notifying the publisher of such). See the accompanying sample Author Warrants clause.

Author Warrants. You warrant to us that the Work you submit to us is your original work and has never been published, that you are the sole author of the Work, that no portion of the Work is in the public domain, and that you have the power to grant the rights granted under this Agreement. For portions of Work that are not your original work, you agree to identify all such material and obtain written permissions, acceptable to us, for any such material owned by other persons, allowing us to use the material as part of the Work. In addition, you warrant to us that the Work will not impair anyone else's copyright or other property or publicity rights and that the material is not libelous, not obscene, or unlawful in any way.

You cannot copyright a title. No matter how creative a title may be, you cannot copyright it. There are many books with the title *The American Dream*. And there will probably be more in the future. The only exception to this is if the publisher can argue that a certain title is actually a *brand* with significant market value and that another publisher's using the same title would cause market confusion and allow the second publisher to take advantage of the first one's considerable goodwill. This is difficult to prove, but it has been done. In such cases, the publisher can trademark the title, making it officially part of the marketing arsenal. (Trademark and copyright are similar but separate areas of law.) In a few cases, publishers have even managed to persuade the courts to support the brand value of untrademarked titles, but this is a costly and risky business probably beyond the reach of a small e-publisher. For all practical purposes, your titles are up for grabs.

You can copy the idea behind a book. Unfair as it may seem, the idea behind a story—even the plot itself—is not copyrightable. As long as the new story is written from scratch without using any of the actual words or characters from the original book, a story can be retold in new words. This is really not so surprising when you think about it. After all, with works of fiction, there really aren't that many new stories to tell. However, as common sense should indicate, copying a book's plot point by point while changing only the names and characters could result in a copyright infringement case. The manner in which a plot unfolds could be successfully argued as being part of the execution of an author's idea, and consequently copyrightable. In the nonfiction world, the structure of a book can probably be copied, provided the copy is not using any actual wording from the original book. The exception is when an idea is, in fact, unique and patented. A patented idea cannot be copied. As an author, it's important to remember that your idea is probably less valuable than the execution of that idea. In terms of copyright, it's the execution and not the idea itself that can be protected. If more authors thought this way, we'd probably have better books.

You can quote from other works, with some restrictions. It's acceptable to quote from other sources. Many people use the following rule of thumb when quoting: One short paragraph of no more than 200 words can be copied and credited to another source without permission. This is a *fair use* permission. Unfortunately, the truth is that there is no official minimum or maximum number of words that can be copied. The general spirit of the fair use doctrine is that a small amount of material can be presented if proper credit is given and if the use of that material is not intended to diminish the value of the original work. Naturally, it all depends on the original work and the way in which material is used. One of the key factors is the proportion of material being quoted—taking 200 words from a 400-

page book is different from taking them from a 400-word newspaper article. Another is the impact of the quoted material in the original—presenting the key point in an argument, the best line in a poem, the end of a story, all might genuinely reduce the market value of the original—regardless of the intent of the person doing the quoting. (Note that quoting from works of fiction, poems, and songs tends to be much more subject to restrictions than quoting from nonfiction works. Based on bitter experience, many publishers insist on specific written permission from the copyright holder for any quote from any work of fiction.)

Publishers usually don't want material that has already been published. Most publishers don't want to republish material that has been published before—even if that material is not encumbered (that is, it's free to be sold to the publisher without violating anyone's copyright). With the exception of publishers who are in the business of re-releasing out-of-print material, publishers want to know that what they are publishing is new. Likewise, material in the public domain is generally not wanted by publishers. Most publishing contracts include language to this effect, such as in the sample Author Warrants clause discussed earlier in this section.

Lawsuits and Plagiarism

If you happen upon a book that contains material you published or wrote, and it's clear you have been plagiarized, then you have the right to pursue legal action against the publisher of the book. Your first step should be to contact an attorney to help you with the legal process of bringing a claim against the culprit. The attorney will probably follow a standard procedure, perhaps beginning with a cease and desist letter, and if that is not effective, a lawsuit. Since you are suing somebody for money, it's possible the attorney will work on *contingency* (collecting as payment a percentage of the funds the court may award), but this kind of case is risky enough that attorneys often prefer to work for cash up front.

However, bear in mind that lawsuits are no fun at all, no matter which side you are on. If you are suing somebody, the opposing party will secure an attorney to fight for their interests. That may mean their calling you to give a deposition, at which point you will come under fire by their attorneys outside of court, but in a courtlike setting, with a courtroom stenographer recording everything you say. This can be a frightening experience, although your attorney will be there to help you. Further, unless your attorney works on contingency, you could really run up some big bucks paying for the lawsuit. Also, even if you win, that doesn't automatically mean you'll get any money. If the defendant doesn't *have* any money, you certainly can't *get* any money. And a defendant who does have the money may well refuse to pay, meaning you have to pursue further legal channels to get it. And finally, you might not win the case, leaving you to pay heavily for a lost fight and possibly risk a countersuit for allegedly harassing the defendant.

Unless you thrive on fights, we suggest you avoid lawsuits. Definitely talk to an attorney about it, and let the attorney help you decide if you really do have a strong case before going forward with it. And remember that it will be a stressful struggle for you as well as the defendant.

Now suppose you are on the other side of the fence. Although the person doing the suing may be under a lot of stress, that's nothing compared to what the one being sued will go through. Lawsuits tend to drag on for months or years, especially at the federal level (where copyright suits are heard). They can cause serious fights and arguments among friends working in the company, and people will have the tendency to blame each other. This is often enough to cause the company to collapse. And remember, if your company does collapse, most likely the suit won't end there. Plaintiffs often name individuals as well as companies on the lawsuit. So even if the company is gone, the lawsuit lingers on, and you'll likely be paying for it out of your pocket. And you can't just make it go away.

When someone sues you, you probably won't find a lawyer willing to work on contingency. This means you will be forking out major bucks month after month until the suit is finished. And of course, you could lose the suit, meaning the plaintiff will be pursuing you for a settlement in the form of cash or stock in your company. Despite what we said earlier about a defendant's chances of getting away without paying, the effort to escape a judgment is distressing and far from certain to work. You do not want to deal with it.

So what do you do? Don't get sued. Do everything you can to protect yourself. Do everything you can to make sure that your authors don't submit somebody else's work. If you hire editors, make sure the editors are always on the lookout. You can't guarantee that someone won't sue you, but you can make that option far less tempting by making a successful lawsuit so unlikely that the other side's time and cost aren't worth it.

At the same time, remember that most people are honest. If you make the assumption that writers are dishonest and you are always threatening them, you will not be a popular publisher, and you will lose authors left and right. Remember there's a fine balance between protecting yourself and going crazy paranoid over the exposure.

So what do you do if you do get sued? Your attorney will tell you what exactly to do, but one thing you will strongly want to consider is a settlement. Your life may be a whole lot easier if you can easily pay out some money to the plaintiff or offer them common stock in your company, end the book, and move on. Although most attorneys won't admit it, most people hate being sued. Even if they are innocent they may still settle, because lawsuits are hell—so much so, that even if the defendant didn't do whatever-it-is the plaintiff claims, they will probably want to come to some settlement. That's because if you don't settle, and the plaintiff doesn't give up and drop the case, and the judge doesn't throw it out, the suit *will* go to court. So if you want to avoid that, your only option is to settle. As a defendant you have little power to have the case closed up and thrown away.

So don't get sued. Don't plagiarize.

How to Register Copyright

Under current U.S. copyright law, you do not need to register your work with the Library of Congress to have a copyright. All you generally need is to insert a copyright notice. However, if you are involved in a copyright dispute, it's best that you do have the work registered, primarily because if you don't, the monetary damages you could otherwise collect won't be awarded to you if you're successful. Here's a sample copyright notice that contains all the elements required under U.S. law and in many foreign jurisdictions:

Copyright 2000, Jan Sman, All Rights Reserved.

It's actually easy to register a copyright. Copyrights in the United States are handled exclusively by the Library of Congress, which provides all the necessary forms that you can fill out, and they can let you know the current fee. (At the time of this writing, the fee is $30, and the Library of Congress guarantees this fee will not change before June 2001.) The next section, "More Copyright Information," contains contact information for the Library of Congress, as well as other resources.

More Copyright Information

As we've said, there's a lot to know about copyright. You don't have to become an expert, but it will help if you know some basics. Here are some great resources:

The **Library of Congress Copyright Office** Web site is located at http://lcweb.loc.gov/copyright/. It contains everything you need to know about copyright, including some easy-to-understand explanations of the basics. It also has all the details about registration of copyright for various types of publications. This should be your first stop to discover more about copyright issues and registration. See Figure 11.1.

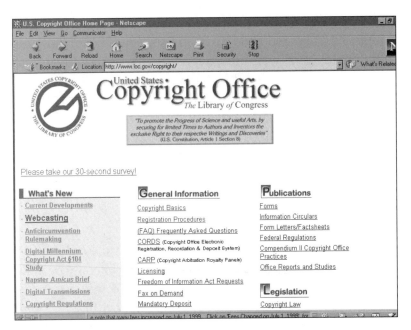

Figure 11.1: The Library of Congress site has plenty of information to take you through all types of copyright issues. It's a great place to start your copyright lessons.

The **Publishing Law Center** at http://www.publaw.com/legal.html has many articles and publications dealing with contracts and copyright law, including information about the fair use doctrine, discussed in the "Cans and Can'ts of Reuse" section earlier in this chapter, and work made for hire contracts, discussed in the "Work-for-Hire Agreement" section later in the chapter. Figure 11.2 shows one of the articles at this site.

The **Yale University Library** site at http://www.library.yale.edu/~llicense/liclinks.shtml contains links to a number of copyright information resources, both national and international, including plenty of information about electronic rights and Internet copyright issues.

Stanford University has a page at http://fairuse.stanford.edu/ with articles and legal papers dealing with copyright statutes, regulations, international treaties, and the Constitution. After you have a grip on the basics, check this information out for some interesting reading.

Pamela Samuelson, a professor of law at the University of California at Berkeley, has a site with a number of papers that she's written on the subject of copyright, digital data, and cyberlaw. You can find her papers online at http://www.sims.berkeley.edu/~pam/papers.html.

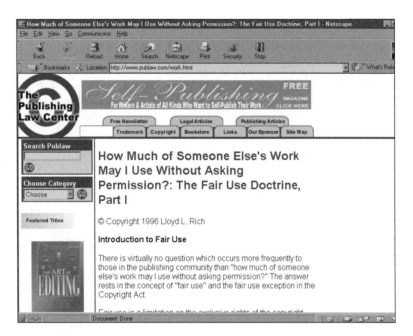

Figure 11.2: This article on the fair use doctrine appears at the Publishing Law Center site.

Non-Exclusive E-Book Deals

A non-exclusive publishing deal allows the publisher to create, publish, and market an e-book, perhaps at the same time as numerous other e-publishers or other types of publishers. No single publisher has exclusive rights to the book, but must share the rights with others. In essence, the author sells the publisher the right to sell *its* version of the book as best it can from its own site or other methods, while other sites are able to compete with it. Kind of like one bookstore competing with another. Does that mean you could have several different versions of your e-book out there on the Internet? Yes, it does. One non-exclusive publisher might ask you to create a certain type of file for it to distribute, while another will create a file for you in its preferred format. It all depends. But it's not as messy as it sounds. One version of an e-book is probably not all that different from another—from a reading experience standpoint that is. And at the present writing, most e-book readers do not let you read e-books in various formats. Rather, they are exclusive to a particular e-book format. So a person with an old RCA RocketBook is probably only going to be able to see one version of your e-books—the one in Rocket Edition format.

Non-exclusive publishers are a cross between publishers and distributors. Basically they are distributors that get their books directly from authors, rather than from publishers. Some sell their books to other online stores, such as **Amazon.com** (http://www.amazon.com/) and **Borders.com** (http://www.bordersbooks.com/) who, in turn, sell to the public. Other publishers are more like a cross between distributors and bookstores in that they make their books available to the public and sell direct to the consumer. They may get their books from authors directly, or from other publishers.

At any rate, one thing you can almost count on is that the non-exclusive publishers will probably *not* make a huge investment in your book—neither in terms of author advance nor in terms of production investment (preparation of the book). They may or may not put much into marketing your book. Some of these publishers are really just fulfillment services for your e-book, offering a Web presence with thousands of books that attracts customers whom you theoretically would not be able to access on your own. They also provide order processing and payment collection—things that not every e-book author with a floppy disk full of the great American novel has the know-how, time, or energy to do online. It's often more worthwhile to pass these tasks along to one of the Web publishing services and share part of the pie with them. For a more in-depth look at the publishers and what they offer, refer to Chapter 6. "Checking Out the E-Publishers," and Chapter 7, "Assembling Your E-Publishing Venture."

What Do the Contracts Look Like?

So let's get down to it. What kinds of non-exclusive terms and conditions can you expect to see in a non-exclusive publishing deal? The answer at this point in the game is, "almost anything." But it's not all that bad. The non-exclusive contract is usually pretty simple. There are really only a few things with which to be concerned.

Grant of Rights

As in exclusive publishing deals, the Grant of Rights is the key element of non-exclusive publishing deals. This part of the contract defines what the publisher is getting from the author, how long the publisher will get to keep it, and whether anybody else gets to use it too. Thankfully, the Grant of Rights in a non-exclusive deal is much simpler than that of an exclusive deal. That's because what needs to be said is essentially "you're giving us rights to publish this book, but not exclusively."

Some publishers have other minor issues to add to the non-exclusivity of their deal. For example, here's a Grant of Rights clause from a publisher that wants exclusivity within its own field, but grants non-exclusivity for everything else.

That is, it doesn't want any of its direct competitors to get your e-book, but you can sell it to anybody outside the field of competition.

> *Grant of Rights. You assign and grant us all worldwide non-exclusive rights in and copyright to the Work, its parts, and all versions and revisions of the Work, for the full term of copyright and all renewals of copyright, including the right to print, publish, distribute, and sell the Work online, in all countries and including all of the rights set forth in paragraphs 6 and 13. You also grant to us the non-exclusive right to license or permit others to do the same. You also grant us an **exclusive right** in the copyright for the field of online content distribution that is competitive with our business model as well as other competitive online content syndicators. The copyright shall be registered in your name.*

Notice that this publisher wants to be able to license your work in various ways, but only wants exclusivity in one area. This way, you are selling the publisher a single, exclusive right to your work, along with the privilege of sharing the rest of the rights with you or whoever else you choose to sell them to. Be aware, if you actively pursue other rights deals for this book, you should be careful to manage the rights you are vending. You don't want to end up with conflicts down the road and angry publishers ready to sue you for copyright conflicts. As a quick reminder (this was covered in the preceding chapter), this publisher could end up selling a license to your work for a print version while you are out there selling the print rights yourself. If you're not careful to make sure that both contracts are non-exclusive, then you could end up with conflicts.

Here's a different Grant of Rights philosophy. In this case, the publisher wants exclusivity for a limited period of time so as to get a head start on the others. After this exclusivity term is up, you're free to sell the e-book to anyone else— even competitors.

> *Term and Termination. The term of this Agreement will continue until the Material is removed by Author, unless terminated earlier as provided herein. After the exclusive electronic rights period, either party may terminate this Agreement at any time with or without cause upon 30 days notice. Publisher's rights to the Materials listed below shall be exclusive electronic rights for the first 12 months from delivery of the material.*

This is one of the most non-exclusive (or is that "least exclusive"?) Grant of Rights clauses we've seen. That's probably because this publisher sells to a particular group of customers directly and only needs a limited period of time to get your book sold through to its customer base. Its managers figure that other publishers will probably be focusing on other markets.

Non-exclusive e-book publishing deals should (and generally do) have a time limit. That is, they end at some point, or at least come up for renewal. This is to protect both the publisher and the author. Often distribution and non-exclusive publishing terms automatically renew if both parties are in good standing with each other. Sometimes the agreement converts into a completely open, non-exclusive deal after a term of exclusivity. The fact is, non-exclusive publishing deals are a new ball game and anything is possible. If the contract has a normal Grant of Rights clause, such as the one shown earlier, then a separate Term clause would need to appear in the contract. As an author, you want to be on the lookout for a favorable term. If you're happy with the publisher after the term is up, you should be able to renew.

Promotion

Since a non-exclusive publishing or distribution deal is really giving a company the right to promote and sell your book, you want to be clear about what the company is able to do to promote your book. Some companies attract authors and small publishers with the traffic they attract to their Web site. Although promotional promises usually don't make it into the publishing or distribution agreements, you can do your own research to find out what the company offers.

Then there are e-publishers who feel that *any* distribution is good distribution and are willing to work with just about anyone. The theory is to get books out to as many people through as many channels as possible. As long as the distribution agreement does not restrict the publisher from making other deals, then why not give anyone a chance at selling books?

As an independent e-publisher, how you approach distribution is up to you. As an author, keep in mind that you might be better off working with a publisher who has established relationships with distributors and booksellers—giving you more time to write more books.

Royalties and Discounts

Some non-exclusive publishing deals are really distribution deals in other clothing. The idea is that another company or Internet organization is going to take your e-book and sell it to its various customers—usually direct to consumers through its online bookstore and to other online booksellers, such as Amazon.com. Whether you are given a royalty or whether the distributor-publisher takes a discount, the bottom line is that you'll end up with a portion of the cover price—usually from 40 percent to 60 percent. Amazon.com, for example, requires a 55 percent discount from its publishers or distributors. You might find that non-exclusive distributors end up taking even more than this, so as to sell to Amazon.com at 55 percent and still make a small profit too. Whether couched as a royalty or a distributor discount, you should be clear what you'll be receiving for your e-books from these publisher-distributors.

Contracts You'll Need

Business is business. And when making deals, it's important to have good contracts that protect both sides from possible problems. We provide some wording in Appendix C, "Sample Contracts," that you can use as a starting point. Here we'll give you an overview of the types of contracts you'll need and why. Those types of contracts include:

- Publishing agreement
- Work-for-hire agreement
- Collaboration agreement
- Revision letter

Publishing Agreement

The publishing agreement is the contract you'll use most often as a publisher. It's the contract between the author and the publisher for the transfer of rights from the author to the publisher. It gives the publisher the right to publish a given book. In the preceding two chapters we talked a lot about the various clauses and terms associated with publishing agreements. If you decide to work with the example contract we've provided in Appendix C, then it's important that you understand the basic issues involved—because no single contract can work well for everyone and every occasion. You'll almost certainly want to modify the sample contract to make it more suitable to your situation. The publishing contract should cover the following issues at the least:

Transfer of rights to publisher. This includes issues such as which rights, specifically, the author is transferring, what the publisher is able to do with those rights, and for how long the publisher can exploit those rights. This includes rights that the publisher is personally exploiting as well as rights that the publisher may or may not transfer to a third party.

Amount of payment from publisher to author for the rights. Clearly, this should specify the amount of advances and royalties that will be paid for the work and any licenses (transfers) of the work to third parties. It also can specify any exceptions that require more or less payment to the author. For example, the publisher is usually allowed to give away promotional copies for free without payment to the author, while copies sold directly from the publisher to the consumer often result in higher payment to the author.

Non-Negotiable Is a Dirty Word—Every e-book is different. And every author–publisher relationship is different. It's impossible to imagine every publishing agreement being the same. So how can a publisher create the same contract with the same terms for every single e-book and every single author? But "non-negotiable" is what you'll hear from most e-publishers regarding their contracts. Perhaps they feel that they are already offering such wonderful terms that authors should not need anything else. Or perhaps e-publishers have an aversion to negotiating deals. Most likely, publishers just don't have the capability to track differences among their many book deals and want to minimize the hassle in calculating royalties differently for each book (for this problem, we offer our "Royalty Accounting" section later in this chapter). Whatever the case, the best authors will almost certainly request changes to a publishing agreement. And "it's not negotiable" is a turn-off to anybody. Check out the complete publisher listings at E-Publishing Opportunities (http://www.myplanet.net/vanburen/epublishers-full.html) to see just how many publishers say their contracts are non-negotiable. We invite you to stand out from the crowd and negotiate your contracts.

When the publisher will pay. Most publishers create quarterly royalty reports and pay authors within 30 days after the final day of the quarter. An increasing number of publishers pay monthly and a few still pay twice per year (a very old standard in publishing that should be dead by now). If a publisher wants to pay once per year, an author should consider working with a different publisher.

Guarantees from the author. These author *warranties* are promises from the author, ensuring that the work is original, that the author is legally able to enter the contract, that the author will not sue the publisher for certain things out of the publisher's control, and that the author will retain original copies of the work. Certain publishing situations require other promises between the parties.

Guarantees from the publisher. These publisher promises include such things as that the work will be published within a certain amount of time, that the publisher will put the author's name on each copy of the work, that the publisher will register the copyright, and that the publisher will keep accurate records of account. Other publisher promises may be appropriate for certain situations.

Ways in which the contract can terminate. Contracts terminate naturally when term limits run out or if the book is considered "out of use." Contracts can also terminate when the author or publisher breaks a promise. The basic details of how and when the contract can be terminated should be covered.

How the author can purchase copies. It's customary for the publisher to give the author a certain number of free copies of the work in all its editions. It's also customary for the publisher to offer the author a special discount to purchase additional copies. Some publishers encourage authors to purchase copies for resale and others do not. It depends on how the publisher chooses to market its books.

Avoiding a Fight Between Co-Authors—When purchasing copies for personal use or resale, it's common that authors do not receive royalties on those copies. Instead, the author receives a discount on the purchase of the books. But in some cases, it might be best to trade the discount for normal royalties on these author purchases. In particular, when there are two or more co-authors associated with the work, it's better to accept a smaller discount in exchange for receiving royalties on author-purchased copies. Why? Because if one author has an avenue for selling tons of books while the other does not, the second author will receive no compensation for the copies purchased and sold by the first author.

Work-for-Hire Agreement

Also known as a contractor agreement, a work-for-hire agreement indicates that one party is paying the other for a specific job. The results of the job are the property of the party paying for the work. Concerning creative works, it's important to note that a work-for-hire agreement means that the writer will not have any rights in or to the work after accepting payment. The copyright in and to the work is the property of the buyer. Normally, publishing deals are not work-for-hire deals, since the author is technically "loaning" rights to the publisher in exchange for an interest in the work's revenue (that is, a royalty). However, in some cases it makes sense to use a work-for-hire agreement. Here are some instances:

When contracting editors to alter the work. Editorial work is usually not considered a royalty-generating contribution—even when the editorial work includes heavy revisions and alterations. A work-for-hire contract is useful for hiring editorial assistance.

Promotional text or book cover material. The material written for the front and back cover of a book is not a royalty-generating part of the project. If you hire writers to contribute this marketing information, it's important to use work-for-hire agreements so that all rights are the property of the publisher.

When the publisher has a large creative participation in the work. Some publishers have book series or brands that may add as much to the final work as the writing itself. This is common with travel guides, for example. Most publishers with strong book brands hire writers with work-for-hire contracts, avoiding the payment of royalties. This is often considered unfair to authors, who receive a flat fee for writing a book, while the publisher receives ongoing income from sales. Indeed it *can* be unfair if the publisher's contributions do not really add creatively to the project. On the other hand, if the flat fee is decent, then trading in your future royalties for up-front cash is not such a bad idea.

When hiring writers to create revisions or adaptations. Often the original author will not be available to revise a work and the publisher may hire a second writer to do the revision. The same is true with adaptations, such as translations or the creation of anthologies or condensed editions. In such cases, a contract can also be written so that it is partially a work-for-hire and partially an advance-and-royalty arrangement.

When a writer is contributing a small portion of a book. Sometimes a chapter or small section of a book requires a special expert other than the author. The publisher may end up hiring the collaborator outside the publishing agreement with the author. In such cases, a work-for-hire agreement may be appropriate. This is more common with nonfiction works.

Collaboration Agreement

A collaboration agreement is generally used between two authors—when one author originates a contract with the publisher and the second author joins the project later. Rather than create a new publishing agreement to add the second author, it's easier to create a collaboration agreement between the two authors. The collaboration agreement can include royalties for the second author or it can be a work-for-hire agreement, depending on the situation. The important thing about a collaboration agreement is that it protects the publisher from work being done by an author who is not on the original contract. Publishers should contractually demand that their authors use collaboration agreements when working with others or hiring the services of contributors. Typically, the original author–publisher agreement prohibits reassignment of authors' obligations without the express written permission of the author.

A typical problem scenario might look like this: An author signs up to write a book about coffee. Halfway through the project, the author decides to hire a collaborator to write a section describing how coffee is prepared after picking. Unknown to the first author, the collaborator plagiarizes the entire section from information that appears on the Internet. The publisher finds out before publishing the book and as a result decides to terminate the original contract.

The original author pleads with the publisher, saying that the problem section was written by another person and was not the author's fault. The publisher is justifiably angry that the author hired a collaborator without a proper contract and is not confident that the book can be published without risk to the company. Fixing the problem may not be an option. Everyone loses.

Whether you're an author or a publisher, when hiring collaborating writers, it's critical to use a proper collaboration agreement to protect yourself from problems.

Revision Letter

Certain types of books must be revised and updated now and then. Computer and technical books, travel guides, and other types of nonfiction works become almost worthless within a fairly short time. If you publish such books, you need to consider how to handle these revisions contractually. For such books, it's important to include a revision clause in the main publishing agreement. This clause stipulates how revisions are to be handled. Following is a typical revision clause:

Revised Editions. When and if Publisher considers revision of the Work necessary to render its continued publication profitable, the Author agrees to revise the Work within a reasonable time mutually agreed upon. After receiving a notice of request for revision, the Author shall advise Publisher within 60 days whether he or she will prepare the revision. If the Author does not advise Publisher within such 60-day period of intent to prepare the revision, or if the Author is otherwise unwilling or unable to prepare the revision, Publisher may have the revision prepared by a competent third party and may deduct the reasonable cost thereof from the Author's royalty account.

First, it's important to note that it's the publisher's choice whether to publish a revised edition of the book. Authors usually don't like this. They want to be able to publish a revised edition whenever they feel it's time. But the publisher ultimately decides what it wants to publish, including revisions of existing books.

Happily, since e-books are not expensive to publish, most e-publishers should be able to create revisions quickly and easily whenever the author feels strongly that one is needed. Nevertheless, the revision clause should give the publisher the final decision. In some cases, the publisher may want to create a revision for a book before the author does and, depending on the situation, may even want to retain the right to create a revision with or without the author's participation. Naturally, the author should be consulted first of any such desires by the publisher. Notice in the preceding Revised Editions clause that the original author is given first option to revise the work when the publisher chooses to publish a revised edition and only if the author is unwilling or unable to revise the work (or does not respond to the publisher's request) is the publisher able to proceed without the author.

Royalty Accounting

Probably one of the biggest fears authors have is that their publishers are somehow tricking them in the money department—making errors in royalty accounting or outright hiding things. It's true that publishers have traditionally been some of the most creative folks when it comes to accounting, finding loopholes and gray areas where royalties can be diminished. "After all," publishers jokingly comment, "this would be a great business if it weren't for the authors." Imagine yourself as a publisher, seeing a large sum of money come in from sales of your books, then remembering that an awful lot of it has to be paid out to the authors. Ouch! That hurts. Plus, most of the large publishers develop a "reduce costs and expenses" attitude when they have stockholders to please and the accounting department reports clearly reveal that the largest single outflow of money (next to the printing bill) is paid to authors in royalties. All this adds up to publishers' seeking ways to reduce royalties to authors. And authors, not surprisingly, end up developing a rather suspicious attitude toward publishers, particularly after hearing horror stories like those that follow.

> **Foreign Intrigue**. A publisher opens several foreign offices to print and distribute books in foreign languages. The publisher then sells its domestic editions to the foreign divisions for an amount well below the norm for foreign sales. The foreign division ends up with a fantastic deal, paying low advances and royalties on the translations. The publisher ends up with extra profits from foreign language sales—through the foreign divisions. Since the author has no power to audit the foreign publisher, there is really no way to know if anything is wrong. And publishers have the power to enter into third-party agreements for the author's work at their discretion—without the author's approval (or even the author's knowledge) of individual deals.

> **Dizzy Discounts**. A publisher has the opportunity to sell a large number of copies of a book to a retail store. The discount has been negotiated to 54 percent off list price. But the publisher calculates that if it gives the store an extra 1 percent discount, it will be able to gain money from the author's royalty account in exchange for giving up one point to the store. How? This happens through the *deep discount* clause in the publisher's contract. In this example, the author's royalty is cut in half when the discount is 55 percent

or greater. In many cases, it's actually in the publisher's interest to increase the discount to the sales outlet to reduce royalties to the author. Everyone wins but the author.

Sleight of Hand. A publisher pays its author a fee to reuse a portion of a book in another publication. The contract stipulates that the publisher is purchasing the right to reuse the work in exchange for this fee. The publisher then ends up reusing portions of the new book in yet another book and the author's original work now appears in two adaptations. The publisher claims that it had the right to reuse the work a second time, since it purchased this right for the first occurrence. Depending on the details of the reuse agreement, a publisher could be able to get away with this— without payment to the author. Tricking authors in the contract department is a long-standing practice with some publishers. Most authors do not know enough about the publishing business to know how to spot potential problems. Frankly, most lawyers don't know enough about publishing to spot these problems either. What's needed is an expert in publishing contracts—a good publishing attorney, professional publishing auditor, or literary agent.

Revision Rustling. A computer book publisher determines that it's time to revise a book about a popular program, since a new version of the software is due in a few months. Rather than asking the author of the original volume to create the revision, the publisher works with a completely new author and creates a completely new book with the same title as the old book. The new author, perhaps, is willing to work for a smaller advance and royalty than the first author. The publisher correctly argues that the title is not copyrightable and that it has the right to create a new book from scratch—without taking any material from the old book. Okay, fine. Publishers must be able to make these decisions if necessary. But what really hurts the original author is that this deal makes it impossible to revise the original book and sell it to another publisher. The old manuscript is essentially dead, but the author does not have the right to bring it back to life—until the publisher decides to put the old book out of print. Unfortunately, the publisher does not put the old book out of print until it's way too late for the author to write a competitive book for another publisher.

These are only a few of the nasty tricks that publishers have been known to commit. There are hundreds of areas in publishing contracts and accounting that can be twisted in the publisher's favor. Authors generally get the right to audit the publisher's records of account using a professional accountant or other representative. But an audit is usually not profitable unless there is plenty of money at stake (that is, if the book has sold a great many copies or the author has several books with the same publisher).

Thankfully, e-book contracts are much simpler than traditional print publishing contracts—and so is the royalty accounting. A simple system should be enough to track the various discounts given to the distributors and booksellers—as well as the various royalty rates given to authors (assuming the publisher has negotiated its royalty rates). Plus, with e-books, most resellers pay publishers on sales made—that is, actual downloads from customers. In the print publishing world, a publisher would sell, say, 500 copies to a reseller and account for 500 sales. But the reseller might not actually *pay* for those copies for quite some time and half of them might eventually come back as returns.

E-books and Print On Demand copies are generally created when a sale is made, so accounting for e-publishers is more current and "actual" than for print publishers. Most e-publishers pay a simple percentage based on net income from e-book sales. So regardless of the wholesale discount or whether the book was sold directly from the publisher's site, the publisher simply adds up the income on a particular title and gives a percentage of this figure to the author. The same is true for POD sales, although the royalty percentage for POD is usually different. Finally, a third royalty rate may be paid for third-party sales and licenses. Figure 11.3 shows a sample royalty statement with these types of issues displayed.

Notice that the statement does not display every transaction, only the sum of all the transactions of a particular type. That is, the statement does not show the author what each outlet purchased and what the sale was. That would be a bit excessive, although authors drool for this information. Most publishers regard these details as their private business and not for anyone outside the company to know. Only in a direct audit of the publisher's records will anyone gain access to individual transactions, to check them against the

Royalty Statement
For period ending March 30, 2002

TITLE: Taking Responsibility
ISBN: 00092252x
AUTHOR: John Smith

Description	Units	Amount	Author Royalty	Total
eBook standard sales	1200	9600.00	50%	4800.00
eBook direct sales	85	1275.00	30%	382.50
Print On Demand sales	500	6000.00	20%	1200.00
Licenses				
French Translation Rights		1000.00	50%	500.00
Total net sales				$6,882.50
Returns	1	8.00		-8.00
Advance balance from prev statement				-200.00
TOTAL DUE				$6,674.50

Figure 11.3: This publisher's royalty statement tracks the various different types of income from sales of the author's work.

royalty statements the publisher has issued. And then, only the accountant or other agent gets to see the information—not the author.

Business Tips for E-Publishers

We close this chapter with a few friendly tips for the new self e-publisher and Internet entrepreneur. We take this opportunity to remind you that we are not business consultants and encourage you to check out other resources for information about starting and running online businesses and general business management.

Get ISBNs for your books. Most publishers are not taken seriously if their books don't have ISBNs. And most distributors demand ISBNs on books before they'll distribute them. The investment of time and money required to get a series of ISBNs is something you'll find well worth it.

Focus on making good books. Nothing calls attention to a company like excellent products. Some publishers are in the business of accumulating as much electronic information as possible, dumping it online, and creating the impression that they have vast archives of electronic documents for their customers to enjoy. In the end, people want good books, just like always.

Do not underestimate the power of appearance. Remember that everything is bought and sold on the basis of its presentation. A book, like anything else, must make a good first impression. That means it should have an attractive cover and compelling cover copy.

Remember that you are running a business. Get a good accountant to help you with the financial issues; secure a good attorney to help you with the legal and obligatory state, county, and city processes and paperwork. And making even an informal business plan would help you define your values and goals—and the steps toward achieving them.

Learn about online business tactics. There are plenty of resources out there to help you run a successful online business. It might be an interesting notion to consider that you are not in the publishing business at all. Rather, you are in the online information business. Here are a few more books to get you started: *Starting an Online Business For Dummies,* by Greg Holden (Hungry Minds, 2000); *Millennium Intelligence: Understanding and Conducting Competitive Intelligence in the Digital Age,* edited by Jerry P. Miller (Information Today, 2000); and *B2B.Com: Cashing-In on the Business-To-Business E-Commerce Bonanza,* by Brian O'Connell (Adams Media Corporation, 2000).

Relationships are everything. It's often said that people do business with the people they like. So strive to form lasting and powerful alliances with others in your industry. This includes distributors and booksellers as well as authors and other suppliers.

Don't forget to sell. Don't make the mistake of many Internet start-ups and assume that just because you have a Web site online, you're going to get people to visit your site and buy your products. No, you have to sell, sell, sell. Even after getting your e-books into the online bookstores, it's usually necessary to promote and market your titles to attract attention.

PART V
Real-Life Success Stories & Future Trends

CHAPTER TWELVE

Personal Success Stories

It's always nice to know that you're not alone out there. Although the world of e-publishing is relatively new and uncharted, there are plenty of folks who have passed this way before you and are willing to give you some firsthand advice. This chapter provides a few personal stories from some e-publishing adventurers. We hope you find them both inspiring and informative. In this chapter you'll find the following:

Give Up on Giving Up, by M. J. Rose, shows how an unknown self-published author can break into the big time publishers on the merits of her work. It should provide some inspiration as to what's possible in the online world.

Fantasy and Fiction in the E-World: Perspectives of a Writer, by Xina Marie Uhl, demonstrates how two writers with great ideas and plenty of optimism went around the print publishing community to create an e-publishing company to sell their works.

Perspectives of an Author-Founded Publishing Company, by W. L. Warner, shows how e-publishing can be particularly great for authors serving special niche markets. It also provides some details about how one publisher approaches the issue of multiple e-book formats.

The Essence of E-Publishing, by Mary Westheimer, is a perspective from a publisher and publishing service company. It gives an interesting overview of e-publishing opportunities past and present and several ideas about how to approach an e-publishing venture from scratch.

You Can, by Daniel Newman, provides a view of a different type of e-publishing venture that combines print and free electronic files that can be read online.

Give Up on Giving Up

M.J. Rose
http://www.mjrose.com

In 1996 I thought about giving up my dream of becoming a published author. I had written two novels, found a wonderful agent, and by her account had the best rejection letters any writer could wish for.

I asked my agent what I should do. I didn't want to give in and change my style to fit the publisher. I actually thought about giving up and tried to figure out what I'd do if I couldn't be a writer. I made lists of alternative careers. But each one suggested a character in a novel and I'd wind up making notes on possible plots. All I wanted to do was write. "So, why not just keep writing?" a friend asked.

Well, if all I needed to keep writing was readers, how many did I need? Perhaps not the multitudes I'd wanted. What about just one? Ten? Twenty?

If I couldn't do it the traditional way and have my readers find me in a bookstore. . .maybe I could self-publish my *Lip Service* on the Web as an electronic download and find those readers myself.

Little did I know the derisive laughter that would greet my decision by everyone I'd ever known connected to the field of writing. To a person, everyone

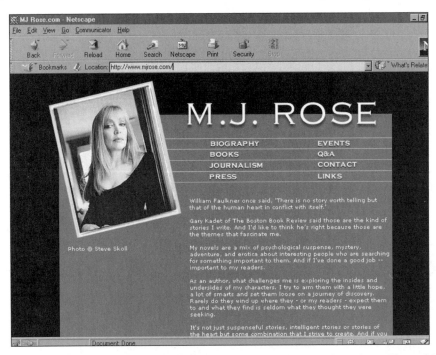

Figure 12.1: M. J. Rose's site displays her many books and her tips for other self e-publishers.

said self-publishing is nothing more than a huge ego-trip. All of them thought the concept of an electronic file was ludicrous. (This was in 1997, still three years before Stephen King's *Riding the Bullet* made e-books something like a household word.)

What did I have to lose? What was so crazy about downloading a book to your desktop and then printing it or reading in segments? And what was so terrible about self-publishing? Independent filmmakers who finance their own movies are lauded. Indies even have their own film festival at Sundance.

But it is different—self-published authors, my well-meaning friends told me, are writers whose books are not good enough to get published by the big New York houses. Whereas indie filmmakers are iconoclastic visionaries who make gems of movies.

But despite them all . . . or to spite them all—I'm not sure which—I took to the Web.

Taking to the Web

I had a Web site built and a book cover designed. And then I spent four months figuring out where my kind of readers lived online. It took over 2,000 hours to research and develop a marketing plan, learn about self-publishing, make mistakes, and then correct them. I offered hundreds of free books to webmasters who might like to review my novel. I joined endless lists and newsgroups to talk to other writers and readers about what I was doing. I lived online.

And then slowly, very slowly, I started to get reviews. And then I got my first reader. A month later I had ten. Three months later I had 500. I was finally a writer. I knew I was okay. I would be able to write my next novel and my next.

About 16 months after my Web site went live, in February of 1999, *Lip Service*—the little book that could—was discovered online by an editor at the Doubleday Book Club, who bought it as an alternate book club selection.

It was the first time a major book club had bought a self-published novel. The first time a book had been discovered online. And two weeks after that Pocket Books offered my agent a contract. At that point *Lip Service* became the first e-book to cross over to become a mainstream novel. *Lip Service*—the book no one wanted in 1996—has now sold over 60,000 copies and has been published in England, Germany, Israel, The Netherlands, France, and Australia. The trade paperback version has just gone into a second printing.

In January 2001, my nonfiction book, *How to Publish and Promote Online* (co-authored with Angela Adair-Hoy), was published by St. Martin's Press and my new novel, *In Fidelity,* was released by Pocket Books. How ironic. The very reason I couldn't get published five years ago was because I didn't fit in. Now it's an accolade.

These days, you can find me at the laptop, working on my third novel or writing about e-publishing for Wired.com. And if all this isn't enough of a reason to convince you that giving up are the only two words all writers should erase from their vocabulary—then I give up.

Fantasy and Fiction in the E-World: Perspectives of a Writer

Xina Marie Uhl
Co-founder of XC Publishing
http://www.xcpublishing.com/

The road that led to the decision to become an electronic publisher was a long and winding one for me and my friend and business partner Cheryl Dyson. It began when Cheryl and I met back in high school and discovered that we were both writers. We wrote every chance we could—stories, comic strips, novels, and about a million silly, giggly notes and letters to each other. We started writing fantasy novels at the same time and encouraged each other to continue. We were—and still are—each other's number-one fan. Together, we've experienced all the typical pitfalls of the writer's life: critique groups, rejection slips, writer's block, and boring, yucky day jobs. It took both of us years to learn to write and by the time we did we both had really great manuscripts. We began sending them out to traditional publishers and waiting months on end for a response. One publisher kept my manuscript for nine months before rejecting it. Since most publishers do not accept manuscripts submitted simultaneously to other publishers, this can stretch the submission process out for a long, long time. Most often the rejection slip is an impersonal photocopied letter, though sometimes an editor would offer a few lines of opinion about the work (scrawled hieroglyphics that writers live for). Competition is enormous. Publishers receive literally hundreds of manuscripts from wannabe writers every week. Only a small percentage of them are published—and it's not because they are the only jewels in the stack. . . but I'll get to that later.

The Rewards of Writing—or Lack Thereof . . .

Reading is an incredibly subjective experience. Regarding the same manuscript, I've had one editor tell me that I have great storytelling skills, while another told me that I needed to improve on my storytelling skills. Many programs, organizations, and books offer to help the would-be writer create publishable manuscripts. But once a writer learns the basics of compiling a compelling, clearly written, grammatically correct story (including proper manuscript format, an active voice, well-rounded characters, and a comprehensive plot)

Figure 12.2: The attractive XC Publishing site shows just how much a couple of self-published authors can accomplish.

there is still a great expanse to cover on the way to finding a home in a traditional publishing house. Is this because publishers are evil people bent on destroying dreams? No. It's a simple numbers game. Publishers cannot afford to publish every good manuscript they find. It's a costly business to produce paper copies, which must be bound and printed, distributed, and subjected to large discounts by booksellers, who ship a large percentage of unsold books back to the publisher and demand a refund.

Even when an editor shows interest in a manuscript, the process of being published is a difficult one. One afternoon a small Canadian publisher called me and asked for the remainder of my novel. I was elated and sent it out immediately. She offered to publish it, but only if I did some rewriting. I rewrote all right, even though I didn't agree with some of the changes. It took me eight months. The editor said she'd offer me a contract "soon." Soon came and went, and I never heard anything.

Cheryl and I knew that our books were really good—we'd been telling each other that for years—and we knew from reading other writers' work that there were many, many other great books out there from unpublished writers that just sat in a drawer after making the rounds at traditional publishing houses. All the hours and all the tears spent on those manuscripts seemed like an incredible waste if no one ever got to read them and if the authors were never recognized for their work. In addition, we've always been avid readers and were often frustrated by the quality of the work being published in the traditional print market. So one day last summer we were e-mailing each other our frustrations when I told her about a recipe e-mail newsletter I received daily that had 40,000 subscribers. From there it was a short leap to "Hey, we can do that, too!"

E-Publishing Rides to the Rescue

It wasn't a spur-of-the-moment decision, though. We spent months shooting ideas back and forth in at least a million e-mail notes until we came up with our business model. We studied the design of other electronic publishing companies. The main shortcoming we saw in many Web sites was not enough detail about each individual title. Some just have long lists of book title names with hyperlinks that take the interested party to a short excerpt. We wanted to have perhaps a smaller list of titles, but make each title stand out—in essence, to make an *event* out of each title.

Our goal at XC Publishing is to build a company with consistently great titles. We want to create a following as a publisher, just as authors have followings of their own. One way we've come up with to do that is to offer many novel-related extras on our Web site—maps, screen savers, artwork, puzzles, articles, quizzes, and games. Another strategy is that we will offer our titles in all available formats—not just e-books but also (a little further down the line) print and audio. We currently offer our e-books in HTML for reading on Internet Explorer or Netscape, PDF for Adobe Acrobat and Glassbook, RTF for any word processing software, TXT (plain text) for many other software programs, and LIT for Microsoft Reader. In addition, we also run a free book review newsletter called **Word of Mouth**, http://here.at/wordofmouth, in which reviewers share their all-time favorite reads of all genres and a little about themselves so that our readers can decide whether they share the reviewers' tastes. Although the focus of Word of Mouth isn't exclusively on e-books, we do include them frequently.

Cheryl and I are both fantasy authors who are releasing our own fiction as well as that of others, but one of the advantages of the new e-publishing industry is that we are able to offer titles that transcend the traditional genres of speculative fiction, romance, mystery, and so on, which many traditional publishers have shied away from because the marketing departments didn't know how to classify them. Genre limitations are not our concern; publishing great stories that are well written is.

To date, we've established our company Web site, released several original titles, and have a growing queue of original titles slated for release. We've also established arrangements for the distribution of several titles by independent authors via our Web site.

The challenges we've faced to get to this point are many. My partner has had to learn how to design, build, and maintain a Web site, produce cover art, and set up a system for evaluating manuscripts from authors and for editing the manuscripts we accept, among many other things. The majority of my time has been spent both learning about the electronic publishing business and applying what I've learned. It is necessary to know what's being offered currently in the marketplace, what changes are occurring, where to find readers, how to write news releases and distribute them, how to format and establish our titles on our own Web site as well as other online bookstores, how to build our Web site traffic, how to fulfill orders, and so on.

Rules to Live By

Growing a business such as this is an organic process. There are no hard-and-fast rules, except for these three:

- Be organized.
- Be flexible.
- Communicate with one another.

I've listed organization first because it is the most important quality to cultivate. The wealth of information on the Internet is so staggering that it's absolutely essential to set up ways to manage it. It's possible to waste months online and not accomplish anything. Daily goals and plans that relate to bigger goals are a must-have.

Flexibility is important because this industry changes on what frequently seems like a daily basis. Being open to new ideas and opportunities is essential to reap the benefits of these changes.

Communication is also integral to success. We've set up systems to facilitate this. For instance, every Monday I send Cheryl a report on what I'm working on, what I need help with, and what I think we should do, and every Thursday Cheryl responds with the same items from her perspective. In this way we create a running dialogue about issues that need resolution.

Although most business books I consulted in the process of starting XC Publishing warned against partnerships because of the potential for discord, I couldn't be happier in my partnership with Cheryl. Cheryl and I are a perfect match. Whatever skills I lack, Cheryl has, and vice versa. Sorting out our responsibilities, as noted earlier, has made our partnership flow smoothly. We know each other well and even though she lives in the Pacific Northwest and I'm in Southern California we communicate effectively through e-mail (one of the benefits when both partners are writers). We've committed to working through our disagreements if and when they arise instead of letting them fester. Honestly, though, we're on the same page in so many instances that I can't think of any issue we've faced that we had completely different viewpoints on.

We believe that electronic publishing is the best chance many writers have to gain readers for their work and earn money from it as well. However, it's not for everyone. Electronic publishing is still in its infancy, so electronically published authors should expect to spend a fair amount of time promoting their work. It takes effort, absolutely. However, the field is growing daily. Why not find out if it's the option for you?

Perspectives of an Author-Founded Publishing Company

W. L. Warner
GLB Publishers
http://www.glbpubs.com/

My partners and I launched our self-publishing venture, GLB Publishers, a decade ago because there seemed no other publisher interested in the work I had in mind. The step was made possible by the early forms of desktop publishing, and predominantly by the laser printer. Our first books were done by offset printing from camera-ready pages that used 300 dpi laser printer output, which now looks rather rough but seemed entirely adequate then. Our covers were mechanical paste-ups. When others of like persuasion saw what we were doing, they wanted us to do it for them, too, and this was the beginning of a cooperative publishing venture that has continued relatively unchanged since 1990. We filled a gap, as most new businesses do; we were publishing gay and lesbian fiction, nonfiction, and poetry that most mainstream publishers would not touch. And we were the only ones publishing bisexual explicit fiction. We still pay 25 percent royalties for print books as a cooperative. The most important change in activities has been brought about by involvement in the Internet and adoption of e-books as a major branch of operations.

We have approached e-books in much the same way we deal with print books. At all times, publishing is a joint venture for the author and GLB. Our cooperative print books are *ours*, the author a partner in the publishing effort, and the situation is similar with e-books. Again we are filling a niche. For e-books we pay 50 percent royalties. We are always cognizant of the gay and bisexual men and women who are many miles away from a bookstore carrying

Figure 12.3: GLB Publishers serves a niche market with a number of books.

gay, lesbian, and bisexual titles and who need our books. The Internet has brought our books within reach of their living rooms and dens and offices, throughout the United States but also in foreign countries.

Formats Aplenty

To enhance the communication we produce all e-books in a variety of formats: eight different ones for fiction and nonfiction. With poetry and chapbooks we recommend sticking to PDF or special HTML because formatting of poetry is more important there and may be difficult to preserve otherwise. The workhorse for most of these forms is WordPerfect 9, which will produce Rich Text Format, Text, XML, HTML, Word, and WordPerfect files easily. At this point there are free-for-download programs for converting work for many of the reader devices, and a few organizations are gearing up for conversion to OEB (Open eBook) format as well as other forms as a service to e-publishers. If the Word and WordPerfect files are done in Times New Roman or some other universally available font, those files transfer quite well—and preserve their appearance without further tweaking if the recipient has those programs. Of course, those fonts are almost never used for serious print publishing and professional designers rightly regard them as dull—but when ease of production is critical, it's still a good idea to use what works for everyone.

For further information on some of these formats, the **Glassbook** system (associated with Adobe) is at http://www.glassbook.com/ and the file for converting Word text to the **Microsoft Reader** format is at http://www.overdrive.com/readerworks/. We had some inconsistent results with the Microsoft Reader conversion of large files (a 128,000-word novel just wouldn't convert, while smaller files seemed okay), and we finally had to give up on that format for the long book as Microsoft never got around to answering our service requests. The situation for the Rocket eBook is fluid, I think; two new models of the devices were recently released and their compatibility with older models has been questioned. We originally downloaded the file for converting HTML files to .rb from http://www.nuvomedia.com/, and this worked okay, but the current status is uncertain.

What's Up With Rocket?—*The situation really is fluid here. As we pointed out in Chapter 4, "The Production Process," the new owners haven't released conversion software for the successor to the Rocket eBook reader–see the note titled "More About RCA" in that chapter. In Chapter 7, "Assembling Your E-Publishing Venture," you'll find contact information for services that can still convert text to .rb format.*

The Print On Demand production of e-books is becoming more popular by the day, it seems. These books are produced from scratch and shipped to the customer supposedly within 48 hours of receipt of the order. As with many other approaches to publishing, the requirement for the publisher is to become proficient with Adobe Acrobat and the PDF file format for both text and covers, usually for the Docutech machine. We have found that producing text with margins appropriate for this application are not as easy as expected and we do not have easy answers to some setup questions as yet. The two main players in POD are the **Lightning Source** division of Ingram at http://www.lightningsource.com/, and the **Replica Books** division of Baker & Taylor at http://www.replicabooks.com/. The manufacturing costs of a POD book are several times that of a copy in even a modest print run.

We have some reassuring contacts with our e-readers from time to time. When one lady didn't know which format she should order, we inquired about the programs she had and sent one that she could work with successfully. In another case (in Scotland or Singapore or some such place), customers reported that they had, over a period of time, downloaded all the works of one of our writers, had used 3-hole punched paper for printing out the PDF files, and were binding them in volumes, using the cover art that we supplied. Of course that is what we hoped would be done.

Small Is Beautiful

In e-book publishing there is also a spirit of pioneering in a nascent industry. Almost daily the differences between the large e-publisher interested only in the bottom line (it seems) and the small entrepreneur—interested in satisfying a community's needs—become further defined. The advantages of the small publisher are obvious in many ways in e-publishing. Through the Internet, the publisher can deal more directly with the reading customer, an advantage never imagined or sought by mainstream publishers. The large publisher tends to think of sales as the function of a special division or of an outside agency, a third party who is expecting a share of the purchase price. For the small publisher, especially the e-publisher, the hat rests on fewer heads.

Of course, relationships with authors are also more direct in the small organization, and devoted e-authors are a somewhat different animal from the traditional print author. The expectations of many authors have (realistically) decreased recently, it seems. The potential for popular exposure of e-books is vast and worldwide, but rarely is more than a tiny fraction of that achieved. And now with Print On Demand (POD) as an e-book choice, the two worlds of print and download can coalesce to a larger extent. The work involved for the small e-publisher in preparing a POD edition is essentially the same as for the regular print version, so to offer a large assortment of download formats plus a POD edition requires considerable effort. The cost of most of this is not passed on to the author, and so we are all gambling on a good sales pay-off.

There have been some systemic problems associated with this developing industry of downloadable e-books that involve the entire print-publishing segment as well. The question of ISBNs is probably the most irritating for many of us. While we all may subscribe to the need for identifying books with a unique code for archival purposes as well as sales simplification, questions arise when the same book is presented in 8 or 9 or 10 or 20 formats, generically divided into downloads, print (POD), CD-ROMs, floppy disks, and so on. In the print world, the same book presented in both casebound and paperback editions is assigned an ISBN for each edition, but many of us believe that it is ridiculous to carry that over into the huge variety of presentations employed in e-books. This was complicated by the unexpected rise in the cost of blocks of ISBNs from Bowker, the supplier of the numbers for the United States. At this point I am not aware of a uniform number-handling system for e-books accepted throughout the industry.

We have taken the position that the "senior" edition (which is the POD edition if there is one, or the PDF edition for downloads only) is assigned the ISBN, and the other "junior" editions are considered subsets. That may change.

Discussions are under way with various groups, and the Association of American Publishers is active in this regard, exploring other systems that may be more practical for the burgeoning world of electronic publication. We try to keep the interested groups aware of developments through our e-mail discussion list, ind-e-pubs@egroups.com, which includes about 120 e-publishers and others particularly interested in e-publishing, and I believe our voices are being heard.

This is certainly not a standard success story of a small company that made it, because we are still struggling—just struggling in new ways to match new challenges. I sometimes think that most publishing success is more persistence than perspicacity, but I haven't had to dig down into personal savings lately to meet a royalty deadline. Come visit us anytime at the **GLB Publishers** site, http://www.glbpubs.com/.

The Essence of E-Publishing

Mary Westheimer
CEO, BookZone, Inc.
http://www.bookzone.com/

If anyone had told me ten years ago that I'd be in the thick of the electronic side of publishing, I would have shaken my head and laughed incredulously. In fact, just six years ago when we founded BookZone, I literally looked away when someone brought up the Internet at a writers' luncheon. As a book packager and journalist, I just didn't need anything else on my computer, on my desk, or especially on my to-do list. Today, I'm CEO of BookZone, the Net's largest publishing community, which serves 3,600 publishing professionals with Web hosting, design, development, and Internet promotion. That means, of course, that we're now as involved with e-publishing as almost anyone could possibly be.

How does someone go from skeptic to disciple? For me, the answer is all about value. The first time I saw the World Wide Web—which was just a year old when we started BookZone—I felt a shiver go up my arm. That's what I call "The Chill," and it's always proven to be an indicator of something extraordinary.

At the time, I wondered if we were behind the curve. After all, this Internet thing was worldwide and there was already one big book site, Charlie Stack's Book Stacks Unlimited, as well as a couple of bookstore sites such as Moe's Bookshop. The more I saw and learned, however, the more I realized that this medium would change business, change the world, and, with it, change all of our lives immeasurably. Now I realize that, despite the remarkable strides in the last six years, the Net is nowhere close to fulfilling its potential and taking its intrinsic place in our lives.

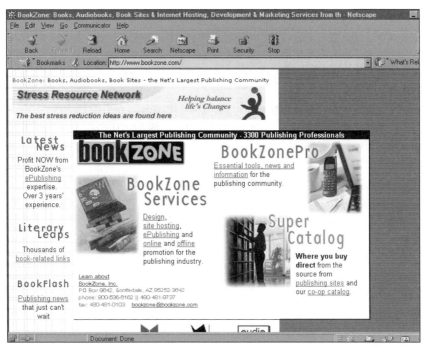

Figure 12.4: BookZone is a highly visible site with its own publications as well as services for other e-publishers.

What I saw initially, though, was a welcome answer to an ongoing challenge in the businesses of the publishers and authors I knew from my involvement with the Arizona Authors' Association and the Arizona Book Publishing Association, who were having trouble getting into distribution channels. Now they had a direct line to their customers! The ability to sell and to reach buyers directly would have a huge impact on these authors and publishers as well as their buyers. After all, if you can interact directly with your customers, they can (and will) tell you what they want, and you can get it to them cost efficiently. This is especially important because existing clients are your best prospects and, if you're publishing in a specific niche (say, gardening, business, self-help, or philosophy), previous buyers are likely to want your new books, too.

"I Want It and I Want It Now"

The immediacy of the Internet clearly offered yet another benefit. If someone wanted information and they wanted it now, what better way to deliver it than electronically? The possibilities became even more focused in 1995, BookZone's second year online. One day, we got a call from a fellow who wrote elegies. He wanted to know if we had some way to deliver these sensitive materials on demand. "When someone dies, most of us are emotionally distraught, so we put off writing a tribute," he reasoned. "Suddenly, it's the night before the funeral, and we could use some help." He figured that people would be more than willing to pay for sample elegies that could be readily adapted. A lightbulb went on in my head.

As the Internet grew and more and more publishers began creating their own sites, it became increasingly obvious that publishers don't sell books. They sell *information*. From that perspective, the entire landscape changes.

That means the information that publishers package by printing on paper and binding with glue needn't be limited to that medium. Just as material can be offered as audiobooks and videotapes, it could be delivered in other alternative media. Could just parts of that information be sold as reports? Could portions be delivered as a printed newsletter? An e-zine, or e-mail newsletter? How else could technology improve delivery and value?

At that time, the ways to present information online were limited. Adobe's PDF, or Portable Document Format, provided consistency of presentation between the printed and electronic versions, but it required visitors to use the Adobe Reader. The reader was free, but even so it meant installing yet another piece of software and using it outside the Net to view the material, a hurdle that impeded many visitors. Even if it only added a little work, any work might put off someone who didn't want to take extra time to install and learn a program. (By the way, the Adobe Reader has come a long way since then. It's no longer a stand-alone and specialized program that each user has to hunt up and learn; instead, it's integrated as a seamless experience within the browsers, and nearly 200 million copies are in use. The Adobe format is now a known quantity in a field brimming with newcomers. And it's still free!)

Another obvious choice was HTML itself, the format used to create Web sites. That's what we used initially to deliver the reports of self-publishing guru Dan Poynter on his **Para Publishing** site, http://www.parapublishing.com/, in early 1999. We created a payment interface that required customers to pay before they got a look at the document (the document didn't even exist until payment was made to prevent anyone from putting in a link to the reports themselves), then delivered the material on a Web page. The only downside for Dan was that, if someone really wanted to copy the material, it was as easy as highlighting the code that created the page. Today, we've converted all of Dan's reports to Adobe PDF, using the same payment interface and security measures to make the documents unobtainable without payment. The site has real-time credit card processing, too, so that Para Publishing employees don't need to reenter card information.

Breaking It Down: Granular E-Publishing

In 1998, BookZone had tackled another project that spotlighted the importance of seeing the product as information rather than its package (a book). One of our clients, the Audio Publishers Association (APA), had established a strategic alliance with R.R. Bowker, which publishes *Books In Print* and its companion volume for audiobooks, *Words On Cassette*. Working with APA and Bowker, BookZone designed what is now sometimes called a "granular e-publishing" system. The term *granular* sounds mysterious and, well, rather grand, until you realize just how appropriate it is. It simply means breaking down the whole into parts that can be sold separately. In this case, and as with many directories and reference works, it makes far more sense to allow users to purchase the material incrementally.

Think for a moment how you use such a book. Let's say you want to find out what Stephen King books are available in audio format, or what other books your favorite voice talent has available. You don't need the whole book, you just need *the specific entries that provide that specific information*. So, based on our clients' input, we set up a system that permits people to buy a subscription, a single search, or a set of ten searches of the entire text of the book. Those publishers who are APA members have special icons beside their names to communicate their affiliation, and visitors can click through to their Web sites. APA members also get a discount on subscriptions and searches.

To me, this is the ultimate way to sell information: Give people just what they want at a lower price than the entire collection of information (what is found in the printed form) but at a higher price per bit of information than that information would cost as a subset of the whole. In other words, although buyers are proportionately paying slightly more for the information they want, they're shelling out far less cash overall because they're not buying information they don't want. The customer has saved money, and the publisher will make more in the long run. And this doesn't even address the fact that the book (in this case actually a set of volumes) is far more valuable when it is more easily searchable by computer than it is in printed form.

We've created other granular e-publishing projects since then, including one that is used by libraries. Our proprietary payment, delivery, and reporting system, which can be placed on a customer's own Web site, has since been named and marketed as the BookZone EDGE. It's used by publishers, distributors, and others to sell full-length books as well as special reports, booklets, and other information. We offer single-title listings, too, for those publishers and authors who don't want or need the more elaborate, customizable approach. Looking back while looking forward, it's projects like enabling 58 online universities to offer their documents to students electronically that confirm for me the value of offering information to people the way they want it, when they want it.

The Year of E-Publishing

Who woulda thunk that the entire book publishing industry would go bonkers over e-publishing? Not many people, until precisely that happened in 2000. It was almost as if the stars aligned in just such a way as to illuminate what people saw for the future. No more printing! No more warehousing! No more books damaged in shipping! Well, they didn't quite make it, though all those things may happen someday—but it was amazing to watch the near mania with which publishers, authors, and distributors rushed to convert everything into electronic format. Although there may be some disappointed people out there when the dust settles, the industry's willingness to embrace change is impressive.

What happened to effect such change? I believe a few things conspired to bring about the frenzy. First, with the arrival of Adobe's PDF Merchant system, material can be encrypted (also known as digital rights management) and thus protected from being passed around by attaching it to an e-mail note or putting it on a disk and sharing it with friends. With the apparent assault on the sanctity of intellectual property rights by sites like Napster and MP3.com, this answered an understandable concern of publishers. Second, enough people are now sufficiently adept on computers to suggest there may be a receptive audience out there. Third, electronic readers are becoming an accepted concept. Finally, though, was the acceptance of Stephen King's *Riding the Bullet* electronic novella. When citing the last as a success story, most people forget that many of the 400,000 copies downloaded were purchased by e-tailers who then gave away copies, but the fact that 400,000 people even wanted to read them was encouragement in itself.

Will it be full steam ahead for all e-publishing now? Probably not. We still need a cost-effective handheld reader that makes sense for a critical mass of readers. We need consensus on format, something that will be undoubtedly affected by the arrival of Microsoft Reader. And the maturing of the generations that can't remember a time before computers will contribute to the obvious acceptance of a technology that seems penny-bright to many. Without a doubt, e-publishing is a viable concept that is here to stay, and I believe it will quickly prove to be to the benefit of us all.

You Can

Dan Newman
President, Say I Can, Inc.
Author and Speech Recognition Expert
http://www.sayican.com/

My company publishes the leading how-to books on speech recognition software—software that lets you talk to your computer instead of type. Our books are available in bookstores nationwide and are sold by mail order through our Web site and other online stores. We also publish a free e-mail newsletter to keep customers and interested site visitors up to date on the latest developments in this fast-changing field.

Why We Published Online

As a small company, we are always looking for innovative ways to attract attention and serve our customers better. I decided to make the bold move of offering our best-seller, *The Dragon NaturallySpeaking Guide,* for free on our site as an electronic book. Publishing the book electronically and for free made sense for a number of reasons.

Figure 12.5: Say I Can has a few publications in both print and free online versions, plus a number of products to serve a specific market—a classic example of a small e-publishing venture.

- We thought that we could gain publicity and increase traffic to our site by offering such a valuable resource for free. The *Guide* has sold over 10,000 in bookstores at $19.95. We put the entire text on our site for anyone to read.
- We expected that people who read the electronic book online would be more likely to buy the printed version. They did not have to purchase a product through the mail, sight unseen.
- We decided to display advertising banners along with the book to earn an additional revenue stream, beyond sales of the printed book.
- As the author of the book as well as the publisher, I was excited at the prospect of making the book available to the widest possible audience. By placing the book on the Web for free, we hoped that the book would reach more than just people who would buy the printed version. Everyone could benefit from the information we had created, even those who didn't or couldn't make a purchase.

How We Did It

The key criteria of deciding how to put the book up on the site were making sure that the banner advertisements would be consistently displayed (so that the book could earn revenue) and making it inconvenient for the reader to print the book from the site or download it to their computer. I also wanted to produce the online book as quickly and simply as possible. These goals conflicted somewhat. The best solution for both banner advertisement display and inconvenience to the user who wanted to print the book would probably be to display the book in HTML format, a separate Web page for each book page, with the banner advertisements at the top of the HTML page.

However, the book is in a Word 97 file and I did not want to recode the entire book into HTML. The book is well designed with many illustrations, type styles, and tables, and it would be tedious to put these into HTML format. Also, displaying the book in HTML would obscure the graphic design quality of the printed version, which is a selling point to potential purchasers. So we put the book up as an Adobe PDF file.

I used Adobe Acrobat to create separate PDF files for each chapter, plus additional files for the index and the table of contents. I could have put the entire 288-page book in one PDF file, but I felt that this would make it too easy for people to download the book and distribute it without authorization, depriving us of Web-site traffic and advertising revenue. With more than 20 separate files to cope with, downloading the book is still possible for a determined freeloader, but it is cumbersome.

Adobe Acrobat has built-in security that allows you to control the level of access to your document. I set the book chapters so that they cannot be printed or modified, and the text cannot be copied using the usual copy and paste commands. (I did allow printing for the table of contents and index sections.) This way users can read the book on the screen as much as they want, but it is still less convenient than having a paper copy.

For the Web page design I created two frames. The bottom frame contains the PDF file with the book, and the top frame, which is small and stretches across the top of the screen, contains three elements. In the center is a banner advertisement, on the right are links to each of the book chapters so that the user can easily navigate between them, and on the left are links to products and other areas of our speech recognition Web site, including a link to our free electronic newsletter. This top frame automatically reloads every 30 seconds, so that different advertisements are displayed as the user browses through the book.

I included a "gateway" page to the book, explaining that the free Adobe Acrobat reader was required, and asking people to click our banner ads to support our free publishing experiment. Later, we added a "Troubleshooting Tips" page after receiving daily e-mail from people who had trouble viewing the book. The most common problem was that their browser was set to automatically download the PDF file instead of display it.

We have not yet made a printable electronic copy of the book available for sale, due in part to security concerns. If we do decide to sell printable PDF downloads, we are considering using a product called PersonalPublisher to sell access-controlled PDF files (see **FileOpen Systems** at http://www.fileopen.com/). Once you purchase this product, which costs about $200, you can sell secure files without paying royalties, avoiding the onerous fees of up to 50 percent from content aggregation sites.

Advertising Provides Income

For our advertising banners, we use a service called **Advertising.com** (http://www.advertising.com/), which sells the banners and serves them to our site. Advertisers pay per click, and we receive a percentage of what the advertiser pays. Typically we earn about 16 cents each time one of our site visitors clicks a banner ad.

High credibility is a key part of our business. At first I was concerned that including advertising in a portion of our site might damage that perception. However, by using Advertising.com, we avoid both an actual conflict of interest and appearance of conflict of interest. If we sold and showed paid advertisements from speech software companies, it might create a perception of bias. However, Advertising.com advertisers do not know where their ads will show up, and the ads served to us run the gamut of products and services. In fact, having advertisements on our site actually increases our credibility. Advertisers include well-known names such as Dell Computer and the *New York Times,* and the banner ads are invariably well designed graphically, making our company seem bigger and more established than it would without the advertisements.

Achieving Results

After putting up the online book, we sought to spread the word about it through a news release and mentioning it in our electronic newsletter. The publicity was extremely successful. People like to tell other people about things they can get for free. We were mentioned in several popular e-mail newsletters with total subscribership of over 200,000 people. Also, we are now able to easily get listed in Web directories of speech recognition resources. Previously, we were "just another Internet store," so it was harder to get listed, but now our site contains an essential resource for speech recognition users. No other sites have a professional-quality, 288-page book on speech recognition available for free.

So far, displaying the book for free has not appeared to hurt our print book sales. The number of unique visitors to our site doubled in the few months after we put up the book, and the number of new daily subscribers to our free e-mail newsletter has increased by 10 times. Advertising revenue so far has been modest, comparable to the profit from selling a dozen print books per month, so I do not recommend advertising by itself as a revenue stream. On the whole, publishing our book for free has been a tremendous success for the business as well as a personally satisfying endeavor. It continues to give me great satisfaction knowing that I can share our created knowledge with the widest possible audience.

Six months after this experiment began, Advertising.com terminated our account. No one there would give us specific information about why our account was terminated, but I suspect it was because we are one of their smaller sites (we're not, for example, *U.S. News & World Report*). The lesson I learned is this: In the Internet Age don't count too heavily on a new revenue model, and don't expect business alliances to last long. We plan to replace the Advertising.com ads with advertisements for products we sell, such as microphones and recorders. I expect this new approach will be more profitable as well.

CHAPTER THIRTEEN

A Look at Trends

Y̲ou're pretty much ready to start your e-publishing venture—whether as an author, self-publisher, or full-fledged e-publisher. In this final chapter, we take a look at the trends that occur in the electronic publishing industry—past, present, and future.

How We Got Here

Although the e-book industry is young, hints of it appeared as long ago as the early 1970s, when Michael Hart launched Project Gutenberg and began putting public domain texts (such as classic novels) online. The original goal was to make such books available for anyone who had access to a computer. Back then, Michael Hart probably didn't predict that in 30 years nearly every household in America and many across the planet would have computers and would be able to read such texts. But he no doubt figured that by now people would be reading books online.

Not much happened in the e-book world until the early 1990s, when personal computers became powerful enough to put software documentation online in the form of online help and online manuals. Early versions of Microsoft Windows had an online help system that looked like a simple form of today's Web browsers. You could click an underlined word and it would take you to a new page; there were even occasional pictures.

Meanwhile, **Adobe** (http://www.adobe.com/) created Acrobat in the early 1990s, along with the popular PDF format, which we have discussed throughout this book. Acrobat was one of the first attempts to put books online that actually looked like printed pages of a book. As soon as CD-ROMs started becoming widespread in the mid 1990s, some software manufacturers decided to forgo printed manuals and simply put PDF versions of the manuals on their CD-ROMs.

As the 1990s went on, small companies began to realize that text could be transmitted over the Internet in a form called hypertext—essentially text combined with rudimentary formatting such as bold, italics, colors, and fonts. This concept grew into what we all know as the Web browser, using the *hypertext transfer protocol*, HTTP, which basically refers to a computer procedure (known as a *protocol*) for transferring hypertext over the Internet from one computer to another.

One such company created a product called Internet Explorer. This company was purchased early on by Microsoft, and we have all seen the product's descendant. Another—a research organization called the National Center for Supercomputing Applications, or **NCSA** (http://www.ncsa.uiuc.edu/)—created a browser called Mosaic. The people who built Mosaic left NCSA and started Netscape—another name everyone knows.

Around 1998 and 1999, people finally started realizing there was a technological place for e-books. Companies and individuals began formulating ways to put books online, using various types of encryption software in attempts to prevent copying. At the same time, several people involved in hardware began coming up with ideas for e-book devices.

Within the publishing industry, one major trend prior to 2001 was to ignore e-books altogether. The technology was too new and it was impossible to say just how much of the world would embrace it. Further, as we have discussed throughout this book, copy protection was a major concern of the larger publishers because of their desire to protect their intellectual property.

Fortunately for the e-book industry, a similar industry, e-music, moved a little faster and made mistakes that the e-book industry can learn from. The path was similar to that of the e-book industry: People wanted music on their computers, and they began coming up with ways to record music onto a computer and copy it between friends over the Internet. Companies began creating technologies to ensure that music could exist on a computer and not be copied. But that's where things got horribly messy. The people resisted the notion of copy protection in music and made it clear they would not tolerate such a thing. So various groups got together and created the MP3 format, which is a way of storing CD-quality music on a computer. With high-speed Internet connections becoming common, people could quickly and easily share music. Underground organizations began to form whereby people were illegally copying copyrighted music. The recording industry got upset and began filing lawsuits, and court battles were fought.

In the end, nobody won. Whereas people could previously download music quite easily, they no longer could because the companies providing such services were under fire, entangled in lawsuits. And if people were willing to pay a buck or so per song, they really couldn't, because there wasn't a standard that both the recording industries and the consumers could agree on and live with. As of early 2001, it's still a mess.

Today's Issues in E-Publishing

The e-book industry has not yet fallen into the music industry's morass. But it has its own messes to deal with, not the least of which is the lack of standards for e-book file formats. Another is the ongoing skepticism about the idea of reading books online, whether on a desktop computer, a handheld device, or any size in between. These and other issues are discussed briefly in the next few pages.

Where Are the Standards?

Each e-book reader has its own file format, with little cross-pollination between packages. The reader devices, too, are generally proprietary. It's a big deal to see some of them supporting HTML files in addition to their own special formats. Honestly, this is along the lines of absurd—fueled largely by the greed and ambition of the reader manufacturers and software developers. Each of these companies wants market dominance, and supporting other companies' software is just not part of the dominance equation. Can anyone imagine Microsoft Reader supporting PDF files? Unfortunately, it seems a bit far-fetched for the likes of Microsoft. Meanwhile, book publishers, those who actually create and deliver the content that makes these reader devices valuable, are not interested in this competition. They simply want flexibility and standardization so as to stop creating six or eight different versions every e-book.

Six or eight different versions—that's if you want to cover all the bases. But two or three leading file formats are not a huge problem. After all, people want to have choice. It's usually not a good thing when one company dominates and standardizes the market. The idea is to settle on a few top file formats (Microsoft Reader, Adobe Acrobat, and Rocket Edition are the first that come to mind) and then see every reader device and all reader software supports all the formats. This way, customers can download an e-book using any of the main file formats and read it on the same device.

In the future, some of this standardization seems likely. When the market demands something, it's usually bound to happen—regardless of the pressure in the opposite direction. Microsoft Reader will have to support other file types, just as Microsoft Word supports WordPerfect files. It's only a matter of time.

To Protect or Not to Protect

Throughout this book we've said a great deal about the various blunders in the music industry, and how it has always been all or nothing—music can either be freely copied, or it's far too tightly restricted—resulting in at least somebody getting angry or walked all over. But what can you expect to see in the copy protection world of e-books?

For one, consumers made it clear in the music debacle that they will not tolerate overly restrictive copy protection. With books, they've hinted that they'll be a little more accepting, probably because while a song might be as little as three minutes of entertainment, an entire book can be hundreds of pages and take hours upon hours to read. Perhaps consumers feel they're getting more for their money. Still, consumers have also made it clear that if they own multiple devices they want to be able to read a single book on all their computers, and not have to pay for multiple copies. As copy protection advances, this capability will undoubtedly emerge.

Publishers, on the other hand, don't like the idea of their books being distributed without any sort of copy protection. While many in the industry firmly believe in the shareware model (where e-books are free and you pay for what you read as a matter of good conscience), the publishers so far aren't standing for it. Their books are their merchandise, and they refuse to risk the lost revenue. They want copy protection, even if it goes against the whole "everything is free" Internet mind-set.

When it comes to the standardization of e-book file formats, software companies and hardware manufacturers are often shortsighted. When it comes to e-book copy protection (digital rights management, or DRM), publishers are also being shortsighted, or at least inflexible and fearful. Most publishers would not dream of releasing an e-book without document protection—despite the fact that customers continually vote against it. Authors tend to be mixed on the issue. Some believe that any barrier that hinders the customer from purchasing the book is not a good idea—especially since e-books face an uphill struggle for acceptance as it is. Other authors feel, as publishers do, that their work should not be copied without payment and don't want to give customers any opportunities to do so.

Many issues and considerations surround the DRM debate for e-books. One thing we'd like to suggest is that it's not a given that DRM and document copy protection are a must for e-books. Some publishers use superdistribution methods and shareware standards for getting their books into as many hands as possible. They believe that the more hands that touch their e-books, the more pockets there are to reach into—and the more money is likely to get paid. It's not a crazy idea at all. When you look at the success of the Linux operating system, which is a totally free, open-source program, it's almost baffling how many people are willing to pay for it and how many companies have made millions selling free software.

Most likely, the years to come will not see a complete resolution of this issue on one side or the other. Things may well split down the middle, with some companies going free-book and others insisting on cash up front. Each method of distribution requires some special marketing expertise and dedication to the chosen paradigm. Meanwhile, copy protection on e-books will probably stay around for a good while. As technology advances, new copy protection methods that are consumer-friendly but do not deprive the publishers of their valuable revenue will come on the market.

Skepticism Remains

People are not yet convinced that e-books will ever really reach computer screens en masse, rendering paper-and-ink a thing of the past—or at least diminish the ways in which paper books are used, as television did with radio. But already, millions upon millions of people stay up past midnight staring at computer screens and reading Web pages, e-mail, and chat room messages. Resistance to onscreen reading is breaking down. And the screens are getting easier to deal with—it's likely that high-speed, low-cost, lightweight, easily readable e-book devices that actually *can* be used at the beach or in the bathtub will be on the market at reasonable prices. Imagine a single sheet of flexible plastic about the thickness of a credit card and the size of a paperback book. It has an antenna that picks up the Internet via satellite, from which you can download just about any book imaginable. You can use it at the pool because it's water resistant and the screen looks just like paper (any color of paper you choose). That could remove some of the skepticism.

Sure, lots of people love the feel, the smell, and the beauty of the printed book. Lots of people collect antiques for the same reason. It's not entirely parallel, though. You can sit on an antique chair just as you would on a modern one, but you can't use an antique sewing machine or charcoal-heated flatiron the same way you'd use a modern version—it takes different skills, and there are some things the antiques simply won't do for you. E-books are more like tools than like furniture. Despite the skepticism, e-books and e-book reading devices will dominate our reading experiences at some point in the future. It's not a matter of whether this will happen or not, it's a matter of when.

So as far as today goes, skepticism is not really the problem. The problem is scarce e-books, clumsy and expensive reading devices, confused e-book format standards, and worry about revenue loss due to unauthorized copies. Chances are, these issues will all be resolved as the technology improves, eventually getting to the point where people are no longer buying paper books.

E-Book Numbering System

Speaking of standards, the International Standard Book Number system was not made with e-books in mind. One of the problems that e-publishers face is the need to use a separate ISBN for each format and each edition of an e-book. For those publishers who release their books in as many formats as possible, that can get to be expensive and difficult to manage. E-publishers are screaming for a new standard numbering system to account for their special needs. Are they being heard? Who knows. But one thing is sure, if the problem gets out of hand, there will be a change—either outside the ISBN system or within it.

Electronic Rights

Another problem in today's e-book industry is the way publishers deal with electronic rights. Most e-publishers understand the issues involved with electronic rights and the differences between the various types of e-rights. Many e-publishers purchase only the e-book rights to a work, leaving other electronic rights available to others. But publishers coming from the traditional print world have little understanding of, and even less flexibility with, electronic rights. Some publishers who have electronic rights to their books account for e-book sales as they do normal book sales—paying authors normal royalties. They claim that an e-book sale is the same as any other book sale and therefore demands the same royalty as the printed book. Other publishers put e-book sales under subsidiary sales and pay authors a split of net receipts.

You can expect to see legal battles over this issue. Publishers who try to take advantage of their old contract language probably have some lawyers' fees ahead of them. It's critical that all publishers, agents, and authors learn to deal with the details of electronic rights—and not lump everything together into one simple paragraph in their contracts. That just will not do any longer.

Looking to the Future

Moving further into the new millennium, technology and culture will certainly continue to change and evolve. Technology will adapt itself to the needs of the people—or perhaps more correctly to the demands of the market. Technology will most likely make fewer demands on how people work—while people will have more demands on how technology works for them. This is the nature of an evolving industry. Here we explore a few ideas and outlooks on the future in the e-publishing industry.

E-Books in the Classroom

Many e-book publishers and e-book software houses are negotiating deals with schools, from elementary schools through universities, both public and private, to get e-books into classrooms. Most students are keen on e-books, for several reasons:

- They love technology.
- They grew up around technology and computer screens and it's natural to them.
- They don't want to lug around backpacks filled with books.
- They want to be able to get their books quickly and easily.

People who are a bit older (say, over 30) may have trouble adjusting to the idea of reading a book for hours on end while staring at a computer screen. Yet younger people, who were born after the advent of the PC in the early 1980s (and who are now entering college) have been around computers virtually all their lives and most are perfectly comfortable staring at computer screens.

Those over 30 may scoff at the idea, but think back to the point we made earlier about Web surfing and midnight e-mail. Onscreen reading is already here. And many people use computers on the job so much that their desks are arranged with the computer as the central work point, with everything else around that, in the same way that the average living room is arranged with the television as the primary focal point.

Children won't resist the technology, and it's going to happen. Computers are already in the classroom; many universities and colleges require their students to purchase laptop computers. The next natural step is to put the textbooks online.

But it's more than just putting text and pictures online and forcing young people to adjust. There are, of course, many benefits to having e-books in the classroom. Consider these possibilities:

- E-books could contain interactive multimedia lessons, such as a chemistry e-book showing a rotating molecule or a music e-book playing the sounds of different instruments.
- E-books let students highlight text and make notes—and remove the highlights and notes—without destroying the e-book.
- Teachers could issue special e-books where students' notes are disabled during test taking, allowing for open-book exams where the students are not allowed to bring notes to the exam.
- Teachers could piece together books and articles into a single course packet for the students to download.

The list goes on and on, and these aren't just blind predictions. Companies that make e-books are already planning and implementing such things. E-books are coming to the classroom, and it's likely they'll play a major role there before they make serious inroads in the mass market. Already several online learning companies are putting software into classrooms (such as **Pearson Interactive** at http://www.pearson-publishing.com/interactive.htm); it's only a matter of time before e-books follow suit.

Technology Convergence

The ultimate goal among many computer researchers is to bring different technologies together. When it comes down to it, much of what people do on the computer these days is related: Read Web pages on the Internet; type and read e-mail; use organizing software to keep life in order and help remember dates, phone numbers, and addresses. Online learning is starting to take off, with interactive training materials. And of course, e-books are growing more readily available.

Ultimately, many people want to bring all these technologies together. One question the e-book device manufacturers repeatedly get is: "Does your device include address book and calendar software?" to which most of them (except the eBookMan from **Franklin Electronic Publishers**, http://www.franklin.com/) have to respond, "No." In other words, a business traveler using today's technology has to haul a laptop computer and a Palm Pilot or Pocket PC for calendar and contact info, and now an e-book device for books and newspapers.

Why can't it all be in one computer? There's no technical reason it can't be, and the manufacturers are realizing this. Hopefully the early part of the first decade of the 2000s will see device convergence.

But what about software convergence? Right now even a computer that can deal with all three forms of information has a separate Web browser, a separate calendar, and separate e-book software.

This aspect is a little trickier. In the early days of e-book software, the planners wanted to use Web browsers for e-books—it seemed only logical. They even talked about using the browser's forward and back buttons to navigate through the book. But it turns out that's a problem—and easy to spot, if you think about it: The browser's forward button never lights up until you hit the back button so there's actually a Web page available to move forward to. The Web page cannot program the browser's forward button. The forward button doesn't work for e-books, no matter how much e-book creators might wish they could somehow program the button to allow the user to page through the entire e-book.

Nevertheless, as you have seen in this book, many people have indeed put e-books into Web browsers with varying degrees of success. But some people still like the idea of a single printed page, as opposed to a long page with scrollbars on the right. The usability paradigm between a Web page and a book page is, therefore, quite different. Therefore, today, the options are either to run a Java applet in the Web browser that serves as an e-book reader, or to just put links on a page for navigating and view the e-book as a set of Web pages. Both work, but it's still quite different from, say, Microsoft Reader or Glassbook Reader in the way those packages mimic an actual book with printed pages.

Hopefully within the next few years browsers will be built to handle the e-book paradigm. That's all it will take. Of course, such browsers will also have to deal with issues of copy protection, but you can expect that the browser manufactures will think of that, too.

Self-Publishing Trends

In the past, people who self-published their books were often treated as if nobody would publish their books because they just weren't good enough to warrant paper and ink. Although that wasn't necessarily the case (check out M. J. Rose's inspirational story in Chapter 12, "Personal Success Stories"), it didn't help that many self-published authors were running on a tiny budget, so that the quality of the books sometimes slipped, with books that were clearly photocopies, or filled with typos. Enough of these low-budget self-published books got around to leave a lasting and negative impression on the whole idea of self-publishing.

Today, with e-books, it is far easier to self-publish without sacrificing quality. While self-published e-book authors still need to invest in good editing and layout, the final product can look as good as the e-books put out by the big publishers. This is a major benefit for self-publishers, because first impressions are so important.

Further, with so many outlets that let self-published e-book authors get their works into the hands of consumers, such small-time publishers now present some serious competition for the big-name publishers. So as you can probably imagine, the big publishers are beginning to bite back. They are dumping their own e-books onto the market, and they are sending out press releases and marketing material claiming that they are still the leaders of the market, and that self-publishing is still for the works that are not very good.

When Stephen King decided to self-publish his e-novel *The Plant*, he was faced with such criticism, even though he's a huge name. But in this case, he was a self-published e-book author selling his book through his Web site (with the help of Amazon.com). The publishers were quick to criticize, claiming that the experiment would fail, and that he would still need them.

In the eyes of some people, King's experiment more-or-less failed. He suspended the work, with a promise to return to it in a year or so. But he did leave his mark, and he did make a name for e-books, whether self-published or not. And that's not to say self-publishing cannot work. In Chapter 12 you saw how a few entrepreneurs have made it work.

Because e-book self-publishing is so accessible to everyone, there are bound to be some really bad works out there, but there've already been some great ones as well. The industry will certainly continue to grow, and more and more people will get in on it. The fact that the big publishers are taking a stand and criticizing it shows that they have taken note of it and are a little bit frightened, especially when the really big-name authors start self-publishing their own books, bypassing the big publishers. Naturally, the big publishers see this as a threat to their income (it's all about profit, remember!) and they are going to bite back.

But that shouldn't stop anyone. The self-publishing world of e-books is alive and well and off to a good start, and our humble opinion is that it's only going to get better. Plenty of disgruntled authors out there have had it with the big publishers and are ready to publish on their own. So if you're planning to self-publish, don't be swayed by what *they* tell you; instead, barge forward with your plans.

Big Publishers and E-books

So self-publishing will grow in the world of e-books, but does that mean the end of the big publishers? Certainly some people out there hope so. But the truth is, the big publishers are waking up to the e-book trends and are getting in on the game themselves. They started out a little slowly, carefully testing the waters before diving in. But soon they'll all be in completely, and they are almost guaranteed not to drown—unless their printed book business is drowning as well.

It's no surprise that the big publishers started out slowly. Many of them are over a hundred years old, with correspondingly conservative business practices. They didn't last so long by snatching up the latest technologies. E-book technology is no different. These companies weren't about to invest millions of dollars in an e-book campaign if they thought there was any chance it would fail. But now that they're seeing that it's not failing, they are beginning to invest the big bucks.

Will they survive? Most likely. For every author who hates big publishers, there's at least one who likes the big publishers, respecting the work they do and the services they provide to the authors. The big publishers will never run out of good authors and good work.

Self-Publishers and Big Publishers Side by Side

To most of industry-watchers, it's clear that the big publishers will not go away; they will succeed just fine in the e-book industry, while the self-publishers will also thrive. This is evident if you compare the publishing industry to the software industry. Computers make it possible for one person to build a software package that competes with those put out by the software giants, and so far both have thrived quite well. The same is likely to be true with e-books.

There are, of course, a few people in the industry who predict the demise of the big publishing companies, as authors start to wake up to 50 percent or 75 percent or even 100 percent royalties and begin turning their backs on the big publishers and their 8 percent royalties. But it would be hard to find an analyst who would agree with such a prediction.

It's our feeling that both will thrive, and self-published authors will find a home with niche publishing, as they always have. But with e-books, they will have a much better chance of survival.

E-Publishers

In this appendix, we've provided a comprehensive list of e-publishers and their Web site URLs, where you can find out more about them and, if desired, contact them about your books. The publishers are listed by category, so some publishers appear in several categories. This information is constantly changing, so we also recommend that you check our **E-Publishing Opportunities** site at http://www.myplanet.net/vanburen/ for more current information. Updates will also be posted on the book's companion site at http://TopFloor.com/pr/ebook/ Other online e-publisher listings are presented in Appendix B, "Resources."

Fiction

1st Electric Works
http://www.electricpublishing.com/

Awe-Struck E-Books
http://www.awe-struck.net/

Bell Press
http://www.bell.dk/press/eng/

BiblioBytes
http://www.bb.com/

Booklocker.com
http://www.booklocker.com/

Bookmice
http://www.bookmice.com/

Books OnScreen
http://www.booksonscreen.com/

Boson Books
http://www.cmonlin.com/boson/

Cascade Mountain Publishing
http://www.cascadepublishing.com/

Crossroads Publishing
http://www.crossroadspub.com/

Cybernet Books
http://www.cybernetbooks.com/

Denlinger's Publishers
http://www.thebookden.com/publish.html

DiskUs Publishing
http://www.diskuspublishing.com/

DLSIJ Press
http://www.dlsijpress.com/

Domhan Book
http://www.domhanbooks.com/

Dreamcatcher On-Line Books
http://www.cia-g.com/~jwaldie/

ebooksonthe.net
http://www.ebooksonthe.net/

E-Dition
http://www.e-dition.net/

Electron Press
http://www.electronpress.com/

E-Pulp
http://www.e-pulp.com/

The Fiction Works
http://www.fictionworks.com/

Gemini Books
http://www.lisawrites.com/gem-pub.html

GLB Publishers (Gay and Lesbian themes)
http://www.glbpubs.com/

Hard Shell Word Factory
http://www.hardshell.com/

HyperBooks
http://www.hyperbooks.com/

Indigo Publishing
http://www.wordmuseum.com/indigo/

Mystic-Ink Publishing
http://www.mystic-ink.com/publishing/

New Concepts Publishing
http://www.newconceptspublishing.com/

Online Originals
http://www.onlineoriginals.com/

PocketPCpress
http://www.pocketpcpress.com/

Publish America
http://www.PublishAmerica.com/

Pulsar Books
http://www.pulsarbooks.com/

Random House
http://www.atrandom.com/

Sansip
http://www.sansip.com/

The Reading Edge
http://www.thereadingedge.com/

Wordbeams
http://www.wordbeams.com/

Zeus Publications Australia
http://www.zeus-publications.com/

Humor

1st Electric Works
http://www.electricpublishing.com/

Antelope Publishing
http://www.teleport.com/~writers/books/

Bookmice
http://www.bookmice.com/

Cybernet Books
http://www.cybernetbooks.com/

Denlinger's Publishers
http://www.thebookden.com/publish.html

ebooksonthe.net
http://www.ebooksonthe.net/

The Fiction Works
http://www.fictionworks.com/

Mind's Eye Fiction
http://www.tale.com/

Mystic-Ink Publishing
http://www.mystic-ink.com/publishing/

Random House
http://www.atrandom.com/

Sansip
http://www.sansip.com/

Mystery and Adventure

1st Electric Works
http://www.electricpublishing.com/

Antelope Publishing
http://www.teleport.com/~writers/books/

Awe-Struck E-Books
http://www.awe-struck.net/

Booklocker
http://www.booklocker.com/

Books OnScreen
http://www.booksonscreen.com/

Boondock Books
http://www.boondockbooks.com/

Cascade Mountain Publishing
http://www.cascadepublishing.com/

Cybernet Books
http://www.cybernetbooks.com/

Denlinger's Publishers
http://www.thebookden.com/publish.html

DiskUs Publishing
http://www.diskuspublishing.com/

DLSIJ Press
http://www.dlsijpress.com/

Domhan Book
http://www.domhanbooks.com/

Dreamcatcher On-Line Books
http://www.cia-g.com/~jwaldie/

ebooksonthe.net
http://www.ebooksonthe.net/

E-Dition
http://www.e-dition.net/

E-Pulp
http://www.e-pulp.com/

The Fiction Works
http://www.fictionworks.com/

Gemini Books
http://www.lisawrites.com/gem-pub.html

Hard Shell Word Factory
http://www.hardshell.com/

Indigo Publishing
http://www.wordmuseum.com/indigo/

Mystic-Ink Publishing
http://www.mystic-ink.com/publishing/

New Concepts Publishing
http://www.newconceptspublishing.com/

Nitelinks
http://www.nitelinks.com/

Virtual Publications
http://www.virtualpublications.com/

Random House
http://www.atrandom.com/

Sansip
http://www.sansip.com/

Romance

1st Electric Works
http://www.electricpublishing.com/

Awe-Struck E-Books
http://www.awe-struck.net/

Bell Press
http://www.bell.dk/press/eng/

Booklocker
http://www.booklocker.com/

Bookmice
http://www.bookmice.com/

Books OnScreen
http://www.booksonscreen.com/

Cascade Mountain Publishing
http://www.cascadepublishing.com/

Cybernet Books
http://www.cybernetbooks.com/

Denlinger's Publishers
http://www.thebookden.com/publish.html/

DiskUs Publishing
http://www.diskuspublishing.com/

DLSIJ Press
http://www.dlsijpress.com/

Domhan Book
http://www.domhanbooks.com/

Dreamcatcher On-Line Books
http://www.cia-g.com/~jwaldie/

Dreams Unlimited
http://www.dreams-unlimited.com/

ebooksonthe.net
http://www.ebooksonthe.net/

E-Dition
http://www.e-dition.net/

E-Pulp
http://www.e-pulp.com/

The Fiction Works
http://www.fictionworks.com/

Gemini Books
http://www.lisawrites.com/gem-pub.html

Hard Shell Word Factory
http://www.hardshell.com/

Lionhearted Publishing
http://www.lionhearted.com/

Mind's Eye Fiction
http://www.tale.com/

Mountain View Publishing
http://www.whidbey.com/mountainview/

Mystic-Ink Publishing
http://www.mystic-ink.com/publishing/

New Concepts Publishing
http://www.newconceptspublishing.com/

Nitelinks
http://www.nitelinks.com/

Orpheus Romance
http://www.orpheusromance.com/

Random House
http://www.atrandom.com/

Sansip
http://www.sansip.com/

Starlight Publications
http://www.starpublications.com/

The Fiction Works
http://www.fictionworks.com/

Timeless Treasures
http://www.romancereport.com/timeless/

Virtual Publications
http://www.virtualpublications.com/

Wakefield Publishing
http://www.vnovels.com/

Science Fiction

1st Electric Works
http://www.electricpublishing.com/

Antelope Publishing
http://www.teleport.com/~writers/books/

Awe-Struck E-Books
http://www.awe-struck.net/

Booklocker
http://www.booklocker.com/

Books OnScreen
http://www.booksonscreen.com/

Cascade Mountain Publishing
http://www.cascadepublishing.com/

Cybernet Books
http://www.cybernetbooks.com/

DiskUs Publishing
http://www.diskuspublishing.com/

DLSIJ Press
http://www.dlsijpress.com/

Domhan Book
http://www.domhanbooks.com/

Dreamcatcher On-Line Books
http://www.cia-g.com/~jwaldie/

ebooksonthe.net
http://www.ebooksonthe.net/

The Fiction Works
http://www.fictionworks.com/

E-Dition
http://www.e-dition.net/

E-Pulp
http://www.e-pulp.com/

Gemini Books
http://www.lisawrites.com/gem-pub.html/

Hard Shell Word Factory
http://www.hardshell.com/

Indigo Publishing
http://www.wordmuseum.com/indigo/

Mind's Eye Fiction
http://www.tale.com/

Mystic-Ink Publishing
http://www.mystic-ink.com/publishing/

New Concepts Publishing
http://www.newconceptspublishing.com/

Nitelinks
http://www.nitelinks.com/

Random House
http://www.atrandom.com/

Sansip
http://www.sansip.com/

Starlight Publications
http://www.starpublications.com/

Twilight Times Books
http://www.twilighttimesbooks.com/

Virtual Publications
http://www.virtualpublications.com/

Poetry

1st Electric Works
http://www.electricpublishing.com/

Antelope Publishing
http://www.teleport.com/~writers/books/

Boson Books
http://www.cmonline.com/boson/

Bridge Works Publishing
http://www.atlanticbridge.net/

Denlinger's Publishers
http://www.thebookden.com/publish.html

DiskUs Publishing
http://www.diskuspublishing.com/

HyperBooks
http://www.hyperbooks.com/

Indigo Publishing
http://www.wordmuseum.com/indigo/

Zeus Publications Australia
http://www.zeus-publications.com/

Erotica

Bell Press
http://www.bell.dk/press/eng/

Crossroads Publishing
http://www.crossroadspub.com/

Dreams Unlimited
http://www.dreams-unlimited.com/

Orpheus Romance
http://www.orpheusromance.com/

Renaissance E Books
http://www.rene-books.com/

Self-Help and Spirituality (Body, Mind, Spirit)

1st Electric Works
http://www.electricpublishing.com/

Antelope Publishing
http://www.teleport.com/~writers/books/

Booklocker
http://www.booklocker.com/

Bookmice
http://www.bookmice.com/

Book World
http://www.bkworld.com/

Cybernet Books
http://www.cybernetbooks.com/

Denlinger's Publishers
http://www.thebookden.com/publish.html

Dreamcatcher On-Line Books
http://www.cia-g.com/~jwaldie/

ebooksonthe.net
http://www.ebooksonthe.net/

E-Dition
http://www.e-dition.net/

Gemini Books
http://www.lisawrites.com/gem-pub.html

Hard Shell Word Factory
http://www.hardshell.com/

Mystic-Ink Publishing
http://www.mystic-ink.com/publishing/

Nitelinks
http://www.nitelinks.com/

Petals of Life Publishing
http://www.petalsoflife.com/

Random House
http://www.atrandom.com/

Twilight Times Books
http://www.twilighttimesbooks.com/

How-To and Reference

1st Electric Works
http://www.electricpublishing.com/

Books-On-Line
http://www.books-on-line.com/

Book World
http://www.bkworld.com/

Cybernet Books
http://www.cybernetbooks.com/

Denlinger's Publishers
http://www.thebookden.com/publish.html

Dreamcatcher On-Line Books
http://www.cia-g.com/~jwaldie/

ebooksonthe.net
http://www.ebooksonthe.net/

Gemini Books
http://www.lisawrites.com/gem-pub.html

Mystic-Ink Publishing
http://www.mystic-ink.com/publishing/

Nitelinks
http://www.nitelinks.com/

PocketPCpress
http://www.pocketpcpress.com/

Random House
http://www.atrandom.com/

Computer and Technical

Booklocker
http://www.booklocker.com/

Denlinger's Publishers
http://www.thebookden.com/publish.html

ebooksonthe.net
http://www.ebooksonthe.net/

HyperBooks
http://www.hyperbooks.com/

Nitelinks
http://www.nitelinks.com/

PocketPCpress
http://www.pocketpcpress.com/

Art

Booklocker
http://www.booklocker.com/

HyperBooks
http://www.hyperbooks.com/

Travel

Bookmice
http://www.bookmice.com/

Gemini Books
http://www.lisawrites.com/gem-pub.html

Mystic-Ink Publishing
http://www.mystic-ink.com/publishing/

Nitelinks
http://www.nitelinks.com/

Random House
http://www.atrandom.com/

Sansip
http://www.sansip.com/

Cookbooks

ebooksonthe.net
http://www.ebooksonthe.net/

Nitelinks
http://www.nitelinks.com/

Sansip
http://www.sansip.com/

Business

Booklocker
http://www.booklocker.com/

Bookmice
http://www.bookmice.com/

Denlinger's Publishers
http://www.thebookden.com/publish.html

ebooksonthe.net
http://www.ebooksonthe.net/

Children's Books

Antelope Publishing
http://www.teleport.com/~writers/books/

Booklocker
http://www.booklocker.com/

Bookmice
http://www.bookmice.com/

Books OnScreen
http://www.booksonscreen.com/

Chapter & Verse Publishing for Children
http://www.chapter-verse.com/

Crossroads Publishing
http://www.crossroadspub.com/

Cybernet Books
http://www.cybernetbooks.com/

Denlinger's Publishers
http://www.thebookden.com/publish.html

DiskUs Publishing
http://www.diskuspublishing.com/

Dreamcatcher On-Line Books
http://www.cia-g.com/~jwaldie/

ebooksonthe.net
http://www.ebooksonthe.net/

E-Dition
http://www.e-dition.net/

The Fiction Works
http://www.fictionworks.com/

Indigo Publishing
http://www.wordmuseum.com/indigo/

New Concepts Publishing
http://www.newconceptspublishing.com/

Nitelinks
http://www.nitelinks.com/

Online Originals
http://www.onlineoriginals.com/

Sansip
http://www.sansip.com/

Timeless Treasures
http://www.romancereport.com/timeless/

Educational

Booklocker
http://www.booklocker.com/

Nitelinks
http://www.nitelinks.com/

Legal and Medical

Denlinger's Publishers
http://www.thebookden.com/publish.html

Out of Print Books

Books-On-Line
http://www.books-on-line.com/

Cascade Mountain Publishing
http://www.cascadepublishing.com/

Alexandria Digital Literature
http://www.alexlit.com/

Virtuabooks Publishing
http://www.virtuabooks.com/

Virtual Publications
http://www.virtualpublications.com/

Resources

This appendix contains several Web sites that will help you explore the world of e-publishing. Many of these sites also contain links to other sites. Once you begin exploring, you will discover hundreds or even thousands of pages and sites devoted to e-books—definite evidence that the industry is going places! We have also included other sites that are not devoted to e-books but to areas that would be of definite interest to e-book authors and self-publishers, such as general information about book marketing, plus a couple of actual paper books that will come in handy even though they're not online.

This appendix presents the following sections:

- E-Publishing Business Web Sites
- General E-Publishing Web Sites
- Unions, Groups, and Associations
- Newsletters
- Discussion Lists
- Books
- Copyright Resources

E-Publishing Business Web Sites

The following are Web sites that are devoted primarily to the business side of e-books, particularly the marketing of e-books. Some of these sites contain links to other sites that provide even more information.

John Kremer's Book Marketing Update, http://www.bookmarket.com/. This site is devoted to the business of marketing books—not just e-books, but paper books as well. There is a lot of excellent information here for anybody interested in book marketing.

ePublishing Connections, http://www.epublishingconnections.com/. This site is devoted to e-publishing. It contains a great deal of information, including lots of links to other online resources.

Inkspot Electronic Publishing Resources, http://www.inkspot.com/epublish/. This Web site is devoted to the business of e-publishing. It includes several FAQs (Frequently Asked Questions lists) about the business. It also has several workshops (including resources such as Web links, articles, columns, and other information) and a section on networking.

General E-Publishing Web Sites

Here we list several sites that cover more generic issues and topics regarding e-books. These sites are some of the better ones we've found and, like most sites, many of them contain links to other sites, providing you with a springboard for e-book information. As you dig, you will soon find there are already thousands of e-book sites out on the Web.

About.com, http://www.about.com/. About.com is hard to describe, but we're going to try: It's an online information center filled with hundreds of topics and subtopics, and each topic is hosted by a guide, who is a volunteer knowledgeable about the particular subject. The site is not devoted to publishing, but it has extensive resources relating to publishing. If you visit the site, a good starting point is to type "e-publishing" in the Find It Now search box. You will find numerous pages relating to e-publishing and e-books.

E-Book Reader's Review Board, http://www.delphi.com/ebookreview/. This is an entire online forum devoted to e-books, with both discussion lists and live chats. Although this forum is free, you do need to register, providing a name, password, and some marketing information such as age, occupation, and gender.

ABOUT E-BOOKS, http://www.edu-cyberpg.com/Literacy/ebooks.html. This is mainly a page of a gazillion links about e-books. There's lots of great stuff here.

Independent E-book Awards, http://www.e-book-awards.com/. This is exactly what its title says: a Web site devoted to a particular e-book award. It allows you to submit an e-book to be judged by a professional panel. The award is given once a year.

Unions, Groups, and Associations

For some time, the world of authors and writers has recognized the need for organizing and working together so that the field can grow, so that the people in the field can meet each other and work together, and so that the people within the field can be assured that their interests are protected. The following are Web sites for various unions, groups, and associations that pertain to books and writing in general, or specifically to e-books. You won't find as many links to other sites, but there are some.

Note: As of this writing, it is not yet clear whether the National Writers Union and the Writers Guild of America recognize e-book authors as qualifying for membership. Check with them if you are thinking about joining and have not published anything in paper form.

National Writers Union, http://www.nwu.org/. This is one of the official writers' unions, associated with both the UAW and AFL-CIO. Joining a writers' union has many benefits—including group health insurance, which is something that many freelance authors lack. Joining the union is easy, although you have to meet the basic requirements (which are pretty broad) and you must pay the dues.

Writers Guild of America, http://www.wga.org/. This is another official writers' union. Its requirements for membership are a bit more stringent. This union also provides health insurance for its members, as well as a federally insured credit union based in Los Angeles. As with most unions, you must pay regular dues.

Association of Electronic Publishers, http://members.tripod.com/~BestBooksCom/AEP/aep.html. Although not technically a union, this organization provides a great site for people interested in self-publishing their e-books. It includes information about getting started, marketing your e-books, and finding companies that will help sell your book.

Electronically Published Internet Connection (EPIC), http://www.eclectics.com/epic. This is an organization devoted to e-book authors. It is kind of like a union, and you must be a published author to join.

Newsletters

There are already lots of newsletters, some weekly, some monthly, some more sporadic, that cover various topics about e-books. Although sometimes cumbersome to wade through, newsletters are an excellent source of current news and information, often delivered to you through e-mail. As with any profession, it's important to keep up to date with the latest news, trends, and all that stuff you hear advertised on TV ads for weekly newsmagazines. For e-books, you can find that information here.

eBook Insider, http://www.eBookNet.com/. This site was previously owned by Nuvomedia, maker of the Rocket eBook, and now belongs to Gemstar. Even though it's owned by an e-book device maker, it's quite objective and thorough. It provides a great deal of news and information about e-books, as well as interviews. It lives as both a Web site and an e-mail newsletter.

E-Book Connections, http://www.ebookconnections.com/. This site is by the same people who run ePublishing Connections (see the "E-Publishing Business Web Sites" section earlier in this appendix), but it's a separate site. Whereas the former is devoted to electronic publishing in general, this site is devoted primarily to e-books.

E-Publishing Opportunities Newsletter, http://www.myplanet.net/vanburen/. This is a newsletter created by one of this book's authors, and it covers e-publishing opportunities.

Jeff Cogswell's Beginner's Guide to E-Books, http://www.geocities.com/jeffcogs. This site is created by one of this book's authors, and is a general introductory guide to e-books.

Discussion Lists

Discussion lists are both free and often free-for-alls, where anyone can contribute anything they want to say, provided it is on topic. Some discussion lists have a moderator, a person who approves any messages that get sent out. You can often choose whether to read discussion lists online via a Web page or have them sent directly to your e-mail in-box, much like newsletters. But unlike newsletters, with discussion lists you can add your own contribution whenever you wish.

TEN, http://www.topica.com/lists/ten/. This is a discussion list about e-books and e-book professionals. Anyone is welcome to join it. The group is hosted by topica.com, and the normal sign-up is via the Web site. Alternatively, you can subscribe directly by sending e-mail to TEN-subscribe@topica.com.

Ind-e-pubs, http://groups.yahoo.com/group/Ind-e-pubs. This is a discussion list devoted to the methods of distributing and selling e-books in various formats. The group is hosted by Yahoo!'s egroups.com, and the normal sign-up is via the Web site. Alternatively, you can subscribe by sending e-mail to Ind-e-pubs-subscribe@egroups.com.

All About E-books, http://groups.yahoo.com/group/AllAboutE-Books. A general list that discusses writing, publishing, and distributing e-books. This one is also hosted by Yahoo!'s egroups.com, but to subscribe, you have to visit the Web site rather than send e-mail.

E-books, http://groups.yahoo.com/group/e-books. This is a general list that discusses writing, publishing, and distributing e-books. The list is hosted by Yahoo!'s egroups.com, and the normal sign-up is via the Web site. Alternatively, you can subscribe by sending e-mail to e-books-owner@egroups.com.

Books

We're not vain. Or, if we are, we seem to be in good company. There are lots of great books out there in addition to the one you're holding in your hand, some paper, others electronic-only. Here are two paper books about online courseware, which is related to e-publishing:

Building Learning Communities in Cyberspace: Effective Strategies for the Online Classroom, by Rena M. Palloff and Keith Pratt, (Jossey-Bass, 1999).

The Online Teaching Guide: A Handbook of Attitudes, Strategies, and Techniques for the Virtual Classroom, edited by Ken W. White and Bob H. Weight (Allyn & Bacon, 1999).

Here are two e-books that can assist you in learning about the e-publishing business, along with their Web sites:

Electronic Publishing: The Definitive Guide by Karen S. Wiesner, http://www.avidpress.com/. This is an e-book that includes a huge list of e-publishers, along with other resources. This is definitely a useful resource guide for any e-book author.

e-Lectrify Your Sales: A Writer's Guide to e-Publishing Success by Leta Nolan Childers, http://www.diskuspublishing.com/. This is another excellent e-book about writing e-books. It includes firsthand experience written by a successful e-book author. It takes you through all the important aspects, including understanding publishers, file formats, copyright information, and much more.

Copyright Resources

These sites are devoted U.S. copyrights. There is a ton of information out there about copyrights, meaning there's a lot to learn and understand.

The Library of Congress Copyright Office site, http://lcweb.loc.gov/copyright/. This is where it all happens, at least in the United States. It's a great site, with some easy-to-understand explanations of copyright basics.

The Publishing Law Center, http://www.publaw.com/legal.html. This is another great site containing many articles and publications about the legal issues surrounding publishing, including dealing with contracts. We highly recommend this site.

Links Page, http://www.library.yale.edu/~llicense/liclinks.shtml. This page contains links and descriptions of dozens of sites devoted to copyright information. This is definitely a good reference for such information.

Copyright and Copyleft, http://www.edu-cyberpg.com/Internet/ copyrightleft.html. This is a really good site about copyrights, and it includes sections about copyrights pertaining to self-publishing and lots of links. (Like the remaining listings in this section, this site is housed under The Educational CyberPlayGround domain. However, the sites are distinct sites with their own sets of information pertaining to copyrights.)

Copyright: Where to Begin, http://www.edu-cyberpg.com/ringleaders/ ddcopyright.html. This site has lots of links to resources around the Web pertaining to copyright information, as well as a few articles.

Copyright Permission Form Letter, http://www.edu-cyberpg.com/Technology/ permissionform.html. This page is interesting; it simply shows a copyright permission form.

APPENDIX C

Sample Contracts

The following sample contracts are provided as a start. We suggest that you make alterations as needed. You'll find some places where several choices are available (listed in [square brackets]) and you'll want to select the option best for your particular needs. For more information about how and why you would use these various contracts, refer to Chapter 11, "Business Issues for the Self E-Publisher." The following contracts are provided here:

Publishing agreement. The primary author–publisher agreement, used to acquire works from authors.

Nondisclosure agreement. An agreement to help ensure that trade secrets are kept secret. This is useful in certain cases, when authors or publishers have special information at stake.

Collaboration agreement. An agreement between an author and a contributing writer. It's important to make sure this type of agreement is in place for collaborative works.

Work-for-Hire agreement. A general contractor agreement for various types of work that do not involve a vested interest in the project.

Revision letter. A notice to authors that a revision of their work is desired.

PUBLISHING AGREEMENT

This Agreement is made in the City of _____, this day, _____ between _____ hereinafter called the Publisher and whose address is _____, and _____ hereinafter called Author and whose address is _____. The Author and the Publisher agree to collaborate in the preparation of a literary project, described as follows:

[Insert description of book and tentative title]

hereinafter called the Work, and to undertake and carry out their respective responsibilities as provided herein.

1. Grant of Rights

Subject to the terms and conditions contained in this Agreement, the Author hereby grants, assigns, and transfers to the Publisher the following rights and interests to the Work:

1. The right to publish and sell the Work in any and all e-book formats, including but not limited to PDF, HTML, and Microsoft Reader formats and including the right to market and sell the Work in English throughout the world, or the right to license others to do the same.

2. The right to publish and sell the Work in Print and/or Print On Demand formats.

3. The right to publish and sell the Work in other formats and other media, including [electronic courseware, online database, any and all formats and media] or to license others to do the same.

4. The right to translate the Work into [specific languages, any and all foreign languages] or license others to do the same.

5. The right to condense, serialize, or license the Work or any portion thereof or create adaptations and/or revisions of the Work.

6. The right to exercise or license any other subsidiary rights in the Work, including videocassette rights, broadcast-television and radio rights; free and pay cable rights, film and microfilm rights; photocopy rights; electronic database rights; and any other rights that now exist or that may come into existence during the term of this Agreement.

7. The right to use the Author's name and/or likeness in conjunction with the Work, the promotion of the Work, the promotion of the Author, or the promotion of the Publisher.

8. Any and all rights not specifically exploited by the Publisher within 18 months after the acceptance of the final manuscript shall [revert to the author, be shared equally by Author and Publisher provided that either party shall notify the other in the event of a sale of rights].

2. Manuscript Preparation

A. The Author agrees to prepare and submit a manuscript for the Work acceptable to the Publisher and agrees to follow and comply with the Publisher's *Author Guidelines*. The manuscript shall be delivered according to the following conditions:

1. The complete manuscript shall be delivered on or before _____. This date is hereinafter referred to as the ***Due Date.***

2. The manuscript length shall be approximately _____ pages in standard double-spaced 12-point type with one-inch margins. This length shall include all front matter, back matter, and artwork. The manuscript shall be delivered as an electronic file in the form [Microsoft Word for Windows].

3. The manuscript shall be delivered in form, organization, content, and style acceptable to the Publisher.

4. The manuscript shall be accompanied by clear sketches for artwork, illustrations, charts, and tables, along with any screen dumps, bibliography, and such other materials as the Publisher may reasonably specify.

5. The manuscript shall be accompanied by any necessary written permissions for information included in the Work. These permissions shall be obtained by the Author, without expense to the Publisher, and shall cover any copyrighted materials that are not in the public domain, as well as any other material for which permission is necessary in connection with the Author's warranty in Section 11 of this Agreement. These permissions must be consistent with the rights granted to the Publisher in this Agreement in order that they may cover all the uses to which the material may eventually be put.

B. The manuscript or any portion thereof shall be deemed to be acceptable and satisfactory to the Publisher unless the Publisher notifies the Author in writing within fifteen (15) days after receipt of the full or partial manuscript. Such notice will specify the reasons for the Publisher's determination, and indicate what changes must be made. The Author shall then have fifteen (15) days in which to revise the manuscript in order to render it satisfactory to the Publisher.

C. In the event the Author fails to maintain the Development Schedule for the Work, fails to deliver the completed Work by the Due Date, or fails or refuses to perform any revision or correction within the time specified by the Publisher, the Publisher may elect, in its own discretion, to terminate this agreement. Upon such termination, all rights to the Work granted herein shall revert to the Author.

3. Editing and Publication

A. When the final manuscript is accepted and approved for production the Publisher will:

1. Copyedit the Work, provided that such editing or alteration shall not materially change the meaning of the Work.

2. Publish the Work in one or several formats and in such manner as is deemed best suited to the sale of the Work. If Publisher fails to publish the work within six months after acceptance of the final manuscript, the Author may terminate this Agreement and all rights shall revert to the Author.

3. Establish the title and prices at which the Work shall be sold.

4. Determine the method and means of marketing the Work, the number and destination of free copies and all other publishing details.

B. The Author agrees to do the following:

1. Cooperate with the Publisher in such efforts to prepare the Work for publication.

2. Review the edited manuscript and respond in a timely manner to Publisher's requests for clarifications, additions, and changes.

4. Competing Works

During the term of this Agreement and provided the Work has not sold fewer than 250 copies for three consecutive royalty periods, the Author shall not, without the prior written consent of the Publisher, engage in any activity that could be reasonably construed as competing with the Publisher's right to freely sell and promote the Work. This includes preparing, publishing, promoting, or assisting with or causing to be prepared, published, or promoted, any other version, conversion, or enlargement of the Work, or any other work of a nature that might interfere with or injure the sales or licensing of the Work by the Publisher, or permitting the use of the Author's name in connection with any such work.

5. Author's Copies

Upon publication of the Work, the Publisher shall provide the Author with _____ copies of the Work free of charge. The Author may purchase additional copies of the Work at a discount of _____ percent (____%) off Publisher's prevailing list price. Royalties shall not be paid on copies purchased by the author.

6. Discontinuance of Publication

A. The Publisher shall have the right to discontinue publication of the Work if, in its sole judgment, demand for the Work or any subsequent revision of the Work is no longer sufficient to warrant its continued publication, in which event the Author shall be so advised.

B. If the Work in all its derivations and editions sells fewer than _____ copies in a one-year period, the Author shall have the right to request the termination of this Agreement. Rights to materials prepared by or obtained at the expense of Publisher in relation to the Work shall remain the property of Publisher.

C. The termination of this Agreement shall be subject to the following:

1. Any license, contract, option, or right granted to third parties by the Publisher before the termination will remain in effect for the agreed-upon term, and Publisher will continue to be entitled to its share of the proceeds from such grants as long as they remain in force.

7. Royalties

For the purposes of this Agreement, **Net Receipts** is defined as the Publisher's total proceeds from the Work, less allowances for actual returns, prior to any deduction of distribution fees or sales commissions. The Author shall receive the following royalties in consideration for the Author's grant of rights and performance of this Agreement.

1. As an advance against royalties accruing under this Agreement, the sum of _____, payable as follows:

[list method of payment of advance, if applicable]

2. This advance shall be recovered by the publisher through the author's royalty account and no royalties shall be paid to the author until this advance is recovered.

3. _____% of Net Receipts for each e-book copy of the Work sold by the Publisher through standard wholesale channels and _____% when sold by the Publisher directly to consumers.

4. _____% of Net Receipts for each Print or Print On Demand copy of the Work sold by the Publisher through standard wholesale channels and _____% when sold by the Publisher directly to consumers.

5. _____% of the Publisher's receipts from the sale, assignment, or licensing to others of any rights to the Work or any portion thereof.

6. If the Publisher decides, in its sole discretion, to bundle, combine, or compile the Work with works by other authors, or to offer the work in a custom publishing manner, the Author shall receive a royalty based on the portion of the bundle, combination, or compilation represented by the Work, as determined by the following formula:

$$\text{Royalty due} = \% \times \frac{\text{list price of the Work}}{\text{total list prices of all bundle items}} \times \text{Net Receipts}$$

8. Accounting

A. At the end of each calendar quarter, the Publisher shall prepare a statement concerning the sales of the Work during the quarter. This statement shall show the net copies of the Work sold during the quarter, along with the receipts received for those sales. The statement shall also show how the royalties due the Author were computed for the quarter. The Publisher shall have 30 days following the end of the calendar quarter to prepare this statement.

B. The royalty statement and any settlement due the Author shall be mailed to the Author or Author's representative within sixty (60) days following the end of the calendar quarter covered by the statement and settlement.

C. Any advanced or overpaid royalties paid to the Author, or any other payments due from the Author to the Publisher, may be applied in reduction of any payments due to the Author under this Agreement between the Publisher and the Author.

D. No royalty shall be paid on the following:

1. Copies of the Work provided free to the Author

2. Copies of the Work used for review, sample, promotion, or other similar purposes

3. Copies of the Work purchased by the Author

9. Author's Warranty

A. The Author represents and warrants the following:

1. The Author has full power and authority to enter into this Agreement and to grant the rights granted in this Agreement.

2. The Work is original except for material in the public domain and such excerpts from other works as may be included with the written permission of the copyright owners.

3. Any portion of the work that has been previously published has been identified and the Publisher notified of same.

4. The Work does not contain any libelous material, unlawful statements, or injurious formulas or instructions.

5. The Work does not infringe upon or violate any copyright, patent, trademark, trade name, or trade secret.

6. The Work does not invade or violate any right or privacy, personal or proprietary right, or other common law or statutory right.

B. The Author agrees to keep all notes, papers, and recordings used in the development of the Work for a period of three (3) years from the date of first publication of the Work.

C. The Author shall indemnify the Publisher and its licensees and assignees under this Agreement and hold them harmless from any and all losses, damages, liabilities, costs, charges, and expenses, including reasonable attorneys' fees, arising out of any breach of any of the Author's representations and warranties contained in this Section or from any third-party claims relating to the matters covered by these representations and warranties. Each party shall promptly notify the other of any such claim, demand, or suit, and the Publisher shall have the right to defend and select its own counsel or call upon the Author to defend or assist the Publisher and its counsel. Author will cooperate with Publisher in any claim, demand, or suit including making available to Publisher and its counsel the notes, working papers, and recordings referred to above. Until such claim, demand, or suit has been settled, withdrawn, or finally adjudicated, the Publisher may withhold any sums due the Author hereunder in an amount necessary to cover the costs and reasonable expenses of such claim, demand, or suit. All warranties and indemnities herein shall survive termination or expiration of this Agreement.

10. Miscellaneous

A. This Agreement shall in all respects be interpreted and construed in accordance with and governed by the laws of the State of _____, regardless of the place of its execution or performance.

B. This Agreement may not be assigned by either party without the prior written consent of the other party, which shall not be unreasonably withheld.

C. This Agreement constitutes the complete understanding of the parties regarding the Work and supersedes all prior agreements of the parties relating to the Work, whether written or verbal. No amendment or waiver of any provision of this Agreement shall be valid unless in writing and signed by all parties affected by the amendment or waiver.

In witness hereof, the following parties have executed this Agreement.

Publisher:

_____   _____

Publisher Signature   Date

Author:

_____   _____   _____

Author Signature   Date   SS/Tax Number

NONDISCLOSURE AGREEMENT

This Agreement is made in the City of _____, this day, _____ between _____ hereinafter called the Publisher and whose address is _____, and _____ hereinafter called Author and whose address is _____.

The parties hereby agree as follows:

1. The Publisher is providing confidential information to the Author as part of a possible publishing venture of mutual benefit to both parties. Said information is confidential because its release would financially harm the Publisher and give unfair advantage to its competitors.

2. All information concerning, but not limited to, publishing schedules, proposed titles, titles in progress, title and work subject matter including software, price, press dates, and publishing dates provided to the Author by the Publisher is confidential. The Author agrees not to reveal any information to any non-party to this Nondisclosure Agreement until written permission is obtained from the Publisher or the subject title is published.

3. Author shall not communicate Publisher's confidential information to any third party, and shall use all best efforts to prevent inadvertent disclosure of Publisher's confidential information to any third party. Dissemination of Publisher's confidential information on the part of the Author to other members of Author's organization shall be limited to a "need-to-know" basis for the purposes of Paragraph 1 above, or for any purpose Publisher may hereafter authorize in writing.

6. This agreement shall govern all communications between Publisher and Author during the period from date of Agreement to the date on which either party receives from the other written notice that subsequent communications shall not be so governed.

Publisher:

_____   _____
Publisher Signature   Date

Author:

_____   _____   _____
Author Signature   Date   SS/Tax Number

COLLABORATION AGREEMENT

This Agreement is made in the City of _____, this day, _____ between _____ hereinafter called the Author and whose address is _____, and _____ hereinafter called the Contractor and whose address is _____.
The parties hereby agree as follows:

1. Independent Contractor's Services to Be Performed

Contractor is hereby engaged by Author as an independent contractor to provide services, as Author shall request, including the following:
   [Describe work to be completed], hereinafter referred to as the Contribution.
   The Contribution is intended to be part of a Work to be released by _____, hereinafter called the Publisher and whose address is _____. The Author shall have the right to make such revisions, deletions, or additions to the Contribution that the Author may deem advisable in the interest of space and uniformity of style and presentation, provided that the accuracy of the text is not impaired. Author shall have no obligation to publish the Contribution, but if published, Author shall acknowledge Contractor's contribution to the Work.

2. Compensation

For said Contribution, Contractor shall receive _____. In the event that Contractor's contribution differs from the work specified herein, payment will be renegotiated appropriately and in good faith.

3. Term and Termination

The term of this Agreement shall commence as of _____ and shall terminate on _____ . Notwithstanding the foregoing term, Contractor and Author acknowledge that this Agreement may be terminated by either party at any time, with or without cause, by giving written notice to the other of that party's determination to terminate the Agreement. Should Publisher terminate its contract with Author for this Work prior to its approval of the final manuscript, Author shall have 90 days to resell the Work to another party and all rights in the Contribution remain with Author and all compensation agreed to above must be paid to Contractor. In the event that Author does not place or publish the title elsewhere within 90 days, rights in the Contribution revert to Contractor and no further obligation exists between the parties.

The Author may terminate this agreement in the event that the Contractor does not deliver the final manuscript on or before Due Date or delivers material that is in the Author's reasonable judgment unacceptable in form or style. In such event this agreement shall terminate, the Author shall return the Contribution to the Contractor as soon as practicable and shall simultaneously revert all rights in the Contribution to the Contractor, and thereafter neither party shall have any further obligation or liability to the other hereunder.

4. Independent Contractor Status

The Contribution, including all illustrations, figures, tables, and other materials, shall be considered a work made for hire to the Author, and the Author shall own the copyright and all of the rights comprised in the copyright. To the extent the Contribution or any material contained therein or attached thereto do not qualify as a work made for hire, the Contractor hereby transfers to the Author during the full term of copyright and all extensions thereof the full and exclusive rights comprised in the copyright in the Contribution and any revisions thereof, including but not limited to the right, by itself or with others, throughout the world, to print, publish, republish, transmit, and distribute the Contribution and to prepare, publish, transmit, and distribute derivative works based thereon, in all languages and in all media of expression now known or later developed, and to license or permit others to do so. Contractor shall not represent himself or herself as an employee or agent of the Author or the Publisher. Contractor agrees to comply with applicable laws, rules, and regulations in respect to self-employment. Contractor agrees to defend, indemnify, and hold Author and Publisher harmless against all losses, liabilities, claims, and/or proceedings, and all costs and expenses in connection therewith, arising out of Contractor's failure to comply with this paragraph 4. The provisions of this paragraph 4 shall survive termination of this Agreement.

5. Warrants by Contractor

Contractor represents and warrants that the materials so provided will contain no matter that is defamatory or otherwise unlawful or infringes any copyright or proprietary right of another, or that invades the privacy of another. Contractor further represents and warrants that Contractor has not previously assigned or granted to, or otherwise created in, any other person or entity any right in the materials to be provided hereunder. Contractor shall indemnify and hold the Author harmless from any loss, expense, or liability, including reasonable attorney's fees and expenses, occasioned by any claim, demand, suit, or recovery arising out of any breach of the representations and/or warranties contained in this paragraph 5. The provisions of this paragraph 5 shall survive termination of this Agreement.

6. Miscellaneous

This Agreement shall in all respects be interpreted and construed in accordance with and governed by the laws of the State of _____, regardless of the place of its execution or performance.

This Agreement may not be assigned by either party without the prior written consent of the other party, which shall not be unreasonably withheld.

This Agreement constitutes the complete understanding of the parties regarding the Contribution and supersedes all prior agreements of the parties relating to the Contribution, whether written or verbal. No amendment or waiver of any provision of this Agreement shall be valid unless in writing and signed by all parties affected by the amendment or waiver.

Publisher:

_____   _____
Publisher Signature   Date

Author:

_____   _____   _____
Author Signature   Date   SS/Tax Number

WORK-FOR-HIRE AGREEMENT

This Agreement is made in the City of _____, this day, _____ between _____ hereinafter called the Publisher and whose address is _____, and _____ hereinafter called the Contractor and whose address is _____.
The parties hereby agree as follows:

1. Independent Contractor's Services to Be Performed

Contractor is hereby engaged by Publisher as an independent contractor to provide services, as Publisher shall request, including the following:

[Describe work to be completed], hereinafter referred to as the Work.

2. Compensation

For said Work, Contractor shall receive _____. In the event that Contractor's product differs from the Work specified herein, payment will be renegotiated appropriately and in good faith.

3. Term and Termination

The term of this Agreement shall commence as of _____ and shall terminate on _____. Notwithstanding the foregoing term, Contractor and Publisher acknowledge that this Agreement may be terminated by either party at any time, with or without cause, by giving written notice to the other of that party's determination to terminate the Agreement.

4. Independent Contractor Status

The Work, including all text, illustrations, figures, tables, and other materials created by Contractor, shall be considered a work made for hire to the Publisher, and the Publisher shall own the copyright and all of the rights comprised in the copyright. To the extent the Work or any material contained therein or attached thereto do not qualify as a work made for hire, the Contractor hereby transfers to the Publisher during the full term of copyright and all extensions thereof the full and exclusive rights comprised in the copyright in the Work and any revisions thereof, including but not limited to the right, by itself or with others, throughout the world, to print, publish, republish, transmit, and distribute the Work and to prepare, publish, transmit, and distribute derivative works based thereon, in all languages and in all media of expression now known or later developed, and to license or permit others to do so. Contractor shall not represent himself or herself as an employee or agent of the Publisher and shall not be entitled to any employee benefits from the Publisher. Contractor agrees to comply with applicable laws, rules, and regulations in respect to self-employment. Contractor agrees to defend, indemnify, and hold Publisher harmless against all losses, liabilities, claims, and/or proceedings, and all costs and expenses in connection therewith, arising out of Contractor's failure to comply with this paragraph 4. The provisions of this paragraph 4 shall survive termination of this Agreement.

5. Miscellaneous

This Agreement shall in all respects be interpreted and construed in accordance with and governed by the laws of the State of _____, regardless of the place of its execution or performance.

This Agreement may not be assigned by either party without the prior written consent of the other party, which shall not be unreasonably withheld.

This Agreement constitutes the complete understanding of the parties regarding the Work and supersedes all prior agreements of the parties relating to the Work, whether written or verbal. No amendment or waiver of any provision of this Agreement shall be valid unless in writing and signed by all parties affected by the amendment or waiver.

Publisher:

_____   _____

Publisher Signature   Date

Author:

_____   _____   _____

Author Signature   Date   SS/Tax Number

REVISION LETTER

Dear [author]:

[Publisher name] has determined to prepare and publish a revision of [Work]. This revision shall be prepared under the terms of the Publishing Agreement for the Work dated _____. All terms of said contract shall remain in full force and effect for this revised edition.

Please notify us within _____ days of your willingness to perform this revision. In the event that you are unwilling or unable to perform said revision, [publisher name] shall contract a third party to perform the revision in your stead and deduct the reasonable payment from your continuing royalty account.

We look forward to working with you again on this important work.

Sincerely,

[publisher's signature]

GLOSSARY

Acquisitions editor. Editor responsible for finding and acquiring *rights* to manuscripts. Acquisitions editors generally negotiate contracts with authors or agents.

Adaptation. A reuse of a literary work after changes or alterations. The new work is considered a unique work, different from the original. Foreign translations are considered adaptations, as are condensed versions or otherwise altered editions. Usually, the author of the original work receives a percentage of the proceeds from sales of the adapted work. See *Royalties*.

Books in Print. A standard guide published by R.R. Bowker, which lists all books that have an *ISBN*.

Compatible. In terms of e-books, the concept of whether content created for one device or software can be displayed on another device or software.

Casio E-100. A PDA created by **Casio** (http://www.casio.com) that runs the Microsoft PocketPC operating system. Newer models made after late 2000 include *Microsoft Reader* software.

Collaboration agreement. A publishing agreement used to include a second or subsequent writer on an existing project. A collaboration agreement protects both the publisher and the original author from potential problems arising from the collaborator's efforts.

Consumer. The final human being who purchases and (hopefully!) reads the e-book. See *Customer*.

Content. The material in an e-book or other publication, including the text and the figures, and any other material included in the publication.

Copyeditor. Editor responsible for checking and improving the grammar and clarity of a work.

Copyright. The registration mark for a literary work, which indicates that the work has been registered with the U.S. Copyright Office or a similar authority in other countries to prove its authorship.

Courseware. Online instructional courses that usually involve some level of interaction with the student, such as online tests, interactive videos, and e-mail feedback from an instructor.

Custom publishing. The business of breaking up books into their chapters or other individual parts and allowing customers to assemble original books from the combination of chapters from other books. Generally, these books are then sold as *POD* or e-books.

Customer. A generic term referring to one who purchases something from another. Compare to *Consumer.*

Deep discount. A high discount given to special resellers or corporate customers who purchase a large quantity of books. In print publishing, books sold at deep discounts usually result in lower *royalties* for authors.

Digital Object Identifier (DOI). A number that uniquely represents a digital content item, such as a book, or a chapter, or a collection of books. The DOI works together with directory software so that the content item can easily be located on the Internet.

Digital rights management (DRM). The business or technology of protecting a literary work from being copied or reused without permission from the publisher. Several DRM schemes exist for e-books, some requiring the customer to read the book online and others built into the e-book file format used on a handheld device or personal computer that is not hooked up to the Internet.

Distributor. A business entity that performs the task of getting books from the publisher to the retailers.

DOI. See *Digital Object Identifier.*

DRM. See *Digital rights management.*

E-book. A book represented to the final consumer in electronic format, either on an e-book device or through e-book software on a traditional personal computer.

E-book device. A small handheld computer whose primary purpose is displaying e-books. Compare *Personal Digital Assistant.*

E-book format. The type of electronic file used for an e-book. E-book formats include Adobe Acrobat *(PDF)*, Microsoft Reader *(LIT)*, Rocket Editions *(RB)*, and others.

eBookMan. An e-book device created by Franklin. It includes the Microsoft Reader e-book software as well as organizational software.

E-book software. A computer program designed to display e-books. When aimed at the desktop market, such programs usually run on either a Microsoft Windows or a Macintosh computer.

EBX. See *Electronic Book Exchange.*

Electronic Book Exchange (EBX). A standard created by Glassbook (now owned by Adobe), which details how e-books can be purchased or borrowed while maintaining the integrity of the copy protection.

Electronic content. *Content* that is published electronically.

e-Matter. A trademarked term used by MightyWords to define short electronic documents available for sale at the **MightyWords** site (http://www.mightywords.com/).

Electronic publishing. The act of publishing a work and presenting it in electronic format.

Electronic rights. The right to produce electronic documents from a given literary work. Electronic *rights* include e-book, custom publishing, interactive multimedia, online database, and others. At the time this book is being written, most traditional publishers do not distinguish among these various different electronic rights—while e-publishers generally do.

eXtensible Markup Language (XML). A markup language that includes features not available in *HTML*. HTML can be thought of as a subset of XML.

Extensible Rights Management Language (XrML). A standard created by **ContentGuard** (http://www.contentguard.com) for specifying *rights* within a document.

Fair Use. A set of rules that dictate how and when copyrighted material can be reused without violating the copyright. Fair use is intended to encourage scholarly and literary endeavors by removing some of the restrictions on using other people's work.

File Transfer Protocol (FTP). A method, or technology, for transferring electronic files over the Internet.

Foreign agent. A *literary agent* who represents works from other countries to publishers in the agent's country.

FTP. See *File Transfer Protocol*.

Fulfillment. The process of getting books into the hands of the customer, once orders have been placed. Fulfillment traditionally involves receiving a customer order, checking payment information, receiving payment or processing a customer invoice, shipping books from the warehouse, and tracking unpaid balances. In e-publishing, fulfillment has more to do with the electronic payment side of the equation than shipping books.

Gemstar. The company that purchased Softbook press (former maker of the Softbook Reader) and Nuvomedia (former maker of the Rocket eBook).

Genre. A category, usually in fiction, such as science fiction, romance, or Western.

Grant of Rights. The section in a publishing contract that deals with the transfer of *rights* in and to the work.

HTML. See *Hypertext Markup Language.*

Hypertext Markup Language (HTML). A simple programming language for creating Web pages. HTML can also be used as an *e-book format.* HTML e-books can be read over the Internet or downloaded and read on a personal computer with any Web browser software.

International Standard Book Number (ISBN). A number used to identify information about an individual book. Publishers purchase ISBNs in blocks from R.R. Bowker Inc. and assign them to their books, using separate numbers for each type of publication, hardcover, softcover, and so on. E-publishers are currently seeking a more advanced numbering system to account for the large number of different formats in which a single e-book can be delivered.

International Standard Serial Number (ISSN). A number used to identify an entire serial, such as a magazine or journal. Individual issues carry the serial's ISSN; they do not get a new one.

ISBN. See *International Standard Book Number.*

ISSN. See *International Standard Serial Number.*

Knowledgebase. An online source of information, usually in encyclopedia format, which generally includes an easy method for users to look up information for a specific topic.

License. A transfer of *rights* in and to a work from one entity to another.

LIT. See *Microsoft Reader.*

Literary agent. A party acting as a representative to the owner of literary *rights* (usually an author) to assist in the transfer or sale of those rights to a publisher.

Markup. A special code, inserted into a document, which provides formatting information for a document. For example, in HTML the markup <I> means the words that follow will be in italic, while </I> means the words that follow will not be in italic.

Metadata. A set of data that describes a book or work. Metadata includes, for instance, the title, author name, and publisher name.

Microsoft Reader. An e-book software package created by Microsoft, which runs under a Windows system or on a Franklin eBookMan. It uses files that are stored in a special LIT format specifically for the Microsoft Reader.

MobiReader. An e-book software package that runs on palm-size computers. It is available from **Mobipocket** (http://www.mobireader.com).

Newsgroup. A specific form of online discussion list.

OEB. See *Open eBook.*

ONIX. One of several forms of information exchange. For the one used in this book, see *ONline Information eXchange system.*

ONline Information eXchange system (ONIX). A standard for digitally communicating book *metadata.* It is handled by **EDiTEUR** (http://www.editeur.org/onix.html).

OP. See *Out of Print.*

Open eBook (OEB). A standard for specifying the contents of an e-book using *XML.*

Out of Print (OP). A contractual term referring to when a publisher no longer prints a book. Typically at this point the rights of the book can revert back to the author.

PDA. See *Personal Digital Assistant.*

PDF. See *Portable Document Format.*

Peanut Reader. A software package created by **Peanut Press** (http://www.peanutpress.com/) that runs on small palm-size computers, including Palm Pilot and PocketPC.

Personal Digital Assistant (PDA). A special palm-size computer that includes organizer software such as time management and contacts programs.

POD. See *Print On Demand.*

Portable Document Format (PDF). An online format created by Adobe for storing books. This format includes full page layout.

Pre-production. The process of getting a book ready for publication. Pre-production tasks include manuscript preparation (editing and proofing) and cover design.

Print On Demand (POD). A xerographic technology for printing books from electronic files (usually *PDF* files). Books can be printed in small batches, even one at a time, with no change in the per-book cost.

Production editor. Editor in charge of taking a book from manuscript to a finished product. Often the production editor works with other editors to get the entire job done.

Project Gutenberg. One of the original efforts to convert thousands of public domain books into a simple online format. More information is available at the **Project Gutenberg** site (http://www.gutenberg.net/).

Publishing agreement. The main publishing contract between an author and a publisher, which grants to the publisher certain rights in and to the work.

Publishing agreements should be drafted to protect both the author and the publisher.

Publishing service. A publisher that offers manuscript preparation, publishing, and distribution services to authors and small publishers for a fee. Also known as a subsidy publisher or vanity publisher.

RB. See *Rocket Edition.*

Repurpose. To reuse all or part of a book to create another book or literary work.

Rights. In reference to *digital rights management,* authorization to use specific capabilities available for an e-book, such as copying text, printing the text, copying an image, or lending the e-book to someone else. Each of these capabilities is a right. In general, the term applies to anything one can do with a publication, from quoting some of the words to selling the physical object.

Rights broker. A service specializing in selling (and sometimes buying) rights to literary works. Online rights brokers place *rights* to books on their sites for other publishers to purchase.

RocketBook. One of the original e-book devices, created by Nuvomedia, now owned by *Gemstar.*

Rocket Edition. A file format that stores e-book information specifically for the Rocket eBook reader, or its successor the REB1100 from Gemstar. Files are referred to as *RB* files for their .rb filename extension.

Royalties. Money that is paid to an author from a publisher for a work, typically as a percentage of the net profits on the book.

Secure transaction. An Internet technology that uses a secure server and security features to help prevent computerized theft. Often used for monetary transactions.

Secure format. An *e-book format* that includes *DRM* features for preventing illegal copying of the work.

Shopping cart. A technology for allowing customers to shop a Web site and purchase items as they browse. Items placed in the shopping cart can later be purchased, removed, or changed.

SoftBook Reader. One of the original e-book devices, created by Softbook Press, now owned by *Gemstar.*

Softbook Edition. A file format that stores e-book information specifically for the Softbook Reader, or its successor the REB1200 from Gemstar.

Spam. Unsolicited junk e-mail sent out en masse in the hope of a small favorable response and without regard to the large amount of irritation it is likely to evoke.

Subgenre. A category within a literary *genre*. For example, historical romance is a subgenre of romance.

Subsidiary rights. *Rights* to a literary work that are outside the main publisher's purview. For example, the right to create a foreign language version of a book is a subsidiary right.

Superdistribution. A business model that relies on the fact that digital content can easily and quickly be copied to many people. For instance, when a person shares an e-book with five people, and half of them pay for it and then give it to five more people each (some of whom also decide to pay for it, and so on), the business is relying on the concept of superdistribution to generate profits.

Vanity publisher. See *Publishing service.*

Work-for-hire. A method whereby a publisher hires an author to create a work, and the author is paid a flat fee for the work with no royalties. Typically the author's name does not appear on the cover of the book.

XML. See *eXtensible Markup Language.*

XrML. See *Extensible Rights Management Language.*

INDEX

Other Titles in the Poor Richard's Series

NEW! *Poor Richard's Internet Recruiting*
Easy, Low-Cost Ways to Find Great Employees Online
Here's how to use the Internet to find employees fast—using industry sites, professional organizations, state and city job banks, search engines, mailing lists, and much more.

NEW! *Poor Richard's Home and Small Office Networking*
Room to Room or Around the World
Whether your're in the next room or across the world, this book shows you how to easily and inexpensively build a network that will help your small business or home office stay in touch with employees and shara data.

NEW! *Poor Richard's Internet Marketing and Promotions, 2nd Edition*
How to Promote Yourself, Your Business, Your Ideas Online
Hundreds of proven techniques for getting attention online.

Poor Richard's Building Online Communities
Create a Web Community for Your Business, Club, Association, or Family
Create a *loyal, active* audience with an online community.

Poor Richard's Web Site, 2nd Edition
Geek-Free, Commonsense Advice on Building a Low-Cost Web Site
How to build a Web site without spending lots of time or money and without having to learn a complicated programming language.

Poor Richard's E-mail Publishing
Newsletters, Bulletins, Discussion Groups & Other Powerful
Communications Tools
All of the information and tools needed to start and maintain an e-mail newsletter.

For more information or to place an order
Visit: http://TopFloor.com/
Call: 1-877-693-4676
Or visit your local bookstore.

For lots of FREE information about setting up a Web site and promoting a Web site, visit http://PoorRichard.com/. You can also sign up for the FREE newsletter, *Poor Richard's Web Site News*. With more than 45,000 subscribers, this is one of the most respected newsletters on the subject.